THE OUTSIDER

www.transworldbooks.co.uk

Yes, sir, I had been at Farnborough that day when John Derry at the controls of the prototype de Havilland 110 had plunged into the hillside. No more grins; some serious sideways glances, but approving. Then dismissed. Cannot salute; no flat hat. But I will have one some day.

Five days later another buff envelope. Report to RAF Kenley to be kitted out with flying suit, boots, leather helmet. Then start at Bluebell Hill Flying Club, Rochester, in June. One technical problem: school starts in May. I could do it, but I needed transport.

Dad came to the rescue again. He bought me a second-hand Douglas Vespa scooter. It was British-built, licensed from the Italian Vespa company, and it was a load of rubbish. It had a kick-start pedal and would cough for fifty kicks before sparking into life. Still, it was my first motorized transport. With a learner's licence and a red L-plate front and back, it was legal on the road. Dad ran me to Bluebell Hill to get introduced and see what I would be learning on.

It was a silver Tiger Moth, a biplane like something out of the First World War and the standard workhorse of flying schools back then. Open cockpit, a speaking tube to communicate with the instructor, wind-in-the-hair sort of stuff. Marvellous, intoxicating. The only problem was Tonbridge School. The authorities there had already made plain my passion for flying was juvenile madness. I would never get permission. So I got a shed instead.

Of course it was not on school grounds. It was down in Tonbridge town, on one of those small gardens called allotments, leased for a peppercorn rent by the municipality to those with no garden but who wished to raise their own vegetables. The kindly gardener allowed me to keep the Vespa in it, out of sight and out of the rain.

Back at Parkside for what I hoped would be my last term, I had no more exams to pass so I was put down for GCE 'S' levels. The S stood for state scholarship but it was a forlorn hope. State scholarships were means-tested and my father could now afford university fees without state help, so it would never be awarded. But no one wanted me hanging idly around. Actually I had another exam in mind – my private pilot's licence. But I would not take that until 26 August, the day after my seventeenth birthday. Still, I had thirty hours of pre-paid flying tuition waiting for me up at Rochester and could certainly not wait for school to break up. So I amazed Parkside by becoming a cross-country runner.

Until then I had loathed cross-country running, usually awarded as a punishment for some misdemeanour, or practised by those stringy youths who resembled stick insects. I was still short and stocky and would not start to shoot up until the next year. I regarded cross-country as pure misery. Yet I suddenly started volunteering for it, and not just the five-mile Junior run but the eight-mile Senior Cross. My only condition: that I would run alone.

So, twice a week, I would don white shorts and spotless T-shirt and jog out the gates to the street. It took fifteen minutes to get to the allotment shed where I would put on the canvas flying suit, boots and leather helmet. Thus disguised I could putter past the school gates and out on the highway to Bluebell Hill and its flying club.

After six hours' dual instruction I went solo and experienced the intoxication of flying free, high over the winding

Medway, looking down on Rochester and its towering medieval cathedral. Up there I could roll and twist among the clouds, turning, climbing, diving, ripping off the helmet and keeping only the goggles to protect the eyes.

In my boyish imagination I was over the fields of Flanders, circa 1916, in formation with Bishop, Ball, Mannock and McCudden, with a cheery wave for the French aces Guynemer and Garros, hunting for the Germans Von Richthofen, Boelcke and Immelmann. I had read all about them, researched their stories, their victories and, one by one, their deaths. By the end of school term I had logged twenty-seven of my permitted thirty hours, saving three for the final tests at the end of August.

Parkside never solved the riddle of the cross-country-running schoolboy. The bullying ebbed away as there were now other new boys to persecute. The caning continued. I think I managed to collect seventy-four strokes from the rattan cane over my three and a half years, always administered in the bending position, head under a table, protected only by thin pyjamas.

I never contrived to develop those strange deviances so often attributed to the English, but only two things in their place: the ability to take pain in silence and a contempt for harsh and arbitrary authority.

Summer term ended in July 1955. Bluebell Hill promised to welcome me back for the flying tests in late August. Meanwhile one of my few mates at Parkside, John Gordon, and I decided to hitchhike from Newhaven on the Sussex coast across France to Ventimiglia on the Italian border, via the length of the Côte d'Azur. John was fifteen to my sixteen. We thought it might be an adventure. It was.

A Long Hike

HITCHHIKING IS RARE nowadays but back in 1955 for a youngster with no money it was common. Middle-aged men, mindful of their own impecunious teenage years, would take pity on the figure by the roadside with right fist extended, thumb erect, and slow down, pull over and ask the face appearing in the passenger window where he was heading.

National Servicemen in their uniforms, heading home to Mum and Dad with a weekend pass or struggling back to camp, could usually expect some help. Most middle-aged men had once done it themselves. John Gordon and I, though we did not know it, had an even bigger advantage than a uniform.

John had an aunt who lived at Cooden, close to the Sussex coast and not far from Newhaven. There was a ferry across to Dieppe. I ran down to Cooden on the Vespa and the aunt took us to Newhaven the following morning for the first ferry. We had two return tickets and a very tiny budget.

We firmly expected to sleep rough in sheds, outbuildings and even ditches and eat the cheapest of foods, probably bread and cheese. We were in tough hiking boots, short khaki drill pants, knee-high socks and canvas shirts. That plus a haversack. I had taken the precaution of tacking a Union Jack on the back of my rucksack. We would march in Indian file with me at the rear so that motorists coming up behind could see it clearly. It turned out to be the game-changer.

By mid-morning we were out of Dieppe ferry terminal and heading for the highway to Paris when a car swerved up behind, tooted, and a voice asked, in French of course, where we were heading. I replied in French and within seconds the haversacks were in the boot. John telescoped into the rear seat and I was beside the driver, answering his question as to how I spoke such fluent French. Then we learned the reason for the rapid pick-up.

In 1944, only eleven years before our hiking jaunt, the Allied armies curved out of Normandy and proceeded to liberate France. The British and Canadians turned north for Holland and Belgium, passing through all of northern France. Anyone over twenty-five would clearly have remembered the German occupation and the liberation. It was the British flag that did it.

There were no motorways back then, just the usual Route Nationale, narrow and winding, with one traffic lane each side and occasionally a central and pretty lethal overtaking lane, disputed by cars approaching each other at a hundred miles an hour. It was encouraging if the driver would stop looking side-ways and keep his eyes on the road ahead. In three rapid lifts I believe we made it to Paris ahead of the boat train.

Once in the city we took the métro and arrived unannounced at the flat of the Princesses Dadiani. Completely unfazed, as if teenage hitchhikers were always turning up at their door, the lovely ladies welcomed us in and gave us supper. At ten I parked John on the sofa and went back into the night.

I had worked out that there was a very long haul from Paris south to Marseilles and there was one way in which, if it worked, we could cover the distance in a single day. Every day thousands of trucks, big snorting rigs with trailers that we would now call juggernauts, brought fruit and vegetables from the subtropical south, the Midi, to replenish the stomach of Paris. And then they went back empty.

The gigantic fresh-produce market they made for was in the district called Les Halles, long since moved to the outer suburbs. But then it was right at the heart of Paris, a square kilometre of sheds and warehouses, blazing with light and activity through the night, its bars, restaurants and bistros the haunt of the workers and the social night owls. I began to enquire and had no luck.

I went from café to café, asking perfectly politely if anyone was a truck driver heading south in the morning. The answer was always no, until the proprietors chased me out for not spending anything. Then I got a tap on the shoulder from someone who had followed me out to the pavement.

It was a small and scruffy market worker, an Algerian, who said he had a friend who was exactly what I sought and was sleeping at his small flat a few hundred yards away. I should follow him and he would lead me there. Like a fool I fell for it.

The streets became narrower and dirtier, mere alleys between blocks of slum. Finally he led me through a door and up one flight of stairs. He unlocked his own bedsitter and gestured me inside. The filthy little room was empty. I turned. He had closed the door and locked it. He gave me a snaggle-toothed smile and gestured at the grubby bed.

I reckoned there was not much point in calling for help. This was obviously not that kind of community. I shook my head. He gestured again, adding in French, 'Pants down, over the bed.' I just said, '*Non.*' He ceased smiling, fumbled at his flies and produced his penis. It was semi-tumescent. He repeated his instruction.

I am not homophobic but just have a personal aversion to sodomy. I repeated '*Non*' and then added, 'I'm leaving.' Then he produced a knife. It was a lock-knife that needed two hands to open it. The blade was curved; I assumed it was mainly used for cutting fruit. But it would do just as well on a human body.

By great good fortune my father, several years before when I used to camp out in the fields of Kent, had given me a hunting knife, horn-handled with seven inches of Toledo steel blade. It was for paunching and skinning rabbits brought down with my air rifle, cutting twigs for the camp fire or trimming branches for a hide.

I was carrying it horizontally across the small of my back. I fumbled under the shirt. The Algerian thought I was loosening my belt. When the hunting knife came out his eyes widened and he came forward.

There was a scuffle, quite short, really. A few seconds and it was over. I found myself in the doorway, the door open, my hand on the handle. The market porter's knife was on the floor. He had sustained a long gash to the right biceps about which he was making rather a fuss. In Arabic. I saw little point in waiting around in case he had friends elsewhere in the flop-house, so legged it down the stairs and out into the alley.

The incident was not entirely without benefit because on

my way back to the streetlights I came across what I needed, a sort of elephants' graveyard: row after row of parked juggernauts, waiting for the dawn. The drivers were saving their overnight allowances by bedding down in their cabs. I found one relieving himself against the rear wheel of his truck and when he had finished approached him with my problem. He thought it over.

'It's not allowed,' he said. 'Company policy, no hitchhikers. It's more than my job's worth.'

But again luck cut in. He was from Marseilles, which had never been occupied by the Germans. But his wife was from the north and her father had been in the Resistance in Amiens. He was in jail, destined for execution, when Group Captain Pickard led his Mosquitoes on the Amiens jail raid. They had ripped open the cell block with precision bombing and destroyed the outer wall. His father-in-law had escaped and was still alive.

'I'll have to lock you in for the whole trip,' he said. 'If we are caught you say you stowed away during the night while I slept. Agreed? OK, be back here at six.'

It was still dark at six but the graveyard was slowly stirring. Our new friend cleared a space at the rear of the trailer, near the door, piling the empty crates further to the front to create a cubbyhole about eight feet by eight. Once John and I were curled up inside he locked the doors and went to his cab. By six thirty we were rolling.

There was a distinctive odour to the crates that had once contained his cargo. Melons. At seven in the southern suburbs the sun rose. By eight we were out on the Route Nationale One, heading for Marseilles, eleven hours away. By nine it was getting hot; by ten it was a small furnace. By eleven the melon smell had become an overpowering stench. John was white as a sheet and complaining of advancing nausea. By midday he was on his knees trying to deposit what remained of his Russian supper through the crack where the doors joined the floor. The stench of the melons joined that of human puke in a heady cocktail.

There was no way of contacting the driver, way up front in his cabin. At one he pulled into a roadside halt for fuel and lunch, but with other drivers milling around he did not approach the trailer or let us out. After half an hour he resumed the run south but we had not a clue where we were and John was very sick indeed. He had ceased bringing up and was just moaning.

At first he thought he was going to die and then he feared he wouldn't. I was lucky in having a fairly strong stomach, whether for open boats on an angry sea or journeys by road. And I had just spent June throwing a Tiger Moth all over the sky above Rochester. Our misery ended around 6 p.m. when the truck pulled on to a wayside layby and we were let out.

John retired to the verge to put his head in his hands. I produced a map of France from my haversack and the driver pointed out where we were. South of Avignon but north of Marseilles. I thanked him profusely, we shook hands and he left, presumably to head for his melon farm and a large bucket of disinfectant.

But such is the recovery of the young that within half an hour we were up and marching along the verge. By eight as the sun set we had found a farm with a friendly barn full of straw and hay. Despite being ravenously hungry we collapsed in the bales and slept for ten hours.

On the following day we discovered as we marched, rigid thumbs erect for a lift, that the Union Jack did not work any more. The Midi had never been occupied. It was part of Vichy France, notorious for its enthusiastic collaboration with the Germans. Even the Allied invasion of August 1944 was seen locally as an assault rather than a liberation. No cars stopped. We turned along the coast at Marseilles and, for three weeks, thousands of cars, vans and trucks sped by without stopping.

We lived off crusty baguette bread and cheap cheese, slaking our thirst and filling our water bottles at the public drinking fountains in the villages. There was no Corniche Littorale motorway (where hitchhiking would have been forbidden anyway), just the shoreside road that wended through every village and hamlet as well as the great cities of Toulon, Nice and Cannes.

Marching along it, we found tiny non-tourist bays and creeks where we could strip off and dunk over-heated bodies in crystal-clear cool water. We slept in the workers' sheds in the olive groves and once on the cool marble of a mausoleum in a cemetery. We saw the grandeur of Monaco and Monte Carlo where all the cars seemed to be Rolls-Royces and where I would many years later be the guest of Prince Albert. Finally we came to the Italian border at Ventimiglia.

Just to say we had been to Italy, we went across and trudged to San Remo. Then time and money ran out. We had just enough for two third-class tickets back to Marseilles and there we bought just one single ticket for Paris. We spent the whole journey in the lavatory. Three times a ticket inspector came to the door and rapped. Each time I opened a fraction, explained in French that I was not very well and had the ticket clipped.

Each time John stood on the lavatory seat behind the door and out of sight.

We hitched back to Dieppe and used our return halves to get to Newhaven. No mobile phones back then, so we used a public phone booth and four one-penny coins to alert John's aunt to our presence and then waited to be collected.

We were very brown and rock-hard. We had each grown an inch and still, in old age, laugh at some of the tricks we got up to. The Fifties were a good, carefree and uncomplicated time to be a teenager, before drugs and worries and political correctness. Materially we had infinitely less than youngsters today but I think we were happier.

A few years back a friend from the same generation, the teenagers of National Service, very few rules and regulations, minimal bureaucracy, basic but healthy food, good manners and masses of walking, remarked to me: 'You know, we had the best of the last and the last of the best.' And that got it all in a single sentence.

But it was mid-August and I wanted something badly. I wanted that private pilot's licence. So the day after my seventeenth birthday I Vespa-ed back to Rochester Flying Club.

And from that holiday on, John Gordon has never been able to contemplate a melon, and I have never seen the need to carry a blade.

A Silly Revenge

THE FLYING TEST was almost a routine. Everything about it had already been covered during tuition.

First came a triangular navigation exercise, in which I had to give a running commentary to the instructor in the front cockpit, describing what I was doing and why. The technology for nav. exercises in a Tiger Moth was basic and there were two. They were called eyeballs.

A map had already been prepared with the route marked in felt pen, folded and strapped with elastic bands to the left thigh. Identification of where one was could be achieved by putting the head over the rim of the cockpit and looking down. Location and direction were dependent on recognizing main roads, railway lines and, above all, rivers with their distinctive curves. Towns and cities were identified by castle, cathedral or other obvious features.

There was one elderly member of the club who was so short-sighted that he used to swoop down to fly alongside railway trains and read the destination board on the side of the front carriage. One imagines commuters might be somewhat surprised to raise their gaze from the crossword to see a biplane outside the window and an old codger peering at them. But no one seemed to mind. It was a rather carefree age.

After the nav. test we repaired to the clubhouse for a sandwich lunch then did the general competence hour. This involved the usual basic manoeuvres – climb, dive, turn, wing-over, sideslip and several pretended emergencies. The routine was for the instructor to suddenly shut down the power and say: 'You have a complete engine failure. What are you going to do?'

The response was to look around for a large, flat, green field away from woods, large trees and buildings. With the landing field selected, assess wind direction and speed and glide down behind the idly turning propeller, line up as if for a real landing and approach the unwary farmer's best wheat crop. At the last minute the instructor would ram the power back on and the Tiger Moth would surge upwards and away.

Landing back at Bluebell Hill I was told that I had passed and my licence would be 'in the bag'. The written test, a two-hour paper exam, I had completed before going to France. But I noticed that of my thirty hours of flying time so generously pre-paid by the RAF, there were still forty-five minutes left. I asked for them as a last solo flight and with a shrug was granted them. There was something else I wanted to do.

Tonbridge town was easy to find by following the river Medway which flows right through it. Short of the town I dropped down into the shallow valley between the school playing fields and Hildenborough, through which I had pre-tended to jog so many times.

I came up out of the valley and approached over the two playing fields known as Martins and Le Flemings. I think I was about six feet up. There was a quick blip to clear the line of elms between Le Flemings and the first XI cricket pitch, the sacred turf of the Head. Then the school buildings were ahead of me: School House where the headmaster lived and Old Big School, the big assembly hall.

The school was still on holiday and therefore empty of boys, or at that hour on a summer afternoon they would have been playing cricket on the Head. A face appeared at a window in School House, staring open-mouthed at the approaching propeller. It might have been the headmaster, the kindly but ineffectual Revd Laurence Waddy, but I was never later in a position to ask.

The owner of the face threw himself to the floor as the Tiger Moth climbed the wall of the Old Big School, nearly clipped the roof, rolled to the north, missed the pepper pot on the chapel roof by a few feet and climbed away into a clear blue sky.

Having completed my asinine gesture to a place I was yearning to leave, I flew back to Rochester, hoping no sharp-eyed citizen of Tonbridge had noted my registration number and reported me, for then I would have been finished.

School would reconvene in a fortnight and to please my father I had agreed to complete the last term of the year and leave at Christmas. At the start of term I half-expected to be summoned to report to the headmaster, but no one said a thing.

A fortnight later my private pilot's licence arrived from the ministry at my parents' home in Ashford. I mailed my flying kit back to RAF Kenley and have never flown a Tiger Moth since, until I was given a ride and the controls at the age of seventy-six at Lashenden airfield in Kent. And she is still a great little aeroplane.

A Gentleman of Clare

W HEN I RETURNED to Tonbridge in early September 1955 I thought I faced a term of filling in time. The previous summer I had fulfilled my wager with my father, whereby, if I passed every exam they could throw at me, he would get me out of there. With great luck I had managed my O levels at fourteen and my A levels at fifteen, about three years earlier than required. In this my fluent French and German, provided by the prescience of my parents, had been invaluable.

In the summer term of 1955, still sixteen, I had sat for a state scholarship. Dad did not want to be the only shopkeeper on Ashford High Street whose son left school at sixteen, so he begged me to stay on for the winter term and leave at seventeen. I agreed, but idleness was not exactly what Tonbridge had in mind.

My obsession with warplanes and flying magazines brought nothing but frowns and I was soon required to attend a long interview with a gentleman from the Public Schools Appointments Bureau, who came down for a day to look over the winter leavers. He was genial enough, a bit of a Blimp, and he sought to interest me in becoming 'something in the City'.

Eyes alight with enthusiasm, he proposed an interview with Shell-BP or a major bank. There might even be an opening as a stockbroker. There was no point in protesting. I feigned enthusiasm, took his numerous career brochures and slipped away. But I had fooled no one. Strings were pulled in the background and I was secured an interview at Clare College, Cambridge. With the Master, no less. For my schoolmasters this was close to a visit to Parnassus.

I was furnished with a rail warrant to London and another from London to Cambridge, return. I set off, crossed London by bus, arrived at Cambridge station and walked to Clare College, nestling by the river Cam, and presented myself at the appointed hour. I was in school uniform but without the absurd straw boater, which I had been allowed not to wear. A porter showed me up to the Master's study.

The luminary behind the desk was studying a file. It appeared to be about me. He clucked several times, raised his head and beamed.

'Still sixteen,' he said. 'Fluent in two languages and conversational in Russian. Sounds like the Foreign Office.'

It was not a question so I said nothing. Undeterred, his beam didn't falter.

'So, do you want to try for the Foreign Office, young man?'

'No, Master.'

'Ah well, never mind. So why do you want to come to Clare?'

There are times when dissimulation has no point and straight-up honesty is the best policy. I decided this was one.

'Actually, Master, I don't.'

This time the beam did falter. It was replaced not by anger but by an intrigued puzzlement.

'Then what are you doing here?'

'Tonbridge sent me, Master.'

'Yes, I see that.' He gestured at the file on his desk, which had clearly preceded me. 'In that case, what do you want to do when you leave school?'

'I am going to join the air force, Master. I want to be a fighter pilot.'

He rose and came round the desk, the seraphic beam back in place. He wrapped an arm around my shoulders and guided me back to the door, which he opened.

'Then may I wish you the very best of good fortune. And thank you.'

The good wishes were agreeable, but . . .

'Why "thank you", Master?'

'Because, young man, you have just given me the shortest and most honest interview I have ever had in this room.'

I made my way back to the station, thence to London and on to Tonbridge. A week later his report arrived and I went under a very large and very black cloud. But tenacity is a rather British trait and Tonbridge certainly had it. They sent for my father.

I was not in the room but he told me about it later. There were four of them: the headmaster (whose summer repose I had ruined), my housemaster, the head of studies and the chaplain. He said it was like a summons to the High Court. They were all in their scholastic robes, graduates of Oxford and Cambridge. The shopkeeper they confronted came from Chatham Dockyard and they knew it.

The lecture was not hostile but deeply earnest. His son, they told him, was making a grievous mistake. Brilliant exam results stemming from an expensive education. The sort of background that could one day, after two more years at Tonbridge, result in an exhibition, possibly even an open major, to Oxford or Cambridge. A first-class degree could open the doors to the Civil Service. Why, his son might even be able to return as a junior master at Tonbridge, something they clearly regarded as the pinnacle of achievement.

And in the face of all this the lad had some weird dream of becoming little more than a mechanic. It was all very *infra dignitatem* – beneath one's dignity, a Latin phrase my dad had never heard.

In the raging snobbery of those days it seemed that Dartmouth College (Royal Navy) or RMA Sandhurst (Army, good regiment of course) was just acceptable, but volunteering for boot camp, RAF, was distinctly bizarre. It was his (my father's) clear duty to do everything in his power to dissuade his son from avoiding those last two years at school and inexplicably declining to go to Cambridge.

My dad heard them out, one after the other. Then he spoke very briefly. He said:

'Gentlemen, if my son wants to become a British fighter pilot I intend to give him every conceivable support and encouragement of which I am able. Good day to you.'

Then he left, drove back to Ashford and reopened his shop. He was a great man. I left school that December, still under a cloud.

Learning Spanish

EVEN OVER THE Christmas break my father had made plain that at seventeen and three months I would have no chance of getting into the Royal Air Force when the permissible age was eighteen. I would be wise to wait until I was at least seventeen and a half before trying.

He also made plain he was not having me mooning about the house doing nothing. Some activity had to be found to fill in the first three months of 1956. We made a study of the terms of the scholarship I had won five years earlier to Tonbridge. Founded by the long-gone Mr Knightly, the Knightly Scholarship involved a large sum of deposited money which, with sound investment, should (and did) generate enough to create one bursary per year. But if there was a surplus, this would be lodged in a separate fund.

This extra fund could, with the permission of the governors, be used to allow a student to study an extra language during his last year at school. It did not insist that he must necessarily be at the school to do this. I made an application to be allowed to take a course in Spanish, with costs paid for by the fund.

The bemused governors, who had never had such an application, found the fund was brimming from so many years of non-use and needed depleting. A little more research disclosed that Granada University in Andalusia, southern Spain, offered a three-month spring course for foreigners to study Spanish language and culture. Again the governors conceded the point and paid the course fee plus a personal allowance of six pounds per week while away from home. In early January I left for Spain.

The course was not actually held in Granada but at Malaga on the coast. Back then the sprawling city of modern Malaga was just a seaside town famous for two things. Before the war (the Spanish civil war, which was the conflict that still consumed Spain), the matador Carlos Arruza had performed in the Malaga ring, while suffering from flu and a raging temperature, a corrida so spectacular that he had been awarded two ears, the tail and one hoof from the dead bull, a feat never matched since.

And Pablo Picasso, still alive and painting but in exile in France after bitterly opposing Franco and painting *Guernica*, had been born there. If it had an airport it must have been a small municipal field and not on any international route. I flew to Gibraltar, hefted my suitcase across the border on foot and took the wheezing old coastal bus from La Linea to Malaga. In Gibraltar I exchanged all the sterling pounds I had into pesetas at the remarkable rate of two hundred to one pound. I did not know enough to realize that I had become a wealthy young man by Spanish standards.

What today is the sprawling Costa del Sol chain of tourist resorts did not exist. Between Malaga and La Linea were four small fishing villages: Torremolinos, Fuengirola, Marbella and Estepona. Today's huge motorway was a narrow track, one lane each side. But as the verges were very pitted, every driver rode the centre line, swerving at the last minute with much hooting, shouting and gestures. I was entering a very different and fascinating new culture.

At Malaga I reported to the local branch of Granada University and met the course director, Don Andres Oliva. He was truly cultivated, a real traditional caballero, a gent. I quickly learned that the fifty or so students on the course were all to be lodged in one communal hostel. It also became rapidly plain that as they were Americans, Canadians, British, Germans, Danes, Swedes and others, they would all have one common language – English. And that was what would be used in the hostel. But that was not what I had come for. I wanted to lodge with a Spanish family who spoke no English, and took my problem to Don Andres.

He considered it with quiet but surprised approval, remarked that no one had ever requested this before, but promised to ask around. Twenty-four hours later he told me he had found a family content to take in a paying guest.

The lady concerned was Doña Concha Lamotte, Vda de Morales. When deciphered that meant Madame Concepcion (or Conchita or Concha) Lamotte, Viuda (widow) of the late Señor Morales. It transpired she was French by birth but in the Thirties had married Señor Morales. He had been executed by the Communists during the civil war and his widow had raised her two children alone.

Not surprisingly she loathed the Communists and adored General Franco, who in 1936 had landed with his Moroccan troops just down the coast to start the civil war as the republic fell into communist hands. Franco, of course, was by 1956 dictator of Spain, running a pretty extreme right-wing government.

I took my grip, walked from the hostel to the Lamotte apartment beside the old Miramar Hotel and introduced myself. My lodging was three pounds per week but Spain then was so extraordinarily cheap that the other three pounds of my weekly allowance would be more than enough pocket money. I would have a room of my own and eat all meals with the family.

Madame's children were her son, at seventeen the same age as me while also awaiting his call-up into the armed forces, and her daughter, two years older and engaged to be married. They spoke not a word of English and had never seen an Englishman, let alone a Protestant. I spoke no Spanish but I had a grammar primer and mercifully Madame could just remember her native French and help me out when we got really stuck.

Malaga was still a sleepy, quaint and intensely traditional community. Each evening the girls of the respectable classes not yet 'spoken for' would slowly parade the length of the palm-lined Paseo, duly chaperoned by mother or aunt. From the sidelines they could be observed by the young men not yet engaged. It was a marriage market of great decorum.

The girls would have high ivory combs in their hair, draped with a black lace shawl, the mantilla. The young men often wore the short jacket, the *traje corto*, and the wide-brimmed black or dove-grey hat known as the Cordobes.

If or when a young man saw a girl he really fancied he would ask around for her name. When he had it, he would go to his father, who would then enquire about the girl's own father, and if he was also of a respectable family in a good house and with a worthy profession the two fathers would meet to confer over a possible union of their offspring. There was no question of the youngsters meeting for a chat.

The girl's father would then invite the young man to his house for tea. The girl's mother and possibly a bevy of aunts, all agog with curiosity, would sit with the girl on one side of the room as tea was served, the young guest and the father on the other. It must have been a very stilted occasion with all sides pretending it was just a neighbourly cup of tea.

In fact, both sides were sizing up the other. Courtship was carried on with the eyes. The young people never touched. If impressions were favourable, the father would later consult with his wife and invite the boy to join them for mass the following Sunday.

While he had seen her during the Paseo when she caught his eye, that first stilted cup of tea would be for the girl her first sight of her new admirer. Her curiosity must have been immense. My new friend Miguel Morales told me all this because he had been through it via his sister.

As chastity was total there had to be some release valve and this was the bordello, of which there were many. At the top of the range these were also pretty dignified establishments. It was far from impossible for the mayor and the chief of police to take a glass of sherry with a leading madame, who was also a pillar of the community (not to consort with wives, of course) and a donor to good causes such as the church and the orphanage, to which her girls, if they were careless, might one day contribute.

From a vantage point of sixty years later it is hard to imagine all this, but that was the way it was. The chief of police was not run ragged by overwork because crime was very rare and violent crime just about unheard of. The occasional knife fight might take place among the gypsies or *gitanos* who lived in a camp out of town and who made a living either tending horses or giving demonstrations of flamenco at private soirées or in cafés with a hat passed round. And that was before the gawping tourists arrived.

To get in trouble with the police, a troublemaker would really have to work at it, but political opposition was a serious concern, and police tolerance was non-existent. But that seemed to be the way the people liked it. They had experienced four years of war and cruelty in the late Thirties when the Falangists (Fascists) fought the Communists and they did not want it back.

Life was cheap, the prices minimal. One could have two large schooners of fine sherry, attended by enough free tapas to constitute a good dinner, for ten pesetas.

The scholastic course was 160 lectures. I attended only the first in January and the last at the end of March. I would have missed that as well but for the fact that a foreign student peered at me nursing a large bumper of amontillado at a café table on the day before and asked me if I was the missing English student. Then she told me about the final exam the following day.

Without a hope of passing it I showed up and met an amused and sardonic Don Andres Oliva. I noticed something quite quickly. The hostel students spoke a grammatically perfect but stilted and awfully accented Spanish. I was rattling away in torrents of street Spanish with an Andalusian accent. Don

Andres had to exercise all his self-control not to burst out laughing.

The examination turned out to be one single essay in Spanish on a subject of the student's choosing, drawn from the five headings of language, literature, culture, geography and history of Spain. And there I had a problem. I did not know anything about any of them. So I chose history.

But that proposed a further problem. Recalling our history lessons at school it appeared that every time British and Spanish history made contact we were fighting each other, especially in 1588. That was when King Philip the Second sent his Armada fleet up the English Channel to invade and subdue the heretical Protestant English. The Devonian seadog Francis Drake, a former pirate along the Spanish Main off Central America, was instrumental in the Spanish Fleet's destruction. It was not very diplomatic but it was the only story I knew that involved a bit of Spanish history. If only I could have stuck to the Conquistadors.

Legend has it that when the sails of the Armada hove over the horizon, Drake was on the expanse of greensward outside Plymouth known as Plymouth Hoe playing bowls. He is supposed to have told those who came to warn him that he would finish his game before taking on the might of Spain.

Then arose the third problem. They play 'boules' in France, virtually the same thing, but no bowls in Spain. So despite my Spanish I did not know how to say 'bowls'. The exam markers must have been somewhat bewildered to be told that when the Armada appeared Francis Drake was playing with his balls.

Anyway, these Andalusian scholars must have been intensely tolerant, for five days later they actually gave me a diploma in

Hispanic studies. At the inevitable sherry party I protested to Don Andres that it was wholly unmerited. He smiled somewhat sadly and said:

'Frederico, mine is not a rich country. We need these foreign course fees. So when you get home please tell everyone what good value this course is.'

And I did. At least, I wrote to the governors of Tonbridge to recommend the Granada University's Malaga course as an excellent avenue for future holders of the Knightly scholarship to perfect their Spanish. But after the reception I had to leave because my father had arrived with Mother in tow, was lodged in the Marbella Club Hotel and wanted to see me.

It was all because someone else, a neighbour from Ashford, had perchance seen me imbibing sherry, again in the heat of the day, at a street café. He had asked me what I had been doing and, being a bit light-headed from the sherry and the blazing sun, I told him. He had scurried back to his hotel and rung Ashford with the news. That was what brought my parents on the next plane to Gibraltar.

I had not spent the middle 158 lectures sitting drinking sherry. After my arrival in January, I had investigated what I had really come for. Bullfighting.

During my last year at school I had come across and devoured Ernest Hemingway's classic *Death in the Afternoon*, and had become fascinated by this brutal but incredibly testosterone-fuelled spectacle on the sand of the arena beneath a glaring sun: a lethal pitting of a man against half a ton of truly wild animal. I had followed up Hemingway with Ibáñez's *Blood and Sand* and various other books. And I was determined that I would see it.

In Spain winter is the close-down season for the corrida –
which simply means 'the running'. But in the deep south it is
still warm and sunny even in January, February and March – or
it used to be. That was the time for the *novilladas*.

A fighting bull suitable for a full-fledged corrida is usually
five years old. Until he trots out of the dark pen beneath the
stands for his last twenty minutes on earth he has led an idyllic
life roaming free on the vast ranches with a herd of lady friends
and all the lush grass he can eat. Not for him a miserable abattoir
at barely a year old. But he is emphatically not sweet-
tempered.

Any talk that a fighting bull has to be provoked to charge is
nonsense. He will charge at anything not on four legs. That is
why the vaqueros on the ranches have to be mounted. Any
human descending to the ground on two legs is committing
suicide. Because the bull is short-sighted and sees in mono-
chrome, it is not the 'red' that he is charging but the cape,
flickering and taunting him. When he has hit it and felt no
impact, he turns and charges again. And again. If the matador
remains motionless beside the cape in his hands he should get
away with it. Some do, some don't, because those huge horns
are absolutely deadly.

While it is still a calf, or *becerro*, the bull will probably be
tested once and briefly so that it does not remember later what
happened. The point is to see if, when taunted by a cape, it will
run straight and true or turn away. If the latter it will be for the
knacker's yard. If it charges it will go back to the ranch to spend
four more years coming to full maturity.

But at three it is called a *novillo* and, in the deep south,
corridas featuring only novillos take place. They are mainly for

young matadors who have not yet graduated to the great summer festivals. These are what I wanted to see in Malaga. The novillo may not be as big as a five-year-old, but he is still a very dangerous brute. When I made enquiries at Malaga's famous bullring for the spring programme I discovered something interesting. There was a training school there as well. I signed up at once.

Basically, it was under the tutelage of a retired matador with a heavy limp. He had stopped one horn too many and his hip had never healed up. This did not prevent him teaching because the matador is not supposed to run around much anyway.

The school met in the mornings out on the sand of the arena beneath the empty stands: about half a dozen young aspirants with hopes of one day starring in the big festivals of Granada, Seville or Madrid. A teenager could still look up and imagine those stands thronged with swooning señoritas and hear the clang of the pasodoble and the roared 'Olé's that greet an impressive passage of capework. Then Don Pepe ended the daydreaming and introduced us to the two capes: the capa and the muleta.

The capa came first, a heavy canvas semi-circle, magenta on one side and yellow on the other. The surprising weight of the capa explains why matadors have immensely strong wrists. The muleta, a smaller, bright scarlet cloth splayed on a sword and a wooden stick, used only for the third and last section of the encounter, would come later.

There was, of course, no real bull. They are expensive and not to be wasted on apprentices. The contraption that charged was a construction of two wheels on a frame. At the front of the frame was a set of two real horns from a long-dead Miura, fearsome artefacts about a yard wide, each with needle tips that would really hurt if they hit you.

Behind the frame were two long shafts and the whole thing was raced across the sand by two boys earning themselves a bit of pocket money. At the start of the charge they held the ends of the shafts high, so that the horns were dipped low, for that is how a bull really charges.

As the horns went through the cape, the running boys would thrust downwards on the shafts, causing the horns to swerve upwards as the bull seeks to gore and toss his enemy. After several mornings it became plain I was never going to make a matador. As the horn tips swept up towards the genitalia I tended to step sideways. This caused great merriment.

The matador is supposed to stay absolutely still, the feet planted, and sway the hips like a ballet dancer so that the rising horn almost brushes the fabric of the trousers. My father later averred that he would have taken a ten-foot leap. But my single step was enough to earn a mocking cheer from the Spanish teenagers and a grin from Don Pepe. Towards the end of my stay I completed the lessons but gave up any hope of ever going further.

That was when the neighbours from Ashford spotted me at the café and rang my father. Within days my parents were in the Marbella Club, then a small private hotel out on the Marbella road. My dad came to collect me from Madame Lamotte's flat after the diploma ceremony. He told me never to reveal to my mother that I had been in a bullring. She would attain her grey hair one day without any help from me.

The only other thing of interest during those ten weeks in the hot, sunny spring of 1956 was a torrid affair with a

35-year-old German countess. She frequented the training sessions and later taught me many things a lad should know as he steps out on life's bumpy road.

She had the quaint habit of singing the Horst Wessel song during coitus. At the time I did not know what it was and only a year later learned it was the marching song of the Nazis. This probably meant she had been involved during the war with something deeply unpleasant, which would explain her migration to Spain which, under Franco, was tolerant of that sort of thing.

My folks spent a week at the Marbella Club, then we all left for Gibraltar and the ferry for Tangier.

Tangier and Commandos

TANGIER IN 1956 was an extraordinary place, my first taste of Africa and the world of Islam. Morocco had been, until recently, a French colony, but Tangier was under tripartite administration between the British (the post office), the French (police and law courts) and the Spanish (general administration).

There was a vigorous independence movement called Istiqlal, which rioted elsewhere, but the Tangerines are known for their civility and tolerance so Tangier was spared the rioting, at least while we were there.

It had a fascinating 'old quarter', the medina, and a large covered market, the soukh, where tourists could browse for bargains in perfect safety. I recall that the French were not liked as they represented the law and punishment, while when we were identified as British it was smiles all round. As we only ran the post office our sole visible presence were the little red vans delivering letters.

Tangier was also a free port into which freight ships would arrive to unload out-of-bond cargo immune from even French or Spanish taxes. The cargoes underpinned the smuggling operation, which was considerable. Lined up at the quay was a line of lean, grey Second World War motor torpedo boats, war surplus bought cheap but easily able to outrun the motor boats of the Spanish customs across the water.

Thus each evening as the sun set they would slip mooring and head towards the Spanish coast, loaded with perfume, toilet soap, silk stockings and, above all, cigarettes, mainly Camel and Lucky Strike, which were contraband but highly prized and therefore expensive in Spain.

They would cruise through the darkness slowly, lights doused, engines rumbling quietly, until the first flashlight on the shore indicated where the mule trains were waiting. Then it was a fast run to shore, frantic hands discharging the cargo before the arrival of the Guardia Civil, and the mules lumbering away into the olive groves. A fast run back out of Spanish territorial waters and a slow cruise home brought them back to Tangier by dawn.

The going rate for a deckhand was 50 pounds per trip, which was a lot of money back then, so I went down to see if anyone would take me on, but was rebuffed. No vacancies. The jobs were extremely sought after despite twenty years in a Franco jail if caught, and anyway I had no seamanship.

Otherwise Tangier was noted for the sumptuous palace occupied by Woolworth heiress Barbara Hutton. It was also a magnet for elderly European gays because the Moroccan boys were numerous, willing and cheap.

My parents played the tourist out of the El Minzah Hotel, but I could not, like them, retire to bed at 10 p.m., so I would steal back out and explore the bars and dives of the port quarter. It was here I met the Marine Commandos.

There was a British warship moored in the outer harbour

on what is called a 'flying the flag' mission. The idea was to spread pro-British goodwill along the African coast. It was in a dockside bar that I came across a group of marines who were having terrible trouble making themselves plain to the bar staff, who spoke only Moorish Arabic and Spanish.

I tried to help and was promptly pressganged as unit interpreter by the senior sergeant. They were all from Glasgow, from, I believe, Gallowgate or the Gorbals; about five feet tall and the same wide.

The problem was not between English and Spanish. That was easy. It was between English and Glaswegian. I could not understand a word they said. Eventually a corporal was discovered whom I could decipher and the three-language enigma was solved. We moved from bar to bar as they spent their shore-leave and accrued pay on pints of beer and triple-Scotch chasers.

Another problem, and quite a big one on a goodwill mission, was that they tended to leave each bar looking as if a bomb had gone off. I solved this by suggesting a gratuity for the staff. Contrary to rumour, Glaswegians are not stingy. When I explained the Tangerines were dirt poor, the marines chipped in generously. But I explained to the bar staff the extra money was the house-repair budget. Smiles all round.

Each morning I was decanted from a taxi outside the El Minzah at about five, just in time for a short nap before joining my parents for breakfast at eight.

On the third day the Royal Navy warship weighed anchor and cruised off, taking the commandos to continue their friendship-building mission somewhere else.

After six days my parents and I went back by ferry to

Gibraltar and then by plane to London. I had reached seventeen and a half and needed to get on with the serious task of wangling my way into the Royal Air Force. But in three months, all on the tab of the late Mr Knightly, I had learned fluent Spanish, collected a Granada University diploma, learned how to handle a cape in the face of two charging horns, discovered what to do in bed with a lady and developed a rock-hard head for alcohol. I was out on the 'dusty high road' referred to in the Tonbridge school song and enjoying every minute of it.

Leopard–skin Solution

April 1956 seemed to be racing by and still I could not persuade the air force to let me in. It was a very odd position to be in. Compulsory National Service was not popular and it was becoming even less so as the mood towards a fully professional army, navy and air force strengthened.

The rumours grew that by 1960 it would be abolished. All my contemporaries were seeking ways of delaying their call-up until abolition. Some invented maladies that would enable them to fail the medical. Much of a generation claimed to have flat feet, fallen arches, defective vision or shortage of breath. If they were all to be believed, one would conclude the young manhood of Britain was the unfittest on earth.

And yet I was trying to get in against an oncoming tide of youngsters trying to get out. I went to two recruiting offices in East Kent and in each the result was the same. The flight sergeant in each welcomed me with something approaching disbelief, a surprise compounded on learning I was not trying to sign up for a whole career but just for the two-year National Service that everyone was trying to avoid.

There was a reason for this. I did not want to spend a

working lifetime in a blue uniform if I could not fly. In fact, the RAF was extremely generous in that regard. If you failed the selection tests you could leave immediately, but I did not know that.

In each office the senior NCO beamed a welcome, drew out a long form and began to fill it in. Everything went swimmingly until the query about date of birth. When I gave it there were several seconds of mental arithmetic, then the sad smile as the form was torn up.

'Nice try, son,' they said. 'Come back when you are eighteen.'

It was my father who cracked it. Ashford had an Air Cadet Corps and the corps had a band and up front marched the big drummer, in both senses. He was a big lad and jutting out from his chest was the big drum. But he had no leopard-skin tabard or poncho. Everyone knows that the big drummer has to have his leopard skin.

Dad was a furrier and in his basement store he had a magnificent leopard skin, deposited for safe keeping before the war by someone who had never come back and probably never would. He took it from the chilled vault, trimmed it, backed it with red baize, cut a slit for the drummer's head and presented it to the corps.

The drummer was in seventh heaven and the corps commander deeply grateful. The point was, the corps had a patron in the form of a retired air marshal who lived out at Tenterden. He rang my father to express his appreciation. The conversation ended with the perfunctory, 'If there's ever anything I can do . . .'

'Well, as a matter of fact there is,' said my father.

The warmth at the other end dropped several degrees. 'Yes . . . ?'

'I have a son.'

'Good.'

'He wants to join the air force.'

'Excellent.'

'There's a problem, Air Marshal. He's just a little bit too young.'

There was a thoughtful pause, then: 'Leave it to me.'

This is where the luck came in, though I only discovered later the story behind the story.

During the war, the air marshal had been a group captain commanding an airbase in the middle of Iraq called Habbaniyah. Serving under him was a certain junior officer, a flight lieutenant. In the intervening years the group captain had become an air marshal and retired to Tenterden. The flight lieutenant had become a group captain and director of personnel at the ministry. To this day I have a fantasy of the conversation between them. Something along the lines of:

'Now look here, Farnsbarns, stop faffing about and send this lad his papers, and we'll say no more about the missing petrol coupons.'

Something like that. Anyway, a week later my call-up papers arrived. The usual buff envelope headed by the letters OHMS. On Her Majesty's Service. I was to report to RAF Hornchurch for aircrew selection tests.

I have little doubt no one knew I had already done that once, and the presumption was that I would fail and that would solve the problem. After all, only about one in a hundred National Servicemen passed. There was a sound reason for this.

Since the end of the Second World War, the procedure had been that those getting their wings during National Service would go back to Civvy Street but remain on the roll of the Auxiliary Air Force, flying at weekends with one intensive two-week refresher course per year.

But it was becoming very plain that weekend warriors were not going to be any match for the Soviet Union's MiGs and Sukhois if it came to World War Three. The economists in London were even then pointing out that training someone to fly fighters, which took two years anyway, then losing him a fortnight later was a waste of money.

Awarding a boy a flying scholarship was going to cost the Air Ministry only thirty hours in a Tiger Moth at six pounds per hour. From zero to wings on a single-seater jet, even back then, cost over one hundred thousand pounds. The system continued, but unwillingly, sustained only by the inertia of all bureaucracies.

The one thing the men in blue could really do was to ensure that National Service trainee pilots were as few as possible and were 'chopped' (discarded) for the slightest inadequacy. I had only one ace in the hole. I had been through the Hornchurch tests the previous year and knew what to do and what was expected.

So I took my rail pass and went up there for the second time. I made no mention of the earlier visit and only divulged to the interview board that I had my pilot's licence, not how I got it. They assumed my father had paid for it and approved the enthusiasm. I also implied I was only a National Serviceman because if I could not fly I did not wish for a life behind a desk. The two officers with wings nodded at that as well. The one with a uniform unadorned by wings looked glum but two outvote one.

A week after returning home I got the last buff envelope. No mention of being seventeen and a half. I was ordered to report in civilian clothes with one small suitcase to RAF Cardington, Bedfordshire, the 'kitting out' base for new recruits, all branches. At last I was in.

'I'm Jesus Christ'

CARDINGTON HAD ONCE been the base of the barrage
balloons that had floated over British cities to deter the
bombers of the Luftwaffe. The gigantic hangars that housed
them proved perfect for the masses of stores needed to transform a generation of young men from civilians to
aircraftsmen.

There was a day of form-filling then haircuts. The mid-
Fifties was the age of the Mods (moderns) and Rockers (bikers).
The former had short hair, wore suits and rode scooters. The
Rockers had long greasy hair, wore leathers and rode motor-
bikes. When they met they fought in 'rumbles', gang fights that
consumed the seaside resorts to the outrage of the citizens. Out
in the early-May sunshine, rows of service barbers gleefully
wielded their electric clippers, reducing everyone to (very)
short back and sides.

There were several thousand young men on the camp, well
over 99 per cent extremely 'bolshy', a short form of Bolshevik,
meaning seriously truculent. After shearing, everyone passed
down the long lines of trestle tables in the hangars, being issued
with boots, socks, undershorts, singlets, shirts, trousers, blouses

and berets. After changing in the dormitory huts, the civilian clothes were packed in the suitcases and mailed home. There was one exception: a very small group destined for flying training and thus immediate junior officer status. There were eighteen of us in a single hut trying to survive the week. Because of the shirts.

All our uniforms were of very scratchy serge, but the shirts were different. Those destined to be airmen or 'erks' had shirts of the same rough serge. Those destined for officer cadet status were issued shirts in lawn, a type of soft cotton. It was a dead giveaway.

As soon as we emerged for 'chow' in the eating hall it was plain to all that if you really wished to thump an officer the next two days would provide the last chance. We retired to our hut and more or less barricaded ourselves in.

You could tell very quickly who had been to boarding school and who not. The former immediately grabbed the beds furthest from the door, standard dormitory lore. When the NCOs came in at crack of dawn to waken the exhausted and fast-asleep youngsters, they would start bed-tipping nearest the door. Those at the far end had a few seconds to wake up and get vertical with a bleary but cheerful 'Morning, Sarge'. It helped the day start without a tangle of sheets, blankets and bedframe. It also meant you did not have to put the whole thing back together again.

The senior NCOs knew perfectly well we were targeted by the rest of the intake and, to be fair to them, stuck fairly close to us. Two days after kitting out, the 'soft shirts' were ordered to assemble with kitbags near Main Gate. We were off to boot camp. Even though we were destined for a flying training base, there was still the ritual of twelve weeks of basic training.

That would mean endless polishing of metal buttons and leather boots, pressing of uniforms, marching and counter marching, rifle drill, running, obstacle courses, physical training and saluting just about everything but the trees.

A blue bus showed up and took us to the nearest rail station. In the late afternoon we were decanted from a branch line on a wayside halt in the middle of the wilds of Lincolnshire, at a place called Kirton Lindsey.

As we stood blinking in the sunlight on the platform, surrounded by our kitbags, a small corporal strutted up and planted himself in front of me. I am no giant but he was much shorter. He wore his flat hat well forward, with the black plastic peak just above the tip of his nose. This meant that to see where he was going he had to hold himself like a ramrod, extracting the most height from his tiny frame.

Even so, he had trouble glancing upward. I was aware of two malevolent sultanas glaring up from beneath the cap's peak. Then he spoke in a shrill and outraged squeak. I learned later he was always outraged.

'Do you know who I am?' he screeched.

'No, Corporal, I don't.'

'Well, I'm Jesus Christ, that's who I am. And that's how you'll bleeding well treat me.'

The tone was set. I had met my first British junior NCO. Corporal Davis.

The twelve weeks of boot camp passed quietly. We polished and marched, attended the gymnasium and the rifle range, practised with .303 rifles and submachine guns, marched again, polished again and saluted everything. And there was the drill.

Hour after hour of it. Up two three, down two three, general salute, present arms, trail arms, porte arms, shoulder arms, left turn, right wheel, halt, quick march. AttenSHUN.

Honestly, we were not a success. Some of us had been in the cadet force at school and pretty much knew the ropes. Others were new to it and quite bewildered. Our course leader was the oldest at twenty-six with university and a doctorate in chemistry behind him. I was the Benjamin, six months younger than the next youngest.

Our drill sergeant was not the monster of comedy films but a kindly flight sergeant who treated us like wayward nephews. At that age, everyone over forty seems elderly. He tried so hard to turn us out like the Brigade of Guards and failed nobly. Once, after we had ended up at the edge of the parade ground in a tangle of limbs, he actually burst into tears. It is a terrible thing to see a grown man cry. (Well, it used to be.) Though we had a few shillings a week pocket money, we took him down to the local pub, the First and Last, and got him well plastered.

Finally there was a passing-out parade and we prepared for the next camp and what we had come for – basic flying training. At this point we divided. The six trainee navigators went off to one training school and the remaining pilots to another. We spent one last evening in the First and Last, downing foaming pint after pint, singing really bawdy songs, knowing the villagers, wives and all, were listening in the neighbouring bar, pretending to be shocked while missing not a word and laughing their heads off.

Then we were gone, the pilots across country to RAF Ternhill in Shropshire. With the transfer came elevation from cadet to junior officer, specifically acting pilot officer. The reason for 'acting' was that if you flunked out you could still be busted back to airman.

But failing that, the scratchy serge was replaced by smooth barathea, the beret by a peaked cap. There was an almost invisible ring round each sleeve, other ranks had to throw up a salute as you passed and men old enough to be your father called you 'sir'. And the pay went up to a staggering 23 pounds a week; being three pounds basic plus twenty pounds 'flying pay'. I would not earn that much again for five years.

I think we all enjoyed our nine months at Ternhill in the lovely Shropshire countryside. Sleeping quarters were in a row of Nissen huts, but divided so that we had a small bedsitter each, which gave some privacy for the first time since the parental home. Eating was in the grand officers' mess building with stewards to wait table.

Much has been written to the detriment of National Service but it accomplished three functions that nothing else could. It brought young men from every part of the country together to meet and share living quarters, travel, adventures and camaraderie, youngsters from Kent in the southeast to Carlisle in the northwest who would never have met each other. It bonded them together and helped unify the nation.

Secondly it also brought together youths from every social group and background and broadened a lot of horizons. It taught those of a privileged background never to look down on anyone else, ever.

And it took millions who had never left the parental home, who would only graduate after marriage to the marital home, away from Mummy's apron strings to an all-male environment where you stood on your own two feet – or else.

The aeroplane on which we trained was the Provost, made by Hunting Percival, now long gone. It was a bulky, fixed-undercarriage side-by-side seater, powered by a single rotary engine. It was stable, docile and without vice. It introduced us to aerobatics and very rarely stalled and fell out of the sky. I do not recall that anyone was 'chopped' on the Provost, though two of our dozen fell ill and had to be retarded until the next course. And two others joined us from earlier courses. We clocked up 120 hours on the Provost before a final flying test and passing-out parade. Then we had a fortnight's home leave with parents before reporting to Advanced Flying Training school at RAF Worksop in north Nottinghamshire. At last, single-seat jets.

Vampire

So we reconvened in high summer of 1956 at RAF Worksop, most of us at Retford station, the better-off in their own cars. Mike Porter came from Scotland in his hugely admired MG TF sports car; Anthony Preston came from his Saxmundham, Suffolk home in his four-seater drophead MG tourer, which, as he was the only teetotaller, would soon become the safest way home from the pub on a Saturday night.

There were no more Nissen huts to live in. We were now lodged in the huge officers' mess, each with a spacious room and each with a batman or personal valet. My own was a civilian who had served at that airbase since the war. It felt strange to be looked after by a man old enough to be my father.

There was a first-night dinner in the spacious dining hall, then we all convened in the bar to meet our new commanding officer, the Wing Commander (Flying), and the instructors. Each of us longed for the morning when we would go down to the hangars to be introduced to what we all longed to fly. The de Havilland Vampire.

It was a flight sergeant who finally led us round the corner of the hangar, and there she was. We just stared and almost salivated. We felt we had come so far and passed so many tests, and there she was. A Mark 9 single-seater version.

She crouched low on her stubby oleo legs, canopy back, cockpit open. To us she exuded power and danger. Short elliptical wings, triangular air intakes, small capsule of a body and twin booms to sustain the broad tail. Somewhere inside was the de Havilland Goblin engine that would throw her through the sky at up to 600 miles per hour.

For years after 1945 the Vampire, along with her contemporary the Gloster Meteor, had been the principal front-line fighter of the RAF. Although relegated to an advanced flying trainer, she was in essence just the same. The four Aden cannon had been retained for the purposes of balance and only stoppered at the front end. The gunsight had been removed from the cockpit but that was all.

We circled, we prowled, we approached as the flight sergeant reeled off the statistics. Length, wingspan, weight, take-off speed, landing speed, maximum altitude over 40,000 feet, way up in the stratosphere.

Finally we looked into the cockpit and marvelled at how small it was. Like a tiny sports car of extraordinary power. Then one of us made an interesting remark.

'Flight, it's got no ejector seat.'

And it was true. The larger twin-engined Meteor had been fitted with the Martin Baker Mark 4 ejector seat, although invented after the aeroplane, because there was room for it. The side-by-side twin-seat Vampire T11 trainer, designed and built specifically for dual instruction, had it. But not the Mark 9, designed and built long before the Martin Baker that would hurl a pilot clear of a doomed and falling aeroplane and save his life.

'That's right, sir,' came the sardonic reply from the senior NCO, who would no more fly one of these things than jump off a cliff. 'It is the only jet the RAF has ever sent into the sky that has no ejector seat. And no one has ever escaped from a dying Vampire. You either fly in it or die in it.'

We retreated to the mess for a rather silent and thoughtful lunch.

But fly in it we did, aware that with dinghy pack and parachute strapped to your rear end, like the bulbous home of a spider on its backside, you could stand up in the cockpit but never get out. The front coaming of the windscreen would jab you in the stomach before the parachute could clear the back of the seat. Like a champagne cork, you were stuck and could only sit back down again.

And that was while stationary on the apron. In the stratosphere, a 300mph slipstream would simply bend you back until your spine snapped.

We started on the T11 dual-control version with the instructor in the left-hand seat (always the left-hand seat for the leading pilot, right-hander for the co-pilot).

It was all learning, a huge curve of new expertise to be ingested and assimilated. And the ground instruction: classroom lessons on aerodynamics, meteorology, aviation medicine, the stresses and strains of G-forces up to six times gravity in the turns and dives, the effects of anoxia (oxygen starvation) if the breathing apparatus packed up.

And the first twenty flights with the instructor at first doing it all, then slowly handing over to the pupil, procedure by procedure until he was satisfied his trainee could handle it all. Then the transfer to the Mark 9 and first solo.

I was forty-four days short of my nineteenth birthday when I took a single-seat Vampire off the deck, and I believe the first and only eighteen-year-old ever to have done so, all because of a leopard-skin poncho.

I sat on the threshold of the runway, engine idling, asking for take-off clearance, waiting for permission, hearing only the low whine of the Goblin behind the small of my back, and the sound of my own breathing and heartbeat inside the rubber mask and the silver 'bone-dome' helmet; and vaguely aware my instructor would be in the tower, gnawing his nails with worry.

'Charlie Delta, clear take-off.'

Slowly forward with the left hand on the throttle, hear the engine moving up from low whine to roaring howl, feel the rumble of the wheels increasing to rapid thuds. Control column neutral, light to the touch. Nose-wheel off the tarmac. Ease back. Rumbling gone, airborne.

Three small green lights on the panel ahead meaning wheel down and locked. Up undercarriage. The lights go red: wheels coming up but not completely. Red lights out. Wheels fully up. One-third flaps, the take-off setting up. She's clean, speed rising.

Switch radio channel, acknowledgement from the calm voice in the tower. 'Charlie Delta, roger.' Then pull back and feel the power, the exhilaration, the adrenalin rush of single-seat jet flight.

One by one, we did it all. Night flying when all England was a vast blaze of lights below, city by city, edged by the pure black of the sea. Instrument-flying with a cowl over the head and vision confined to the panel and no glance outside, the instructor alongside checking instrument readings against the world outside. In northern England there would be cloud, masses of cloud, and once that great ocean of grey cotton wool closes around you, only the instruments will keep you alive and bring you back to a safe landing.

Every emergency procedure was practised over and over again from engine flame-out to loss of radio.

Sometimes we would find an American bomber out of Lakenheath, patrolling towards the North Sea, formate along-side and give the ally a cheery wave. Other times we would find a Soviet bomber over the ocean, probing the defences. Another wave, but they never replied.

Summer ended, autumn closed in, the clouds thickened, we used the clear patches for aerobatics, pulling G until the vision narrowed to a tunnel and grey-out threatened. But we never lost the euphoria. Until November.

You fly in it or die in it, the grizzled flight sergeant had said. And then Derek Brett and his instructor Jonah Jones died in it.

Ironically it was in a twin-seat T11 with ejector seat that they died. They were in dense cloud over the Pennines coming home on a radio-controlled tower-guided descent called an ACR-7. They were ordered to fly away from the base down to 12,000 feet, then turn through 180 degrees and fly back towards the base until final landing instructions. But on the turn they were at 2,000 feet, not twelve. A simple misreading of the altimeter. The Pennines are 3,000 feet high.

In the tower the radio communications simply stopped.

The last known position was noted and an alarm put out. It was the Mountain Rescue Team that found the wreckage the next day. But dinner had been taken in dead silence.

When a fighter impacts into a mountainside at 300mph there is virtually nothing left but a crater and some bits of metal. The scythe-bladed compressor wheel is right behind the cockpit. Still spinning at several thousand rpm, it just comes off the axle and churns forward until it reaches the ground ahead.

The mountain rescue men brought down two stretchers with body bags and the morticians did what they could when transferring the contents to coffins. The family of Flight Lieutenant Jones elected to take his coffin home. Flying Officer Derek Brett was buried at nearby Retford church cemetery.

He was a man on a Permanent Commission, hence his elevated rank. He was older than most of us, married with a baby son. Formerly in Air Traffic Control branch, he had lusted to fly and passed all the tests, joining us at Worksop as others dropped out or were chopped. Our original twelve from Kirton Lindsey were down to six, but increased to about a dozen by late joiners from earlier courses.

It was on a bleak winter's day of sheeting rain that eight of us, chosen for equal height, carried Derek's coffin to the Retford grave and stood in the downpour as the obsequies were completed. Then we went back to Worksop and flew again.

I think that in the lives of most young men there comes a moment when the boy simply has to grow up and become a man. For most of us it was the day we buried Derek Brett. We realized this thing, this Vampire, was not just a great-fun sports car loaned by a generous queen for us to amuse ourselves over the north of England. It was ten tons of aluminium and steel that, if you did not treat it with respect, would kill you.

The remainder of us all got our wings and there was a parade in late March 1958. It was sheeting rain again so the parade was in the largest hangar on the base. An air vice marshal came up from London and one by one took the bright white stitched wings emblems off a cushion held beside him and pinned them on our chests. It was the proudest moment of my life so far.

The thing about wings is that they are yours and yours alone. You cannot inherit them from an indulgent father; you cannot buy them in Savile Row; you cannot win them in a lucky draw; you cannot marry them along with a pretty girl; you cannot steal them on a shoplifting spree. You cannot even earn them in a team event. You fight and you struggle, you study and you learn, you practise and you persevere and finally you do it alone, high above the clouds, in a single-seater.

I could have stayed on, signed the extension, increased the National Service commission to a Direct (eight-year) commission or even a Permanent (twenty-year) career. But I only wanted to fly.

I wanted to be assigned to a Hunter squadron. The swept-wing supersonic Hawker Hunter was then the main front-line fighter of the RAF. I was told very bluntly that there was no hope of a Hunter unit. They were for the alumni of Cranwell College, the life-timers. At best I would get the right-hand (co-pilot) seat in a Hastings cargo plane on the mail-run to Malta; at worst, and most likely, I would drive a desk.

So I decided to go for my next choice of career. I had long

been convinced that there was a lot of world to see. Fifty-seven years later I can still agree with that. There is, and 90 per cent of it is terrific. I had not the money to travel, but I knew people who did: the editors of the great daily newspapers. I would become a foreign correspondent.

And finally I had conquered the bug. The little boy on Hawkinge airfield had not flown a Spitfire, but he had done the rest. He had got his wings. So I opted to leave.

But I still had four weeks of terminal leave and I still had my RAF ID card. There was one more adventure to be attempted. I could use that card to hitchhike to the Middle East, which I yearned to see. I made my way down to the great Transport Command base at Lyneham, Wiltshire. There I mooned about the officers' mess until I found a friendly pilot who would be flying out to Malta as captain of a Blackburn Beverley the next morning. Could he fit in an extra passenger? Why not, came the response. (Things were much more informal back then.)

So I showed up on the flight line that 31 March and found the Beverley was taking a replacement jet engine out to Luqa, the big RAF base on Malta. There were also three other passengers hitching a ride. One was an air vice marshal, a second was an army captain, just appointed aide-de-camp to the British governor, the third was a schoolboy of eighteen joining his parents on the staff of the High Commission.

The lumbering freighter took off and waddled its way across France to the French airbase at Salon, outside Marseilles. There we refuelled and set off again. Not for long. Out over the Mediterranean there was a loud bang and the starboard inner engine blew up. It simply disintegrated. Through the portholes of the passenger compartment we watched several cylinders with pistons attached tumbling lazily down the slipstream.

The skipper, Flight Sergeant Farmer, did brilliantly. He would have closed the engine down but there was nothing to close. Just a large munch-sized bite out of the starboard wing. Running across the void were the fuel lines to the outer engine. If that went as well there would be a one-way flight straight down to the ocean where, with the huge jet engine in the hold, we would sink like a stone. The right wing was suffused with extinguisher foam, the Beverley dived to the surface of the sea and we limped back to Salon.

The schoolboy brought up, the air vice marshal prayed and the exquisitely turned-out army man just sniffed, which I took to be his comment on the RAF generally.

Back at Salon there was a major turn-out of fire trucks, which were not needed. The RAF presence there was a tiny unit of three: one officer and two NCOs. And there was a further problem. The following day was 1 April, the fortieth anniversary of the RAF, founded in 1918. There would be a huge party at Luqa, where we were supposed to be.

The air vice marshal insisted we had to have one anyway. He pulled rank, emptied the RAF reserve of francs and we set off for Salon town. I recall that much good red wine was drunk, I interpreted into French and back, and we all ended up in a friendly bordello, where I think that schoolboy grew up a bit to a round of applause while the army officer just sniffed.

It took three days for a substitute Beverley to be flown out from Lyneham and eventually we made it to Luqa. But it was not to be my week. That evening a sailor was knifed in the Gut;

not his gut, the red-light district known as the Gut. It was the first of the rioting led by local politician Dom Mintoff seeking independence. Everyone was confined to base. I tried my hitch-hiking again and found a skipper prepared to offer me a lift to Cyprus. So I took it.

At Nicosia I got short shrift. The island had been consumed by the EOKA, another independence-seeking group, but for the moment there was a ceasefire operating. I was told there was no room for a spare body hanging about the mess, so the education officer noticed a free offer by Middle East Airlines for a cultural weekend in Beirut. I took that too, and was deposited in the Lebanon. Unfortunately there was another revolution brewing there as well.

I was taking a stroll through the soukh, drinking in the local colour, when there was a sound like tearing calico and two bodies, riddled with machine-gun fire, fell through the awning of a fruit stall. Unbeknown to me, the Druze tribesmen had come over the Chouf mountains and launched what turned out to be the civil war against the government of President Chamoun.

I went back to the St George's Club to find the British press corps lining the bar (where else?), so I gave them my first contribution to the media, an eyewitness account of what was going on outside. The grateful reptiles stood me several rounds of drinks as they filed their copy with long, shouted phone calls to London.

Unfortunately I was so squiffy I went outside to the swimming pool, fell asleep and awoke badly sunburned. Two days later I took the free MEA flight back to Nicosia. And the ceasefire ended. The war resumed. The commanding officer was incensed to see me again and with his impetus I found myself on the 'rumble' (spare) seat of a Canberra jet bomber heading back to Luqa. From thence a Hastings freighter took me home to Lyneham without its engines falling off.

I had been away three weeks, experiencing one mid-air near-disaster, one civil war and two uprisings. From Lyneham, still in my blue pilot officer's uniform, I hitchhiked back to my parents' home in Kent. But before leaving for the Middle East, and after my decision to leave the service, I had applied for a job in journalism.

My father had consulted the editor of the *Kentish Express* as to how his son should best start. That fine man advised against a weekly like his own but recommended what he called 'the finest provincial daily in England'. He referred to the *Eastern Daily Press* based in Norwich, Norfolk. I applied, secured an interview and got a job as an apprentice, starting in May. There would be a three-month trial and, if extended, an indenture of three years.

Returning home from Malta, I stripped off my blue uniform for the last time. I was allowed to keep my stainless steel watch, which kept perfect time until the mid-Seventies. After a fortnight with Mum and Dad, I left for Norwich and a new career.

King's Lynn

AFTER AN INITIAL three weeks at the newspaper's head office in Norwich, I was posted out to the most westerly office within the circulation area, the market and port town of King's Lynn. My trial appointment was confirmed and I spent my three-year indenture there.

The chief reporter was the veteran Frank Keeler, a terrific journalist who became my mentor. He was a stickler for accuracy, dunning into all cubs he ever mentored his personal philosophy: check, check and check again. Then write. I still do.

On a minuscule salary I could just afford a scruffy little bedsitter above a pet-food store on Paradise Parade, the country's most inappropriately named highway. In summer the minced dogmeat stank but in winter the warmth rising from the caged pets below kept my heating bill down.

There was a lavatory but no bathroom, so for hygiene I had to go to the office, in the attic of which there was an old bath that I brought back into commission and used for three years. There was a kitchen, comprising a single gas hob running off a bottle and a cold-water tap. I learned to cook eggs just about every known way and not much else. I am still no use in the kitchen and it is the one room I try to avoid.

But at least, using my RAF savings, I had my first sports car, which was my pride and joy. It was an MG TC model, made in 1949, black with scarlet leather seating. Back in 1949 the technology for making paper-thin sheet steel was not known, or when I crashed it it would have crumpled like a tissue and killed me. Instead it was built like a truck, which enabled me to survive the crash. But we'll come to that.

The apprenticeship I was serving was devised by the National Council for the Training of Journalists. It involved three years of on-the-job training and night school to study typing, shorthand, libel law, constitution and theory of journalism, which is a long way from the real thing. At the end there would be a series of written examination papers and a diploma. Never in the past fifty years has anyone ever asked me for it.

King's Lynn was and remains a bustling market town with rural Norfolk to its east and south, the flat and featureless Fens to the west and the North Sea outside its ancient harbour and port. The port then played host to a constant stream of small freighters plying their trade between the Norfolk coast and the ports of Western Europe, particularly Germany.

Coverage of news concentrated on the town, its council, magistrates' court, police station, chamber of commerce and just about every activity concerning the townsfolk, with further supervisory coverage of the surrounding villages. As training for what came later, it was superb.

Reporters on a national paper, let alone an agency, will never meet their readers. On a regional or local paper they are right outside the door, and come in personally to complain about inaccuracies. So the standards have to be high, and they are. I recall one old buffer, puce with outrage, storming into the office to complain that in the results of the cage-bird show at the Corn Exchange his canary had been wrongly placed. And it really upset him.

In three pleasant but uneventful years, only two episodes remain in the memory. Because of my languages, especially German, Frank asked me to be the new 'port reporter' and keep an eye on ships coming and going. On my first summer vacation, unable to afford a holiday, I managed to be taken on as a deckhand on a German freighter called the *Alster*. She plied between King's Lynn and Hamburg. I spent two weeks on her.

As soon as she docked in Germany I was off to explore Hamburg, starting with the seamen's zone known as Sankt Pauli. This included the famous Reeperbahn and its surrounding maze of streets and alleys which comprised the red–light district. My deckhand wages did not afford much more than a few beers but some of these were taken in the old Zillertal, a beer hall famous for its foaming steins of ale and oompah-oompah brass bands. I went there because my father had told me about it.

In spring 1939, when I was still a baby, he and a friend from Ashford had treated themselves to a short vacation and picked Hamburg, where they arrived by car. They both went to the Zillertal but on emerging heard a scuffle down a side alley. Peering into the gloom, they observed two Nazi thugs beating up an old Jew.

He and Joe Crothall may have just been shopkeepers from

a small market town who knew nothing of the reality of Germany under the Nazis, but it had only taken them twenty-four hours to take a dislike to the strutting young men with their armbands and the sign of the broken cross. Neither was Jewish either, but they just waded in.

In his time in Chatham Dockyard School my dad had been a useful middle-weight and his father had once been boxing, wrestling and bayonet-fighting champion of the Nore Command, which then contained 50,000 sailors. Anyway, he and Joe Crothall (who told me the story ten years later) flattened the two assailants. Then, as a crowd gathered, it was time to get out of there. They ran for their car and sped out of Germany into Holland before getting into any more trouble.

I could not know in 1959 that fourteen years later I would also have to get out of Hamburg in a hurry. It seems to be part of our family history. I just contented myself with sightseeing and enjoyed my stay there.

Then in 1960 I crashed the MG and was lucky to survive. It was one in the morning out on the flat Fenland landscape. I was driving home and, of course, too fast. A friend was beside me in the passenger seat, the roof was stowed and we were enjoying the warm summer wind in our hair when we entered the bend.

It was a right-hander and it turned out to be 90 degrees. I think the MG made eighty of those degrees before losing traction and skidding into the left-hand verge, which was actually a steep bank. The thump threw my mate out of the left-hand seat like a cork from a bottle. He was lucky. He landed on a mound of loose sand left behind by workmen, shaken but unhurt. In my case the steering wheel rammed me back into the seat and when the car rolled, eight times, several things happened.

My left hand, being on top of the steering wheel, hit the road on the first roll and was crushed. The steel-framed windscreen was snapped off and came back into my mouth. The MG came to rest on its wheels with the driver slumped in the seat in a bit of a mess.

By luck the accident happened right outside the house of the village policeman. He woke, peered out and down from the top of the bank, saw the wreck and called an ambulance, which came out from King's Lynn Cottage Hospital.

One of the paramedics found a severed ear in the road, held it up and asked: 'Be this yours?' as if detached ears were to be found all over west Norfolk. My friend, still dizzy on his sandpile, says I replied quite calmly:

'Yes, put it in a dish.' I then passed out into a coma for three days. The ambulance rushed me to Emergency where the first glance by the night-duty sister caused her to think I would not survive till morning. Then the luck set in.

The cottage hospital was not a major unit. It mainly handled domestic and agricultural accidents, plus births and winter chills. On that night Matron was summoned from her bed and began to call in a few favours. The near-body in Emergency was stripped of clothing and X-rayed as a team of four was assembled.

There was a triangular hole in the skull on the left side with the bone fragment embedded inside. A junior surgeon on the staff managed to retrieve the triangle of bone and draw it back into the aperture where it was supposed to be. Then he bandaged it and hoped it would knit back. It did.

A Dr Bannerjee worked on the ear. This was long before micro-surgery. He put it back where it should have been, sutured the meat back into place and hoped the blood vessels and nerves would find each other and reconnect. Miraculously they did. Apart from some puckering, the ear has worked perfectly well ever since.

A Mr Laing, a dental surgeon roused from his bed, worked on the mouth. All five of the top row front teeth had been smashed out and even the roots were in bits. He plucked out every last fragment and sewed the gums closed, leaving tendrils of thread hanging down like something from a horror movie. But the big problem was the left hand. It was pulp.

It just happened that two years earlier one of the finest orthopaedic surgeons in England, after a long and prestigious career in the London teaching hospitals, had retired to his native Norfolk and settled in a village a few miles away. He had met Matron and suggested that, although he was fully retired, if she ever had a really bad one she could call him. That night she did. I believe he was called Mr North. He too left his bed and came to the emergency ward.

He would have been perfectly entitled, I was told afterwards, to amputate at the wrist. Another surgeon told me later, after seeing the X-rays, that he would have done so. That would have been the unchallengeable decision – a clean, thirty-minute removal of what was left of the hand. The alternative was risky. The trauma was so bad that the young driver could easily die on the slab rather than take a six-hour operation. But he took the risk.

Through the night, as the anaesthetist constantly checked the life-signs, the surgeon plucked out the tiny fragments and chips of bone and rebuilt the knuckles and metacarpals. He finished around sunrise. His patient was still breathing. Then he had a cup of tea and drove home.

It was three days later that I finally drifted out of a coma. The head was a large ball of bandages, the mouth a gaping hole with no front teeth. The left hand was a globe of plaster of Paris hung up in the air. My haggard father and mother were sitting beside the bed where they had been for two days. Matron was standing on the other side.

The big worry was that brain damage might have reduced me to a vegetable. But it seems I answered a few simple questions logically, then drifted away for another two days.

Fit young people have amazing powers of recuperation. I was out of commission for about three weeks. The black eyes subsided, the bone fragment in the side of the head resealed itself and hair began to grow on it. The stitches came out of the gums and the ear reattached. Only the left hand was still a globe of plaster. Finally Mr North came back and the plaster was removed.

The hand was still there, uninfected, moving slowly when bidden. Eventually, under the scars, the grip would return but never quite strong enough to hold a golf club again. But a lot better than a stump. Mr Laing came back to assure me that a dental plate would give me a better smile than the one before. Dr Bannerjee was too shy to return to be thanked for his amazing work on the ear. Mr North would accept nothing from my father save a redecoration of the nurses' hostel, which was accomplished. I remain grateful to them all, though, as I was then twenty-one, I doubt any can still be alive.

While I lay in convalescence I was moved from intensive

care to a general ward and found myself next to a middle-aged man recovering from a minor operation. We got talking, as side-by-side patients do, and something very strange took place.

He told me he was a tailor and very diffidently mentioned that he 'used to read palms'. I had no confidence in that sort of thing but was intrigued by the phrase 'used to'. He explained that he had stopped after a nerve-jolting experience. He had agreed to do his fortune-telling hocus-pocus at a village fête.

One of his visitors was a local pillar of the community: wealthy, happily married, healthy, worry-free. Yet in his palm was the unmistakable forecast of his imminent death. He (the narrator beside me) was so horrified he invented a 'fortune' for the man, who left his tent in high good humour.

But the palmist was sufficiently distressed by what he had seen that he went to the vicar and told him. The priest was both horrified and offended, excoriating the palmist and ordering him never to do anything like that again. Two days later the local notable went to the gun room of his large manor house, took a 12-bore shotgun and blew his head off. The palmist beside me said he had never told a fortune since.

Of course, it was like a red rag to a bull. I pestered him until he relented. He wanted my left hand but that was still swathed in bandages. So he studied the less adequate right hand instead. Then he told me what he saw.

I am still unconvinced about this sort of thing. A journalist ought to be a natural sceptic anyway. But I can only report what he said.

He started with my background: birth, family, father's occupation, schooling, the languages, the travels so far, the flying, the lust to see the world, in fact the lot. But I convinced myself he could have learned all this from the staff by cunning questioning. Then he embarked on the future from 1960 onwards.

He told me about successes and dangers, triumphs and failures, advances and reverses, wars and horrors, material success and wealth, marriages and sons. And more or less when and how and where I would leave this planet.

And so far, over fifty-five years, he has been almost completely accurate. Not unnaturally I am quite curious about the next and last ten years.

Two years later I took the final exam. I believe I came second in England for that year. I know little of the chap who came first, save that he was from the north of England and chose to remain with his provincial newspaper. I had other ideas.

I had just turned twenty-three; it was autumn 1961. I was heading for London and for Fleet Street, the capital of British journalism, and I still intended to become a foreign correspondent and see the world.

Fleet Street

I HAD NOT THE haziest idea which newspaper I wished to join when I took that train down from King's Lynn to London in October 1961. I toyed with the idea of the *Daily Express* because my father had taken it when I was a boy, but I had no inside contacts and no introductions, so I just started at the top end of Fleet Street, near the Law Courts, and began walking. I entered and applied for a job at every press organ I came to.

That was when I discovered Fleet Street was a fortress. It did not seem to want any extra reporters and certainly not this one. Walking up to the front desk and asking to see the editor was entirely the wrong tactic. The very idea of penetrating the front hall without a confirmed appointment was out of the question.

There were forms to fill in but pretty clearly they were going to be 'binned' as soon as I disappeared out the front door and back on to the street. I had reached the great black-and-chrome edifice of the *Daily Express* by lunch hour. There was not much point in going in until the editorial staff returned from their liquid lunches. Journalism then had a reputation for heavy smoking and heavy drinking. I repaired for a sandwich and a pint of ale to the Cheshire Cheese pub. It was standing room only.

When the crowd thinned out a bit I took a stool at the bar and thought things over. I was still on the staff of the *Eastern Daily Press*; I still had my tiny flat. I had my return ticket in my pocket. Then the old luck held.

He was sitting down the bar in the now almost empty room, middle-aged, clutching his pint mug, puffing away and staring at me but with a kindly expression.

'You're looking down in the dumps, lad,' he said.

I shrugged. 'Trying to get a job,' I said.

'Any inside contacts?'

'Nope.'

He whistled. 'Off the street? Not a chance. They don't take walk-ins. Any interviews yet?'

'Nope.'

'Any experience?'

'Three years, *Eastern Daily Express*.' I added 'Norfolk' in case he did not know, but I had hit a million-to-one lucky shot.

'I trained with the *EDP*,' he said. 'Long time ago. Which office? Norwich?'

'King's Lynn. Under Frank Keeler.'

He nearly dropped his pint.

'Frank? Is he still there? We were juniors together. Just after the war.'

He held out his hand. We shook and exchanged names. He worked across the road, a veteran of the PA, heading for retirement. The Press Association was and remains the leading news agency in London. I had not thought of an agency, but so what? He led me across the street to the huge grey granite building housing the PA and a range of other companies. Without any ceremony he walked into the office of the editor-in-chief.

Mr Jarvis leaned back in his swivel chair and surveyed the new offering his colleague had brought in. It was difficult to make eye contact because the lenses of his glasses were as if cut from the bases of shot-glass whisky tumblers. There were two eyes behind there somewhere and a very broad Lancashire accent. He gave me the same interrogation as his colleague from the pub.

Age? Where from? National Service? Journalistic training? Any other useful qualifications? I mentioned four languages. He stared fixedly, then said:

'Thee's on wrong floor, lad.'

He took his phone, dialled a number and spoke to whoever answered.

'Doon? I think I've got a live one. He's not for me, I've got no vacancies. But he might be for you. Four languages. I'll send him up.'

I was led to the lift, said goodbye and thank you to the man I had met only an hour earlier and, as instructed, went up two floors. There was a man not much older than me waiting. He led me through swinging doors and down a corridor, knocked and showed me in.

Doon Campbell was news editor of Reuters, a name so prestigious I had not even thought of it. Not just a few foreign correspondents but an entire agency dedicated to foreign news, reported from their myriad bureaux all over the world. He was actually a very kindly man but his first, deliberate, impression was of a no-nonsense sergeant-major. Though he had lived and worked in London for many years, his accent might have come out of the Highlands of Scotland last week. The interrogation was like facing a machine gun. Finally he asked:

'Foreign affairs. Do you study foreign affairs?'

I said I did as best I could from papers, radio and TV. And that I knew France, Germany and Spain, with visits to Malta, Cyprus and Lebanon. He leaned forward, his face close to mine, and snapped:

'Where is Bujumbura?'

A day earlier I would not have had a clue. But on the train down from King's Lynn I had finished both the papers I had bought on the station and spotted a copy of a magazine folded into the cushions of the seat opposite, abandoned by a previous traveller. It was the American magazine *Time*.

I flicked through it and in the centre was a feature about the Belgian protectorates of Rwanda and Burundi, far away in central Africa. Luck again. I also leaned forward until we were almost nose to nose.

'Why, Mr Campbell, it's the capital of Burundi.' He leaned slowly back. So did I.

'Aye. Aye. So it is. All right, I'll give you a three-month trial. When can you start?'

I knew I would get no Brownie points for walking out on the *EDP* without notice, so I told him I would need to work out my month and could join Reuters in December. He nodded dismissively and that was that. I had landed a slot in the world's best-regarded agency for foreign news by a series of flukes. I left King's Lynn a month later and moved to a tiny flatlet in Shepherd Market, whence a Number 9 bus would bring me to Fleet Street in twenty minutes.

Reuters started me in the London editorial desk, charged with covering stories of interest only to foreign newspapers far away. In May I got my break.

The deputy chief of the Paris bureau was diagnosed with a heart murmur and had to be flown home without delay. The British National Health Service was free and the French was not. A head poked round the door of the Home Reporters' room and asked: 'Anyone here speak French?'

I was led to the French-language service whose chief was a real Frenchman called Maurice. My guide asked him:

'Does this fellow really speak French?'

Maurice was bent over his typewriter and without looking up asked in French: 'What do you reckon to the situation in Paris?'

It was back then in a state of crisis. It had just been revealed that President de Gaulle had for months been secretly negotiating with the Algerian resistance at Vichy and had fixed 1 July 1963 for a French pull-out from the disastrous Algerian independence war and Algerian independence for the same day. The French extreme-right and elements of the elite of the army had declared war on de Gaulle personally. France stood on the verge of coup d'état or revolution.

I let Maurice have a torrent of French complete with a brace of slang expressions that a pretend-speaker would never have known. Maurice had served with the Free French in the war, based at first in London with de Gaulle, then fighting his way across his own homeland as it was liberated under Marshal Juin. But he had married an English girl and settled in London. He stopped typing and looked up.

'You're French-born, right?'

'Non, monsieur, completely English.'

He switched his gaze to the man beside me and dropped back into English.

'Better get him over there. I've never heard a Rosbif talk like that.'

My flatlet was on a weekly rent. Living in London I had given up my car. My possessions were one valise and a haversack. I had no ties. I phoned my parents in Kent and was on the morning flight to Paris. A new chapter was opening that would eventually, and totally unforeseeably, lead to a book called *The Day of the Jackal*.

Paris Aflame

THE SITUATION I HAD tried to analyse to Maurice in London was no exaggeration. The uprising against the authoritarian Charles de Gaulle was highly dangerous.

For six years the Algerians under the FLN had been fighting for independence, getting ever stronger and more dangerous. Successive French governments had poured men, arms and wealth into the war, with accompanying cruelties on both sides that were pretty hair-raising. Many French soldiers had died and the mood in France was split down the middle.

In 1958 de Gaulle, who had retired in 1947, or so it was presumed, was recalled as prime minister and the following year was elected president. In his campaign he had used the magic words: 'Algérie Française'. Algeria is French. So the army and the right-wing worshipped him. A few weeks into office as premier he realized the situation was hopeless. France was being bled white in a war it could not win. As president he began secret negotiations to end it. When that news broke it was like a nuclear explosion.

In Algeria vital sections of the army mutinied and marched into exile, taking their weapons with them. Five generals went with them. These were not the raw recruits but the Foreign Legion and the Paras (Airborne), the cream of the cream. The numerical bulk, the military service inductees, wanted to come home so they stayed loyal to Paris. But hundreds of French civilians, settled in Algeria, realizing they would be thrown out or at least dispossessed by a new Algerian government, threw in their lot with the rebels, who called themselves the Secret Armed Organization or OAS. Their aim: assassinate de Gaulle, topple his regime and install the hard-right.

The Paris into which I landed that May 1962 was in turmoil. The biggest communist party in Europe, west of the Iron Curtain, was French, completely loyal to Moscow, which had been arming and funding the Algerians. Hard-left students marched and clashed violently on the streets of Paris with those supporting the right. Plastic bombs exploded in cafés and restaurants.

Between the warring sides was the newly formed anti-riot police, the CRS, whose methods were not gentle. Almost every street corner featured a couple of them demanding identity papers, as in a city under occupation. Surrounding de Gaulle's person and keeping him alive were two forces: the Action Service of the counter-intelligence arm, and his personal squad of four bodyguards, backed by the Gendarmerie Nationale. For a young foreign correspondent it was some baptism and the peak of all the possible postings.

On arrival I reported to the bureau chief, the formidable Harold King. He was a legend. Born German, he had fought in the First World War, but for the kaiser. He emigrated to Britain and naturalized. In 1940 he was Reuters' man in Moscow, following the Red Army deep into Poland, before being repatriated to London. Then he followed the Free French into France and became utterly convinced of the claims and policies of Charles de Gaulle. After the liberation he told Reuters he would head up the Paris Bureau or quit. He got Paris.

When de Gaulle resigned in disgust in 1947 he was presumed to be gone for ever. Only Harold King, like a Jacobite waiting for the return of the king, insisted de Gaulle would one day return to lead France back to glory, and until it all came true in 1958 King was indulgently regarded as a fantasist. Now in 1962 he was the king (literally) of the Paris foreign press corps. His loyalty to de Gaulle was quietly rewarded with tip-off after tip-off.

I walked into his office to confront a burly man in his early sixties, glasses perched high on forehead like accusatory headlights. He was writing and with one hand gestured that I sit until he was finished. I had been warned about him in London. He was regarded by few with liking, by many with fear, and had a reputation for eating young journalists for breakfast and spitting out the pips. Quite a few in London had been sent back within days of arrival and hated him.

He finished writing, roared for a copy boy to take his folios to the telex machine, turned his chair to face me, thrust his spectacles even higher on his forehead where he mostly wore them and glared at me. Then the interrogation began. This was the ritual that could lead to rejection and a flight back to London. Strangely, he took to me and I became his protégé.

I think the unusual reaction was based on two factors. He perked up when told I had actually volunteered for the RAF instead of fighting to stay out of military service, and then got my wings on Vampires. The other factor was that, while never short of respectful, I declined to be browbeaten. Beneath the gruff exterior he hated crawlers.

After an hour he glanced at his watch and asked:

'Do you eat?'

'Yes, Mr King, I do.'

Without further ado, he rose and lumbered out of the office. I followed. He had a Citroën at the door, with his loyal driver at the wheel, a perk he insisted on or he would resign. He growled 'André' or something at the driver, who set off and deposited us at a restaurant called Chez André, clearly a favourite and a regular lunch hole. He was welcomed in and bowed to his regular table.

A new sommelier shimmied up and proposed a bottle of white wine to start with. He raised his specs back to his fore-head, stared at the waiter as one contemplating a boll weevil and growled: '*Jeune homme, le vin est rouge.*'

(Young man, wine is red.) He was right, of course. Wine is red and the other stuff is juice with or without bubbles.

He did not order because the staff knew what he would have. He listened to me order in French and then asked me how I had learned it. Spending schoolboy holidays in the depths of the Limousin, in La France Profonde or Deep France, seemed to please him.

Back then French lunches lasted nearly three hours. We strolled back into the office at close to four. I did not know it but I had been, in a way, adopted, and the friendship lasted until he died. The mentoring that Frank Keeler had started in King's Lynn Harold King completed in Paris, upholding Reuters' house style of rigorous accuracy and complete impartiality

– even though he was very partial to Charles de Gaulle and the compliment was constantly repaid. He was the only Britisher the French autocrat had any time for.

Because I was the youngest and the most junior, and a single man with no family to hurry home to, Harold King gave me a rather unusual assignment. It was to shadow Charles de Gaulle every time he left the Elysée Palace. I was not the only one.

There was an international corps of media people in permanent attendance, tagging along behind his DS 19 Citroën saloon every time he had some journey to make outside the presidential mansion on the Faubourg St-Honoré. He knew exactly what we were there for. It was not to cover his visit to the Senate or whatever. It was for that cataclysmic moment when he was assassinated. He knew and he did not give a damn. He despised his enemies and he despised danger. He just shoved his beak of a nose even higher and stalked through.

Whenever his motorcade stopped for whatever function he was attending, the press group split into two and found cafés in which to while away the waiting time. In one group were the British, Americans, Canadians, Nordics, Germans and all those whose common language was English.

In the other group were the French-speakers – French, Belgians, Swiss and a couple of Québécois. And me. We were often joined by de Gaulle's personal bodyguards, or the pair on duty that day. That was how I got to know Roger Tessier, the Parisian, Henri D'Jouder, the Kabyle from Algeria, and Paul Comiti, the Corsican. I forget the fourth.

Listening to their chitchat and noting the concentric rings of security around the President of France, I became increasingly convinced the OAS would not succeed. There was a large file on every one of them – ex-army mutineers and civilian 'pieds-noirs' from Algeria. Their faces, fingerprints and records were intimately known.

It also became plain – and the security detail was extra-ordinarily loose-lipped – that the OAS was so penetrated by counter-intelligence agents that they could hardly have a four-man conference without their entire conspiracy being quickly blown because one of those present was a grass.

It seemed to me that the only way the OAS would get a bullet through those rings of protection might be if they could find and commission a complete outsider, a professional hitman with no record or dossier known to Paris. Later I would create such a man and call him the Jackal. But that was then. I never really thought to write such a story. So I never told anyone. It was just an idea.

The small flat I had taken on my meagre salary was in walking distance of the office but in the 9th Arrondissement, home of the Moulin Rouge and Folies Bergère, Place Blanche, Montmartre and the maze of streets containing hundreds of smaller cabarets and late-night bars. The 9th was the red-light district and home to much of the 'milieu', the city's criminal underworld. Being kept awake by the wailing of police sirens was extremely common.

OAS sympathizers also frequented the bars of the 9th, and so did I. This was largely because the second day-shift at the office ended at 10 p.m. and I did not need or wish to sleep until well after midnight. So I nursed a beer, stared vacantly at the wall and listened. That gave me some knowledge of de Gaulle's deadly enemies.

I also developed my 'Bertie Wooster mode', an adopted

persona based on P.G. Wodehouse's witless hero: helpless, well-meaning, affable but dim as a five-watt bulb. Affecting to speak little French and with the usual appalling British accent, I was assumed by both bar staff and customers not to understand what they were talking about. The reverse was the case. In the years to come Bertie would get me out of a lot of trouble. This is because the harmless fool with a British passport is what Europeans want to see and believe.

It was a Friday evening in August when the OAS came closest to killing de Gaulle and it was at a roundabout in the outer suburb of Petit Clamart. He was heading from the Elysée Palace to an airbase called Villacoublay, from where a helicopter awaited him to take him and Madame Yvonne de Gaulle across France to their country home in the east: a mansion called La Boisserie in the village of Colombey-les-deux-Eglises.

The couple was in the back of his speeding DS 19. Up front were Gendarmerie driver Francis Marroux and the president's son-in-law. The dozen assassins had learned his precise route and were waiting in a side street. They missed because de Gaulle was late, dusk had come early that 22 August, the convoy was doing close to 90mph and they did not see it until too late. They were going to erupt from the side street, run the limousine off the road and finish off the inhabitants with submachine-gun fire.

They were too late. As the two motorcycle outriders screamed past, they opened up with full-deflection shots on the speeding car, 120 shots in all. Twelve passed through the car but failed to stop it. One passed within an inch of the famous nose.

De Gaulle rammed his wife's head into his lap but remained

ramrod upright. Marroux nearly lost control. Swerved, recovered and drove on. The follow-up car full of armed guards did the same. At Villacoublay the DS 19 slewed to a halt on shredded tyres beside the presidential helicopter amid a cluster of panicking air force officers – word had been radioed ahead.

A pretty shattered Mme Yvonne was helped into the 'copter. De Gaulle emerged, shook shards of glass from the lapel of his Savile Row suit (the only British thing he would have about him) and gave his verdict.

'*Ils ne savant pas tirer,*' he sniffed. They can't shoot straight.

Word reached central Paris about midnight. I and the rest of the press horde got out there and spent the remainder of the night interviewing, observing and filing stories from local pay-phones. Europe's newspapers had already 'gone to bed' but an agency works twenty-four hours a day so there was no rest for AP, UPI, AFP or Reuters.

That October saw the Cuba missile crisis, a hyper-tense four days when it really looked as if the world might come to thermo-nuclear war and be wiped out. To be fair to de Gaulle, rightly described as no admirer of the USA since his blazing rows in the war with General Eisenhower, he was the first in Europe to ring Washington and pledge his total support for John F. Kennedy.

I had turned twenty-four and in January attended the now-famous press conference in the Elysée when de Gaulle vetoed the British application to join the European Economic Community. It was a huge slap in the face to British premier Harold Macmillan who, in Algeria in the Second World War, had 'pushed' de Gaulle's claims to be the sole leader of the Free French.

His conferences were no press conferences at all. He simply planted five questions with five ultra-loyal senior pressmen in the audience, memorized the speech he intended to make in reply and also memorized the placements of the five so-called questioners, because he could not see them.

Harold King was in the front, awarded a question to ask. There were of course no laptops or mobile phones. The Reuters chief would scribble his press story on a notepad on his knee, tear the pages off and give them to a runner from his office. The job of the runner was to pelt to the back of the hall and give them to another colleague, who was holding a phone line open to the office.

He would dictate the story to yet another colleague sitting with headphones in the office typing furiously, and he would give the sheets to the telex operator who would send them to London. I was the runner.

I recall the old buzzard peering down in curiosity at the young Englishman crouched below his podium. Because of his extreme myopia I was about the only person in the room he could actually see and he clearly did not know what I was doing there. In public he was too vain to wear glasses.

His short-sightedness led to several amusing incidents, at one of which I was present. He was on a provincial tour, always against the frantic advice of his security staff, and he had a further habit that drove them mad with worry. All statesmen do it nowadays but back then I think he invented it.

He would suddenly lean forward, tap the shoulder of his driver and order him to stop. Then he would climb out and walk straight into the crowd, shaking hands and playing the friend of the common people. Today it is 'pressing

Ready . . . Here I am in the garden in Ashford aged three in the early war years. RAF Hawkinge and its Spitfires were just down the road (*bottom*).

Steady . . . With my mother and father. My father was a major in the army during the war, but as a member of the fire brigade he was not allowed to go on active service overseas.

Go . . . Off to Bluebell Hill aged sixteen on my second-hand Vespa and then up into the clouds. The knife in my sock came in handy later when I found myself in a tight spot in Paris.

Thanks to my father's efforts, I spent the school holidays abroad learning how to speak French and German like a native. Here I am with Herr and Frau Dewald and their children (*above left*). It was while I was staying with them that I was introduced to Hanna Reitsch (*above right*), Hitler's favourite aviatrix.

Tonbridge School (*left and below*) was not much fun; this is the farewell assembly in Big School in 1952. I hung on until December 1955. At least I had the satisfaction of saying goodbye from the cockpit of a Tiger Moth.

The RAF at seventeen. Heady stuff: flying Vampires in formation. I am number 15 (*above left and right*). Eleven of us made it to the end (*left*). I am second from the right in the back row. Here I am getting my wings (*below left*). I had never been more proud. I was a pilot in the RAF.

To King's Lynn, to work on the *Eastern Daily Press*. I lived in a flat above a pet shop at the far end of the ironically named Paradise Parade (**left**). My mentor, chief reporter Frank Keeler (**right**), taught me the importance of checking facts before you write. Then to Reuters in London where Doon Campbell (**far right**) was news editor and the inspiration for generations of foreign correspondents.

A lucky break sent me off to Paris just in time for the assassination attempt on President Charles de Gaulle in August 1962. He is in the back of the car with his wife, Yvonne, in a reconstruction of the event (**left**). Bullets riddled the body of the Citroën (**right**), and newspaper men rushed to the scene as darkness fell (**far right**).

Nobody lasted much longer than a year in Berlin. I was there from September 1963 to October 1964 and lived on the eastern side of Checkpoint Charlie (**left**). Kurt Blecha was Press Secretary to the Politburo, a nasty piece of work (**right**). When an American spy plane was shot down just outside Magdeburg, I was the first journalist on the scene and managed to get an eye-witness account from a local. The three airmen (see two of them **far right**) had been captured by the Russians.

I joined the BBC in 1965, full of enthusiasm – misplaced as it turned out – and in 1967 was sent to Nigeria to cover what turned out to be one of the cruellest African civil wars. Sir David Hunt (*above left*) was the British High Commissioner in Lagos, a snob and a racist. Colonel Yakubu Gowon (*above right*), a Christian from the north, was the puppet head of state. I went to Enugu and met Colonel Emeka Ojukwu (*below*), an Oxford graduate and military governor of Iboland, who had presided over the declaration of the independent state of Biafra in May 1967.

Soon posters were appearing in Enugu warning of the threat of war (**top**). I was with Ojukwu (**right**) when his soldiers advanced unopposed over the bridge at Onitsha; later they were forced to retreat and blew up the bridge behind them (**above**).

Having terminated my unhappy relationship with the BBC, I visited Israel in the aftermath of the Six-Day War. I went to a kibbutz at Sde Boker in the Negev desert to meet David Ben-Gurion (**top**), founding father of the state of Israel, one of the greatest men I have ever met. I was also anxious to meet Ezer Weizman, one of the first pilots in the Israeli Air Force. Here he is in 1948 with one of his Czech-produced Messerschmitts, the Avia S-199 (**above**).

A chance meeting in a bar led me to the story of the man who drove the truck carrying the explosives that blew up the King David Hotel on 22 July 1946 (**left**).

the flesh'. He called it the *bain de foule*, the bath in the crowd.

On one occasion, as his bodyguards sought desperately to keep up, he plunged on deeper and deeper into the mass, then saw a short, expressionless man in front of him. He seized the fellow's hand and pumped it firmly. Then he moved on. A few yards further, the same man. He did it again. The problem was that more than a yard away a face became a blur. The third time he did it the man reached up and hissed in his ear:

'Monsieur le President, will you please stop doing that. That is my f—ing gun hand.'

It was Paul Comiti, his Corsican bodyguard, who was unable to go for the shooter under his left armpit if anything happened.

The previous March had seen the execution by firing squad of Col. Jean-Marie Bastien-Thiry, the leader of the Petit Clamart attempt, but the OAS did not give up. There were at least three more attempts and they all failed. One involved a bomb under a pile of workmen's sand beside a country road. It failed to explode because it had rained the previous night and the would-be killers had not thought to tarpaulin the explosives.

A second involved a sniper high above the parade ground at the Ecole Militaire where de Gaulle was presiding over a passing-out parade. The intelligence people were tipped off. The sniper, Georges Watin, the Limper, escaped to South America.

A final one had an earthenware jar of geraniums containing a bomb next to a war memorial de Gaulle was due to unveil. In a scene straight from the Pink Panther movies, a kindly gardener, fearing they might wilt, gave them a good hosing and fused the detonator.

In the late summer of 1963, Harold King summoned me, clearly not in a good mood. What had I done wrong? Nothing.

'They want to give you East Berlin, the buggers,' he growled. He meant Head Office in London. East Berlin was a peach of an assignment: a one-man office covering East Germany, Czechoslovakia and Hungary.

Since the building of the now-infamous Berlin Wall in 1961, East Germany had become a pariah state, an outcast from the West. No embassy, consulate or trade mission. If anything went wrong in the harshest of all the Soviet satellites, there would be no back-up, no support at all.

When the Wall went up, all East German presence in the West was expelled, including the East German news agency ADN, which had an office in the Reuters building. East Berlin responded by doing the same, expelling all Western papers and agencies – except one. The Politburo might feed lying rubbish to their own people, but at the top they wanted to know what was really going on. So they retained one Reuters man, with the condition that he had to live in East Berlin and, if visiting West Berlin, be back through Checkpoint Charlie by midnight. No commuting to the office to work and then going West to spend the night.

'I suppose you're going to take it,' grumbled Mr King.

'If you had just turned twenty-five, wouldn't you?' I asked.

'Too bloody right, I would,' he said, then took me out for a slap-up lunch.

Later in September I packed my traps, had a week's leave with my folks in Kent and left by train for Paris and Berlin. Most of the passengers alighted when it stopped in West

Berlin. I remained seated and watched the Wall drift beneath as the train rolled into the communist East.

At the Ostbahnhof station I disembarked and the man I was replacing, Jack Altman, was there to greet me. He had had a year of it and was yearning to get the hell out.

He had a car, which I would take over, and a spacious flat-cum-office in the Schönhauser Allee, which I would also inhabit. After lunch he took me to meet the hatchet-faced officials with whom I would have to deal. I noticed that he spoke good German but would never pass for one. In front of officialdom I made heavy weather of vocabulary and grammar, and affected a clumsy accent. I noticed the officials relaxed at that. This one would be no problem.

He introduced me to the office secretary, Fräulein Erdmute Behrendt, an East German lady who clearly would also be under constant surveillance by the police and the SSD, the formidable Stasi. Two days later he was gone.

Big Brother

I T TAKES TIME to accustom oneself to being under surveillance morning, noon and night. Some people are badly unsettled to know that their office and apartment is heavily bugged; to see the figures in long raincoats pretending to be window-shopping on the streets as they follow you around; to watch the black car with darkened windows moving into position in the rear-view mirror on the highway.

My own recourse was to take it as light-heartedly as possible, to realize that even the goons coming up behind are human beings, albeit only just, and we all have a job to do.

It did not take long to find the main bug in my office. There was a television, a four-valve model that happened to have five. When I removed the fifth there was a television repair man on the doorstep within an hour. Before answering the bell I replaced the fifth valve, then went to make a coffee in the kitchen while he fiddled inside the cabinet. A very puzzled technician left an hour later with profuse apologies for the disturbance.

Opposite the office was an apartment block and right opposite my own windows a single black aperture, which was never closed and whose lights never came on. The poor mutts sitting beside their telescope must have nearly frozen to death in winter when the night temperature went down to ten below. At Christmas I sent over a bottle of good Scotch whisky and a carton of Rothmans king-size, asking the concierge to send them up to the number I figured had to correspond to the window. That night there was a brief flicker from a butane lighter, and that was all. But it was not all fun and games, and yanking the tiger's tail needed a bit of caution.

One of the nastiest pieces of work in the regime was the press secretary to the Politburo, a certain Kurt Blecha. He had perhaps the falsest smile on earth. But I knew a few things about Master Blecha. One was his birthday and another was that in the Thirties he had been a red-hot member of the Nazi Party.

Captured in 1943 on the Eastern Front he had taken no time to convert to Communism, being plucked from the freezing prisoner-of-war camp and installed in the retinue of exiled German communist leader Walter Ulbricht. Blecha returned with the communist veteran on the tails of the Red Army in 1945 to become part of the puppet government, the most slavish of all the satellite regimes.

At Christmas, Easter and on his birthday I sent him an anonymous greeting card at his office. It was bought in East Berlin but typed on a machine in the West Berlin office of Reuters, in case my own machine was checked. It wished him all best, with his Nazi Party membership number writ large, and purporting to come from 'your old and faithful Kamaraden'. I never saw him open them but I hope they worried the hell out of him.

I also learned how to shake the Stasi tail. As the Reuters

correspondent I was allowed through Checkpoint Charlie into West Berlin but the secret police tail was not. They always pulled over to the kerb as I approached the barrier. Once through, I could race down the Kurfürstendamm, from there to the Heerstraße and on to the border leading back into the republic of East Germany at DreiLinden.

It was sometimes thought in the West that Berlin was a border city between East and West. Not so; it was buried eighty miles inside East Germany, with West Berlin surrounded on all sides. Head west out of West Berlin through the Drei Linden crossing point and you were on the autobahn to West Germany, which was also allowed. Once on it I could leave the autobahn at the first off-ramp and disappear into the countryside. With a set of shabby local clothes and an East Berlin–registered Wartburg car, eating at roadside halts and sleeping in the car, I could stay off radar for a couple of days.

There were good stories to be had once outside the cage. In theory everyone was so happy in the workers' paradise that there could not be any dissent to report. The truth was that resentment among workers and students seethed under the surface, occasionally breaking out in strikes and student marches – always short-lived and punished as the Volkspolizei, the People's Police, known as VoPos, struck back.

On returning I would be summoned immediately to the office of Kurt Blecha who hid his rage behind his smile.

'Where have you been, Herr Forsyth? We were worried about you,' was his unconvincing ploy. They felt forced to maintain the fiction that I was free to go anywhere I wanted in their peace-loving freedom-state and being followed was out of the question.

When asked for an explanation, I claimed I was a keen student of church architecture and had been visiting and admiring some of the ecclesiastical gems in East Germany. Back at the flat I had books to prove it. Blecha assured me this was a highly laudable pastime but the next time I left would I please tell them so that they could make introductions?

We neither of us believed a word of it, but I kept playing the bumbling ass and he kept beaming his crocodile smile. As for my filed stories of unrest among the supposedly content proletariat, if the regime wondered where I got them from, I let them wonder.

I arrived in East Berlin in early October. In late November the world was hit by a thunderbolt.

The Death of Kennedy

IT IS SAID that everyone on earth alive at the time recalls where they were and what they were doing when news came through that President John F. Kennedy had been assassinated.

I happened to be dining in West Berlin with a stunning German girl called Annette. We were at the Paris Bar, just round the corner from the Reuters office. It was full and behind the clatter and chatter there was muzak playing. Out of nowhere it stopped and an urgent-sounding voice barked:

'*Wir unterbrechen unser Programm für eine wichtige Meldung: auf den Präsidenten Kennedy wurde geschossen.*'

There was a brief lull in the conversation as the muzak resumed. It must have been a glitch in the music system. A mistake, a joke. Then the voice came back.

'*Wir unterbrechen unser Programm für eine wichtige Meldung: auf den Präsidenten Kennedy wurde geschossen.*'

Then the world went crazy.

Men stood up and swore repeatedly, women screamed. Tables were overturned. Kennedy had been there in June, speaking at the Wall. It is hard to describe to those who came later how he was hero-worshipped, and in this city of all cities. For me there was one priority above all: get back to the office and seek to discover East Germany's official reaction. I threw a handful of West Marks on the table, ran for the car and drove through a panicking city to the Wall and Checkpoint Charlie.

The checkpoint was in the American sector of the four-power-divided city and in their glass booth the GIs were bowed over their radio. You could have driven a herd of buffalo past them and they would not have noticed. The American barrier was up as always. I drove past it and swerved to the East German control sheds. They too had heard.

The East German border guards were the hardest of the hard and politically proof-tested before they got the posting. If needed, they would machine-gun anyone trying to climb the Wall to escape to the West.

The story was still recent of Peter Fechter, an eighteen-year-old student who had got through the minefield and was halfway up the Wall when the searchlights found him. He was hit by a burst of fire from a watch tower. No one wanted to go through the mines to get him down. In sight of the West Berliners, he hung there on the barbed wire, screaming until he bled out and died.

The only good news about that awful night in 1963 was to see these brutes bleating with panic. They surrounded my car asking: '*Herr Forsyth, wird das Krieg bedeuten?*' Will this mean war?

It was 2 p.m. in Dallas, 8 p.m. in London and 9 p.m. in Berlin when the news came through, 10 p.m. when I went through Charlie. All examinations of my car and my papers were waived. I got back to the office in record time and checked the incoming tapes. That probably made me the best informed person in East Berlin.

The media concentration was on a panicking America, but that fear was as nothing to the situation on the Iron Curtain. I rang the East German Foreign Ministry for a comment. They were fully awake with desks staffed but not knowing what to say until told by Moscow. So terrified voices were asking me, rather than the way it should have been.

The point about a communist state, or any dictatorship, is that independent media are out of the question. So despite denial after denial the authorities persisted in the myth that the Reuters man in their midst had some kind of a direct line to the British Government. On each of the two occasions I flew back to the UK during my year in East Berlin I was given earnest messages for the British Foreign Secretary, whom I had not the slightest intention of visiting, nor he me. When I said I was only going to visit my mum and dad, they tapped the sides of their noses and said: *Ja, ja*, we are men of the world. Wink, wink.

By mid-morning word was coming through that the assassin of Dallas was in handcuffs and an American Communist. The panic deepened. On the streets terrified passers-by glanced at the skies expecting to see the bombers of the Strategic Air Command heading east with their nukes. Then Jack Ruby shot and killed Lee Harvey Oswald right in the heart of a police station. If anything was possible to fuel the fires of conspiracy theory, it was that. And indeed the incompetence was pretty hard to believe.

But the USA kept its nerve. The vice-president took over and was sworn in. The bombers remained grounded. The panic slowly subsided to be replaced by grief as the TV pictures flashed up of the funeral with the riderless horse. When another shot showed a small boy saluting his father's catafalque, all Berlin, East and West, was in tears. Extraordinary times.

Christmas came. The two Berlins always reminded me of the fairy story of two hostelries, one ablaze with light, feasting, dancing and laughter; the other, across the street, dark and gloomy. So it was that first and, as it turned out, only Christmas for me.

West Berlin lived in a slightly hysterical mood all those years while the Wall stood, aware it could be snuffed out within a night if the order was given in Moscow, like a partygoer drinking in the Last Chance Saloon. That Christmas it let rip. The East Berliners did their best, but the contrast in prosperity of the two political and economic systems was stark.

It would be another twenty-six years before the Wall finally came down and two years later the Soviet Union simply imploded. But back then both events were simply inconceivable. Yet in all this greyness and gloom, beyond all the bugged apartments and phone calls, behind the headlights in the rear-view mirror, there was one lucky break for the Reuters man, of which I took the fullest advantage.

When East Berlin insisted on keeping the Reuters news service, a deal was struck. East Germany would have to pay 20 per cent of the subscription fee in desperately short, hard Western currency, 80 per cent in virtually worthless East Marks. These would be banked in East Berlin. Problem: they could not be exported or converted – at any exchange rate at all. But no one could stop them being spent – locally.

Before I left London to take up the post, the Reuters chief

Jerry Long explained all this to me and asked me with a straight face if I could try to reduce the blocked account, which stood at over a million East Marks. Even with the office costs and Miss Behrendt's salary, it just kept growing. With an equally straight face I promised to do what I could.

The problem was, there was almost nothing to buy. In communist solidarity, Cuba maintained a shop that sold superb cigars for East Marks. Cuban produce was banned in the USA but quite acceptable as a getting-to-know-you offering to an American officer in the West Berlin garrison.

Czechoslovakia produced high-quality long-playing records of classical music, and Hungary very good pigskin luggage. Both maintained a loss-making 'prestige' shop in East Berlin. Eventually even the East German border guards lightened up. They would say nothing about the cargoes going west in the boot of the Wartburg and I would say nothing when a sack of fresh oranges disappeared while I was in the customs shed on the way back. And there was the caviar.

Each Soviet satellite country maintained a prestige restaurant in East Berlin. There was a Haus Budapest with Hungarian cuisine, a Haus Sofia for Bulgaria and so on. The Haus Moskau served borscht, Stolichnaya vodka . . . and caviar. That first Christmas I really helped Reuters reduce its surplus Marks-pile with a mountain of Beluga and enough Stolly to ensure that all the bugs in my bedroom could record were the snores.

Helping Out the Cousins

SECRET POLICE FORCES reckon that two or three in the morning is the lowest point of the human spirit, when reactions are at their slowest. That was about the hour that the alarm went off on a certain morning in March 1964.

A direct phone line between the Reuters office in East Berlin and West Berlin or Bonn was forbidden. My colleagues could only contact me by telex, which of course the Stasi could monitor and which left a printed record they could read later in case a phone call was so quick it might be over before they woke up.

But in my office an alarm bell was fitted to summon me from bed to machine in an emergency. This was definitely an emergency. The Soviets had shot down an American plane outside Magdeburg.

The armed forces hate to have to ask the media for help, but US Air Force HQ at Wiesbaden, West Germany, was in quite a state. I punched out a quick ticker-tape asking for more details. While I waited I got dressed. So far as sleeping was concerned, the night was over.

What came back thirty minutes later made more sense. The

downed aircraft was an RB66, which I knew from my own air force time to be a twin-engined (jet) light bomber converted to photographic reconnaissance. Less politely put, a spy plane, gorged with long-lens cameras pointing down and sideways.

Its mission had been to patrol along the frontier, training angled cameras at something east of the border, inside East Germany. But in this case it had strayed over the border. Any promotion for the navigator was now highly problematic, though that was not his immediate problem.

There had been a quick panic call, then silence. Seconds later the 'blip' on the USAF's radar had vanished, around 10 p.m. At one thirty Wiesbaden asked Reuters if their man in East Berlin could find it. The reason they needed to know was the Four Power Treaty.

Under the terms of the treaty the Western Allies based in West Berlin had the right to send a patrol car into the Soviet Zone (now East Germany) provided they stated the exact destination. They could not just go a-roving. Without a precise location for their missing spook, they could not leave West Berlin. They also wanted news of the crew: alive, injured, dead, certainly in Soviet hands somewhere.

It was a needle in a haystack but the orders were clear. Get out there and find it. While waiting for my details I had packed a gunny sack with bread, cheese and two flasks of coffee, and written a hasty message for Fräulein Behrendt. Then I left in the Wartburg car for Checkpoint Charlie. As ever with the East Germans, speed was of the essence.

They were methodical and ponderous. They got there in the end but contrary to spy fiction they moved like snails. I suspect I was probably in West Berlin before the tail car had got back to the Normannenstraße HQ to prod the night-duty officer awake. Thirty minutes later I was out the other side of West Berlin on the westward autobahn and swerved off at the sign to Dessau. From there it was bleak, night-black farmland. I used my pocket compass to keep heading west along B-roads and winding lanes.

Dawn came and the country folk awoke while their city-dwelling masters slept on. The first to appear were farm workers. I stopped to ask if anyone had heard of a plane belonging to the 'Amis' (Americans) coming down nearby. I was completely ignored. At the third halt, instead of saying I was the press from Berlin (official and therefore government), I said 'from London'. Immediately the cooperation and helpfulness was unrestrained. I just flashed the British passport to prove my claim and they all tried to help. The denizens of the workers' paradise really hated the place.

At first no one had an inkling, then someone thought it was 'over there' – pointing west towards Magdeburg. A group of road workers told me there had been flames in the sky to the west and mentioned a small village, which I found on my road map.

As a watery sun hung over Potsdam behind me it became clear what the RB66 had been trying to photograph. Outside Magdeburg the Soviet army had mounted a huge war games manoeuvre ground. I found myself weaving between columns of Russian tanks, half-tracks, jeeps and trucks of infantry. With an East German-registered car I leaned out with a broad grin and gave them the V-sign. They responded with the same.

They did not realize that when the first two fingers of the right hand are raised with the palm towards the receiver, that is the Churchillian Victory sign. To the British, the other way round means 'Up yours'. Eventually I parked the Wartburg off the road on a sandy bank and set off through the pine forest on foot. Then I found my charcoal burner.

He was an old man, like something out of a Grimms' fairy tale. I thought he might have a gingerbread house round there somewhere. He considered my request carefully then nodded.

'Ja, it came down over there.' I walked to where he pointed and there it was. Nose down, tail up, most of its fuselage masked by the pine trees but with the tail fin jutting up to the sky. It had clearly been hit by air-to-air rockets and all its ejector seats had been used, so maybe the crew was alive. I marked its exact position and went back to the charcoal burner tending his heap of embers. He was perfectly calm, as one who had lived through two world wars and could cope with the occasional crashing bomber. He showed no nervousness about the authorities but was interested in my passport. I pointed out and translated the bit in the flyleaf where Her Britannic Majesty 'requests and requires' one and all to assist her subject as best they may. Then he spoke quite freely.

There were three crewmen, he said, though he had not seen the first two parachute into the forest. They had been taken prisoner by Russians in jeeps and were lodged in the Soviet army HQ in Magdeburg. His son-in-law, a baker who delivered early bread, had seen them in the jeeps.

The third and last out had landed near him and broken one leg. He was Dutch. No, I said, he was American. The old man tapped his chest on the left side. There was a tab saying 'Holland' and two silver bars on the epaulettes, he said. I recalled the US aircrew wear a name-tag on a white canvas patch, upper chest, left-hand side. So Captain Holland, the pilot of the falling spy plane, had ensured his two crewmen were out before ejecting at the last minute; he landed only two hundred yards from the wreck.

After thirty minutes with my new friend and having delighted him with a pack of Western cigarettes, a universal currency, I had it all. Then the luck ran out. I was stumbling back to where I left the car when I heard voices among the pine trees. I dropped to my knees in the undergrowth. Too late.

I heard a barked *Stoi* and saw a pair of serge combat trousers ahead of my face. An angry Mongoloid face was staring down at me. These Mongol regiments came from the Russian Far East and have always been used as cannon fodder. I stood up. He was shorter than me but the tommy gun pointing at my face created its own very persuasive argument.

Surrounded by his mates I was marched out of the forest to a meadow where a group of officers was standing round a colonel seated at a trestle table studying a map. One of them looked up, frowned and came over. He spoke to the soldier in a tongue I could not understand. Certainly not Russian. So, a White Russian officer from a Mongoloid regiment recruited somewhere way out along the river Ussuri. Or maybe the Amur. A long way away.

The soldier explained where I had been found and what I had been doing. The officer spoke in reasonable German and demanded my papers. Figuring the British passport had served its purpose I offered my East German press accreditation card. He studied it but the name Forsyth did not mean anything to him, certainly not Scotland.

He asked for an explanation. I dropped into Bertie Wooster mode – hapless, harmless and very dim. I told him my car had been run off the road and was stuck in a sand drift. I had been told there was a farmer in the woods with a tractor who might pull me out. Then I dropped my car keys and was scrambling around trying to find them when his kindly soldiers guided me out of the forest.

He took my press card and went to show it to the colonel. There was a jabber of Russian. The colonel shrugged and gave him back my card. He clearly had problems more serious than idiot East Germans getting stuck. The captain came back and handed me my press card, and told me to get the hell out of there. I must have been a bit punch drunk because I said in halting German:

'Herr Captain, it was your trucks that ran me into the sand drift. Your lads couldn't push me out, could they?'

He spat out a stream of orders in the eastern dialect, turned and went back to his colonel. Six Mongols escorted me back to the Wartburg and pushed. It was not stuck at all, but I kept my foot on the brake and when I released it the car shot forward. I turned and waved my thanks at the Mongols, gave them the V-sign and drove away.

I had my story, but how to get it to the West? A laptop would have been useful but I was forty years too early. It was early evening. I needed a phone and a meal. I needed a hotel. Ten miles later I found one, a country gasthof left over from the past.

Presenting my German ID and speaking like a German, I took a room, pleading car trouble for the lack of reservation, went upstairs and placed a call to my East Berlin office.

Fräulein Behrendt had checked in at nine that morning, read my scrawled message, and was still there. With headphones on, she took down my fifteen-page despatch.

I told her to transfer the lot to telex tape but not to connect to West Berlin and Bonn until she had it all, and then run it at maximum speed. She got fourteen pages across to the West before the line very predictably went dead and flashed up *Linienstörung* or 'line disruption'. It always did that when the goons did not want something to go through. But as usual the junior monitors had to check with some senior goon while the story raced through.

I learned later that it had 'gone viral' before that phrase was invented. Client newspapers used it across the globe. Wiesbaden was very happy and a staff car was despatched to Magdeburg to demand the three crewmen back. (They came home pretty quickly. The nervousness caused by Lee Harvey Oswald was apparently still alive in Moscow.)

I should have driven back to East Berlin that night but I was bone-tired and hungry. I ate a hearty supper, went back to my room and slept until morning. After breakfast I paid up and emerged.

Outside the main door I was reminded of those society weddings where the bridegroom's mates all line up in two columns forming a walkway between them.

They were all there. Rural police, city police, forest wardens, People's Police and at the end the long leather coats of the ones who took precedence.

The four Stasi were not happy. They had clearly been slow-roasted all night by their masters in Berlin and now they had the swine responsible. One took over my Wartburg, the other three sandwiched me into the Czech saloon and drove me to their fortress headquarters in Magdeburg.

To be fair, there was no third degree, just a series of very angry interviews and threats. I was not even in a cell but in a bare interview room, with toilet facilities on request. Of course I dropped into Bertie Wooster mode. But, officer, what have I done wrong? I was only doing my job. Me, a spy? Good Lord, no, I wouldn't work for those people; I work for Reuters. I mean, a German correspondent in England would have done exactly the same, wouldn't he? I mean, we all do what we are told to do, don't we? Can I have a widdle?

The senior goon facing me would probably not have had a clue what to do with a hot news story. As he was well over forty I suspected he had been serving the Nazis twenty years earlier and had switched seamlessly to the Communists. Secret policemen are like that; they'll serve anyone.

Years after Berlin the pretty vicious DINA, the secret police of the not-so-saintly Salvador Allende of Chile, transferred without a blip to the service of General Pinochet. They even used the same torture chambers. Only the victims changed.

As he had never lived in a free country at all, asking him to agree with what a free journalist would do was simply embarrassing. I just had to hope my façade of a lucky but gormless fool, and thus too dim to be a spy, would hold up. It did.

I spent a day and a night in that room. In the morning I was ordered out and escorted upstairs. I thought we might be going to the execution wall, but it was only the car park. I was told to get in and follow the two VoPo motorcycle outriders. The black Tatra brought up the rear.

Someone in Berlin had decided they wanted this whole

(for them) miserable affair quashed. We drove fast back to East Berlin but not via West Berlin. As East German drivers swerved off the highway as the blaring sirens came up behind them, we made record time, driving round West Berlin to enter East Berlin from the south. Many never knew that there was a second border separating East Berlin from East Germany proper. It was to prevent Western tourists who were allowed through Checkpoint Charlie from driving straight on into East Germany unmonitored.

As we drove up to the pole across the road, one of the motorcyclists explained to the guards that the Wartburg was going through. They would be heading back to Magdeburg. A figure appeared outside my driver's window and tapped. I lowered the window. There was a face, and not a happy one.

'Herr Forsyth,' it said, 'do not ever come back to Magdeburg.'

And do you know? I never have.

Outbreak of War

I RECALL THE DATE when I almost started the Third World War with exact accuracy for reasons that will become plain. It was 24 April 1964, and it was two o'clock in the morning. I was in my car, twisting and turning my way through the coffin-dark streets of East Berlin back to my flat from a visit to a charming young member of the State Opera Chorus.

I was in a suburb of the sleeping city that I did not know well and had no map, simply heading towards the glow in the sky that was West Berlin, expecting any time to happen upon a major boulevard that I knew would lead me back to the Stadtmitte district where the Reuters office was situated.

I was still about a mile from it when I came to another road junction, a crossroads that I needed to go over. Standing four-square across my path was a Russian soldier. He heard my engine approaching from behind him, turned and held up a hand in the no-mistake 'Halt' signal. Then he turned to face the other way. Because it was chilly I had the windows up, but now I lowered the driver's side window and thrust out my head. That was when I heard the low rumble.

As I watched, the first vehicles appeared, coming from the

right, meaning the east, and heading across the junction towards the west. They were lorries packed with soldiers and it was obviously a very large convoy. It just went on and on. I got out of the car and watched for a few minutes. The trucks were then replaced by low-loaders carrying tanks. Nothing else moved. Apart from the Russians the streets were abandoned.

Wishing to get home, I hung a U-turn and went back, seeking another way past the blockage.

Ten streets further on it happened again. Another fur-capped soldier at a crossroads, arms spread, barring traffic from crossing. More armour appeared, moving east to west, which is to say towards the Wall. Then towed artillery. Now perturbed, I retreated again, found another side street and continued home. By now I was zigzagging all over the place, trying to get through.

The third time, the slowly rumbling traffic on the crossing involved more low-loaders but carrying mobile bridges. Then more mechanized infantry with motorcycle outriders. Though no expert, I calculated what I had seen as between four and five divisions of the Soviet army, in full battle order, moving through the darkness towards the Wall.

During the autumn of 1962 world attention had switched to the Cuban missile crisis but it had been the received wisdom for years that, if war between the Warsaw Pact and NATO ever came, the spark would be the embattled and surrounded enclave of West Berlin.

The besieged half-city was teeming with spy agencies, agents, infiltrators and defectors. One West German spy chief, Otto John, had already been snatched from the streets of West Berlin (or so he said when he later reappeared to explain himself to a sceptical world). In 1948/49, West Berlin had almost been snuffed out when Stalin closed the access motor-ways and tried to starve the Western outpost into surrender. Only a huge airlift had saved it.

The West Berliners lived with the daily fear of the moment the twenty-two divisions of Soviet-based military in East Germany got their marching orders. That was why their mood was always slightly hysterical and their partygoing and sexual mores entertainingly louche.

And finally, with Kennedy dead and Khrushchev locked in a power struggle with rivals in the Kremlin, the spring of 1964 was as tense a time as had ever been. Not long after, the Russian tanks of General Abrassimov and the US tanks of General Lucius Clay would be parked barrel-to-barrel at Checkpoint Charlie with the Reuters man dodging between them.

What I had seen was not merely rolling, it was rolling towards the Wall. In silence, apart from the low rumbling, at 2 a.m. In rising anguish I made it back to the Reuters office-cum-apartment and rushed upstairs. The question running through me was simple: what the hell do I do?

There was no question of calling anyone to consult. Telephonically West Berlin and West Germany were cut off. All the East German ministries were closed.

Do nothing? Say nothing? And what if the worst fears were confirmed by the dawn's early light? Finally I hit upon what I felt was the only thing I could do. Report exactly what I had seen, nothing more, nothing less. No embellishment, no suggestions, no speculation. Just the facts.

So I tapped out the story, watching the yards of hole-punched ticker-tape spool out of the telex machine until there was nothing more to say. Then I hit 'fast transmit' and watched it disappear towards Bonn. By 4 a.m. I was in the kitchen brewing some very strong coffee. I kept returning to the office to check the machine for a response from the Bonn office, but there was none. I suppose their machine was on 'automatic on-pass' to London. Actually, it was. I did not know what was going on west of the river Elbe so I drank coffee and waited for what might become Armageddon as a watery sun rose over Pankow. Only later did they tell me what had been triggered by those yards of punched tape.

It seemed the night staff at Reuters in London woke with quite a jolt. Telephones rang in the suburban homes of the top men in Reuters as the despatch from East Berlin was read out to them. The story was not sent on to the agency's clients worldwide, and thank heavens for that.

Night-duty officers in the British ministries were roused and they awoke their superiors. It was 10 p.m. in Washington when the encrypted calls from London came through. Intelligence agencies were besieged with queries. They were as puzzled as the politicians. There had been no steady deterioration before that date.

Eventually Moscow was contacted and bewildered officials in the Kremlin put breakfast on hold while they checked with their own generals in East Germany. That was when the riddle was solved. Relief surged back across the continent and the Atlantic. Those about to go to bed did so. Those about to get up did that too.

A puzzled Soviet commander-in-chief of Warsaw Pact forces in East Germany explained that it was only a rehearsal for the May Day parade due in exactly one week.

In a rare extension of consideration for the citizens of East Berlin, the Soviets had decided to hold their multi-division military party in the middle of the night when the streets were empty, and being Communists it never occurred to them to tell anybody.

Of course, once the banal and ludicrous explanation was out in the open a rain of derision fell upon the Reuters East Berlin office. My only response was to apologize but with the codicil: well, you didn't know either. Which was grumpily conceded. Eventually it seems a multi-ministry and multi-agency concordat was agreed not to mention it ever again. And so far as I know, from that day to this, it never has been.

Headlights

THE POST OF Reuters correspondent for East Germany involved a very large parish: East Germany itself, with compulsory residence in East Berlin, plus Czechoslovakia and Hungary. Visits to Prague and Budapest were not frequent but mandatory. To Budapest I would always fly but Prague was close enough for me to motor in my ghastly pink East German Wartburg car. This I did in the midsummer of 1964.

As always I checked in to the Yalta Hotel on Wenceslas Square and greeted the bugging devices I knew would be somewhere throughout the suite. Elsewhere, crouched over their turning spools, would be the goons of the StB, the Czech secret police. Mr Stanley Vaterlé, the ever-genial chief of reception, could be relied on to make the right phone call if I handed in my room key and asked for my car key. As I drew out of the guest car park, the StB car would swing in behind me. It was routine procedure and both parties cheerfully pretended not to notice.

There was a sweltering heatwave that July and the Yalta had air conditioning, so after dinner I elected to go down to the basement where the regime permitted a Western-style disco, which took only Western currency and was patronized by Western businessmen. There were also hostesses, usually university students making pin money on bar tips to help themselves through university or some other college. That night I met Jana.

She was gorgeous, a twenty-one-year-old who could have stopped traffic on the highway. Her champagne glass was duly topped up; we got talking, then dancing. I was twenty-five; most of the other males were middle-aged, overweight and beaded with sweat despite the cool air, whether from lust or exercise it was hard to say.

Dancing till dawn was not quite the communist way and at about 12 a.m. a voice announced that the joint would close in a few minutes. I paid up and we went to the lobby. If matters were to go further, as I much wished they could, there was no question of my suite upstairs. Each landing had a gorgon behind a desk outside the elevators, noting comings and goings. Western decadence was not on the menu. But I had a car, even if it was an East German horror. And I knew of some lakes outside the city. To my surprise my suggestion of a night drive was accepted.

I collected my car keys, winked at Stanley who beamed back, escorted Jana to the Wartburg and we set off. I knew Prague by then well enough to weave and swerve my way out of downtown, through the suburbs and into the countryside. After thirty minutes I found the lake. Taking a plaid blanket from the boot, we walked to the water's edge. It was 2 a.m. but still stiflingly hot. So we stripped down and went into the cool water naked.

We skinny-dipped for half an hour before climbing out and

spreading the rug in the long warm grass. Then, like any healthy young animals, we made love; rather extensively to my recall. I used to smoke in those days and after exhausting ourselves I lay on my back with Jana half-asleep on my left shoulder, watching plumes of blue smoke drift up into the starry sky. Then a remarkable thought occurred to me.

I had never driven through Redland, apart from those times in East Germany when I had deliberately shaken my Stasi tail just to annoy them, without the ever-present black-windowed Tatra saloon slotting in two or three cars behind. Even at night, if there were not enough other cars to permit that, and the goons dropped back pretending not to be there, you could always see the wash of their headlights in the rear-view mirror. Except that night; no headlights.

I must have moved in my surprise for a sleepy voice in the crook of my left arm asked: 'What's the matter?' I explained, adding: 'Whatever happened to the StB?'

And the sleepy voice replied: 'You just made love to it.' As I drifted off to sleep I recall thinking: 'If this is the Czech secret police, bring it on.' Well, we all have to make a living.

Beer with a Camp Guard

WEIMAR IS A small and charming town steeped in culture. Composers and writers of world renown worked there centuries ago. But outside Weimar is a hill and on top of the hill is a wood. Unless things have changed, the trees comprising the wood are beeches.

Beech in German is *Buchen* and a wood is called a *Wald*. So when the Nazis built a concentration camp in the middle of it they called it Buchenwald, a place of unredeemed horror. After 1949 the East German government decided to preserve it as a place for public visitation. While I was posted there I motored south from Berlin to see it.

Of course it was a weirdly horrible way to spend a day. There was a car park outside and a place to pay the visitor fee just outside the main gate. Just about everyone else streaming through the gate surmounted by the swastika was in an organized group, quickly taken in tow by the professional guides. Solitaries were rare, for much would be unexplained without a running commentary.

There was a school party just ahead of me so I attached myself to it and no one seemed to notice. Perhaps the officials thought I was a teacher and the teachers thought I was on the camp staff. I could hear the accompanying lecture quite clearly and of course understand it. It was all minutely organized along the permitted paths that made up the tour.

We were led past the parade square with its flogging posts and gallows; through a sample hut (the liberating Allies of 1945 had burned most of them down as they were infected by disease). We were taken to the crematorium where the constant stream of corpses had been disposed of and through the 'medical' laboratory where Nazi pseudo-doctors had experimented on living victims. Over all of us the watch towers looked down, only the old machine guns removed.

By constant repetition the commentary was word-perfect, so eventually it just became a drone without inflection or expression. The children were awed into silence as what had been done there was explained.

I noticed that the guides never used the word 'Nazi' and never ever the word 'German'. Those responsible had been the 'Fascists', even though the Fascists were the Italians. The strong impression being dunned into the children's brains was that the Fascists had in a way, as if from outer space, simply arrived, per-formed their inhumanities and then been hounded out to take up residence in their new natural home, Bonn, the capital of West Germany. No one queried this, nor mentioned that it was actually the Americans who liberated Buchenwald, not the Russians. The whole lecture was a communist tour de force.

By the time it was over and I could escape, thoroughly depressed, back to my car, dusk was falling. At the bottom of the hill, on a side road, there was a gasthof. I pulled in, parked, went into the bar and ordered a stein of beer. I sat alone; I wanted to think over what I had seen. It was probably similar to that flickering film my father had seen at the War Office in 1945. He had told me about it; I had read about it, but never actually seen it (or the remaining evidence of it). Until now. Then there was a power failure, not unusual in rural East Germany.

The landlord came over with a candle. There was only one other drinker in the bar, a middle-aged man glowering over his beer a few tables away. The host asked if I minded if he joined me to relieve the need for two candles. I shrugged and the other drinker came to sit opposite me. The atmosphere by candlelight and with the concentration camp on the hill above us was predictably gloomy, like something from an old Dracula movie.

My new companion did not seem to be drawn from the professional classes: working man's rough clothes, a pocked and coarse face. After a while in silence he asked me:

'*Wo kommst du her?*' Where do you come from?

He used the familiar 'du' form of address, a familiarity that can be either rudeness or an attempt at camaraderie. He had heard me order in German so I supposed he meant from which East German city. I did not feel like being German at that moment, so I replied:

'*Aus London.*'

He stared at me across the beer glasses then shook his head. I must be joking, trying to impress.

'*Glaub' ich nicht,*' he said. Don't believe it.

Sufficiently irritated I flicked my blue British passport across the table. He examined it, compared photo and face and slid it back with something between a mocking smile and a sneer. He jerked his head towards what lay out in the darkness, atop the hill.

'*Und was denkst du?*' So, what do you think?

We both carried on in German. There was something I was beginning not to like.

'What the hell do you think I think?'

He shrugged again, dismissively.

'What happened happened.'

It was a long shot but I asked it anyway.

'Were you there? In the old days?' I did not mean as an inmate, I meant on the staff. He shook his head, then confirmed my suspicion.

'Not that one.'

So, he had been a camp guard but at a different concentration camp. And I was sitting opposite him in the half-darkness drinking beer.

It has long been a puzzle to me which I have never resolved. You take a newborn baby, twelve inches of helpless, chubby innocence. You take a toddler, three years old, a bundle of affection. You take a choirboy, ten and possessed of a pure treble voice, a curly blond angel, singing the *Te Deum* at morning service or helping dad around the farm. Or you take a fifteen-year-old studying to be one day an accountant or architect.

How on earth do you turn that child in a few years into a savage, cruel monster capable of flogging a tethered man to death or throwing a living child into an incinerator or herding families into a gas chamber? What kind of satanic metamorphosis can achieve that?

But it has happened, not just in Germany, but right across the world, generation after generation. Every torture chamber in every dictatorship in the world is staffed by animals like that. And they were all once gurgling infants.

The lights came on. The landlord came over to snuff out the candle. No need to waste wax. I pushed enough East Marks across the table to cover the cost of one beer, mine, and rose to go. The man across the table held out his hand. I left it dangling in mid-air. I had reached the door when his parting shot reached me.

'Killing is easy, Engländer, too damned easy.'

Years later I would discover how right he was.

A Very Unwise Choice

Y DEPARTURE FROM East Berlin was not foreseen but advisable. There were very few places worth visiting after dark. I could stay in but the television was dire, even though I could pick up West Berlin.

This was strictly forbidden for East Berliners and locally sold sets had all been tampered with to make reception of the West Berlin programmes unobtainable. But thousands had a well-paid freelance 'friend' come in to restore the facility. It was wise not to be caught watching the forbidden menu, but in my case they did not even bother.

Or I could read, of which I did a lot. Almost my entire literary education, such as it is, comes from that year. Or I could help Reuters terrible blocked currency problem by consuming caviar at the Haus Moskau restaurant. Or there was the opera.

One of the few civilized things about the East German government that was not an affectation was their love of music, theatre and opera. The Brecht Theatre was justly famous but Master Bertolt Brecht was pretty left-wing and I had enough of that nine-to-five. But the State Opera was famous enough to attract international singers and conductors and the

Politburo spent enough foreign currency to indulge it lavishly. Of course, there was the occasional slip-up.

One occurred during the opera *Nabucco*, which was immensely popular and always in demand. In it is the Slaves Chorus, where the prisoners sing (in German): '*Teure Heimat, wann seh' ich dich wieder?*' Beloved homeland, when shall I see you again? Every time it was played the entire audience rose and sang along. The Politburo members who attended were gratified by the enthusiasm but bewildered that they never did this for any other aria. Then someone pointed out that for them the 'beloved homeland' was not East Germany but the West. It was their only way of expressing a political opinion. After that the authorities discontinued *Nabucco*.

And the opera had the pretty chic Opera Café, for after-performance drinking. That was where I met Sigrid, known as Sigi. She was a stunner, and alone. I checked for an escort. There was none. Move-in time.

An East German had to be extremely careful even taking a drink with a Westerner but Sigi was old enough and sophisti-cated enough to know what she was doing, and even learning I was from the West but living in East Berlin did not deter her. After a drink we shared dinner and ended up at my place. She revealed a remarkable figure matched by a rapacity for love-making. But on my second date I realized there was something odd about her.

She claimed she was married to a corporal in the East German army, who would not have the income to permit her clothes and lifestyle. More, he was permanently based in the garrison at Cottbus, far away on the Czech frontier, and never got any leave. Finally, she refused to let me drive her home but after hours of fun in bed insisted on a cab being ordered from the late-night rank at the Frankfurter Straße station.

One day I saw the same cab driver at the station and for a hefty tip in West Marks extracted from him the address to which he had taken her. It was in Pankow, the very blue-chip suburb where the elite of East Germany had their residences. Further discreet enquiries with some of my contacts in West Berlin revealed whose address it was.

I recall driving back into East Berlin through 'Charlie' that night with the words of a popular song running through my head. The opening line was: the party's over, it's time to call it a day.* I had been sleeping with the mistress of the East German defence minister, General Karl-Heinz Hoffmann.

General Hoffmann was not renowned for his sense of humour. I had just turned twenty-six in October 1964 and hoped for a few more birthdays yet to come. Outside of a prison cell if possible.

I told Reuters I was stressed out and wished to leave rather sharply. Head Office was very understanding; few took more than a year in that place and I had just passed twelve months. Within a week, just before the general returned from Warsaw Pact manoeuvres in Poland, I had handed over job, office, secretary and car and was at West Berlin's Tempelhof airport boarding the British Airways direct flight to London Heathrow.

As the airliner lifted off and both Berlins dropped away beneath the wings I looked down at the divided city convinced I would never return to East Germany. As it turned out, I was wrong about that.

* From 'The Party's Over', lyrics by Betty Comden and Adolph Green, music by Jule Styne.

A Mistake with Auntie

REUTERS SIMPLY SENT me back to Paris to rejoin Harold King and it was in a silent Paris café in the early spring of 1965 that I watched on a TV screen the state funeral of Winston Churchill.

There must have been a hundred or more around me, all Parisians and not world-famous for their admiration of things British, but they sat in awed silence as the bronze coffin of the old Bulldog was taken to its final resting place in a country churchyard.

I had already made my decision that the future of foreign-sourced news journalism was in radio and television, and that meant the BBC. I got a transfer back to London in April, applied for a job with the BBC, attended the necessary interviews, was accepted and joined as a staff reporter on the domestic news side that October. That was probably a mistake.

I learned quite quickly that the BBC is not primarily a creator of entertainment, nor a reporter and disseminator of hard news like Reuters. Those come second. Primarily the BBC is a vast bureaucracy with the three disadvantages of a

166

bureaucracy. These are a sloth-like inertia, an obsession with rank over merit and a matching obsession with conformism.

Being vast, and multi-tasked, the BBC was divided into over a score of major divisions, of which only one was the News and Current Affairs division I had joined. That in turn was divided into radio and TV, then Home and Foreign. All starters began in Home Radio, which was to say Broadcasting House on Portland Place, London.

But there was more. It was also and remains at the very core of the Establishment. The calling of a true news and current affairs organization is to hold the Establishment of any country to account but never to join it.

Then it got worse. The upper echelons of the bureaucracy preferred a devoted servility to the polity of the ruling government, provided it was Labour, and it was.

The icing on the cake was that back then the leadership of the BBC was in turmoil, which prevailed during most of my time there. The former chairman of the Board of Governors had died in office. His deputy Sir Robert Lusty presumed the succession to be his. But Labour prime minister Harold Wilson had other ideas. He wanted an even more tame national broadcaster.

Rather than confirming Sir Robert, Wilson transferred his friend and admirer Sir Charles Hill, almost immediately to become Lord Hill, across from the top of the BBC's fierce rival Independent TV to chair the BBC board. There was chaos.

Sir Robert Lusty resigned. Several lifelong veterans went with him. The powerful post of Director General was held by a former giant of journalism, Sir Hugh Carleton-Greene, brother of novelist Graham Greene, and who had set up North German Radio after 1945 to teach the old principles of rigour, integrity and impartiality. He was the last journalist to head the BBC, and thus to protect the News and Current Affairs division.

The best German news organization for years was the one he left behind him, but twenty years later in London he was being sabotaged and eventually he, too, quit in disgust.

As with any ship when there is chaos on the bridge, the vices were adopted below decks. Talentless little empire builders proliferated using all the Machiavellian tricks of office politics instead of a dedication to the business of news. But at the time this was far above my pay grade and seemed of small interest. Only later did I learn about office politics, just as they effectively destroyed me.

Newcomers began by learning the techniques and technology of tape-recorded radio interviews, working out of Broadcasting House under the aegis of the Head of Home Correspondents and Reporters, one Tom Maltby, a good and honourable man.

Then I secured a transfer to TV news, based way up in north London at Alexandra Palace, whence BBC TV News was beamed to the country. This involved learning about reporting direct into a lens, working with cameramen and sound recordists, being part of a three-man team.

I recall Alexandra Palace, or Ally Pally, with affection. Being away from the hornets' nest it was informal and clubby, consorting with veteran news readers like Robert Dougall and just-arrived young women like Angela Rippon. But I still wanted to go back to foreign reporting and to resume being a foreign correspondent. There was still masses more world I wanted to see.

Still, that summer of 1966, out of Ally Pally, I did cover one good story.

A head came round the door and asked: 'Anyone here ever flown in jets?'

'Yes.'

'Do you get air sick?'

'No.'

'Only we have an invitation to fly with the Red Arrows.'

These were and remain the spectacular aerobatic display team of the Royal Air Force, centrepiece of just about every air display, with visits right across Europe and the USA.

'Are you interested?'

Is the Chief Rabbi Jewish? I was out of the door like a greased ferret.

A Day with the Arrows

MY ASSIGNED CAMERAMAN was the really marvellous Peter Beggin, a veteran who had been all over with his camera round his neck. We drove in two cars to the West Country and found the base of the Red Arrows display team.

Back then they were flying the two-seat Folland Gnat, a converted trainer with twin seats, fore-and-aft, originally for instructor and pupil. We introduced ourselves and were taken out to survey the Gnat. It was very small and very narrow; and, of course, bright red. Near the tails were the canisters that, for the final 'bomb-burst' display, would stream long plumes of red, white and blue smoke.

The tight confines of the cockpit did not worry me but they were a real squeeze for Peter. He was built like a truck, with immense physical strength, which he was going to need.

His hand-held camera was a heavy and bulky Arriflex weighing, I suppose, about ten pounds. Beneath it was a spike and this would slot into a socket embedded in a canvas harness to be worn round the neck and shoulders. With this in place, he could squint through the lens to film the sky, horizon, landscape below and the rest of the squadron flying in tight formation around him.

The problem was the G-forces we would encounter. Pulling 6G, that camera would weigh in at sixty pounds, all dragging downwards on Peter's shoulders.

We spent the morning on extensive briefings in the crew room, being taught everything that would happen and a variety of emergency procedures if it all went wrong. But if either of us brought up, well, that would just be our problem. No stopping for wax-paper bags. We smiled bravely.

It is perhaps a tribute to the informality of those days that there was no proof needed that we were fit to fly at all. No medical, no check for heart murmur. Our role was clearly to be strapped in, then sit tight and shut up. The radios were strictly for those terse instructions from team leader to the rest tucked into his wingtips.

Finally we were led out and slid into the seats. Peter was third down, starboard side, so he could see the rest of the team in formation round him. I was to fly with the leader.

It took time to get Peter settled in. Two sweating flight sergeants stood either side of his cockpit pushing and shoving as he went deeper and deeper. Then the harness. Then the Arriflex into its socket. When the Perspex canopies came down there seemed to be nothing inside his but him and his camera. We taxied out to take-off.

The instructions from the leader, coming through my headphones, were very terse: one syllable, two if he felt talkative. Every manoeuvre was simply a code word and everyone knew exactly what they meant.

There were nine in the team, taking off as a five and a four, then uniting into an arrow formation once airborne. Thus we climbed to about 10,000 feet. The sky was a cloudless blue, the fields of Gloucestershire a patchwork of green. It seemed quite sedate on the way up. When he was ready the leader muttered: 'Close up.' A wingtip appeared a few feet from my left and right eyebrow. I had done formation flying but this was very close indeed. For twenty minutes the two wingtips would not move an inch. Across a few feet of racing air the other two Gnats were as if bolted on. The rest were out behind them.

In deference (I think) to our innocence, the leader began with some gentle barrel rolls and loops. Then the display began.

I heard him say 'Twinkle, twinkle, roll' and the horizon went insane. A twinkle roll is fast, along the axis of the aircraft. The sky went one way, the horizon another and for a split second Gloucestershire appeared above my head. Then we were back where we started. I looked right and left. The wing-tips were still a few inches from my eyebrows.

It went on for about half an hour then, somehow, we were on final approach, wheels down, flaps at the right setting, green grass flashing past, gentle bumps as the wheels met tarmac.

I had long lost the airfield, except twice when it was above my head, but the leader had ensured the whole team hardly left the circuit. That is the point of display flying. The audience has to be able to see it. So it never really leaves their vision. And all the time we had been airborne the assessors had been watching with powerful field glasses to note any imperfection.

We were assisted out of the cockpits to the wings then down to the ground. I went over to Peter. He had probably lost several pounds in sweat but was otherwise impassive. He was probably more concerned for the health of his beloved camera than for himself. How he had taken the strain in the 6G turns I shall never know.

We had a brew with the Arrows, also soaked in sweat, said our goodbyes and motored back to Ally Pally. I was dying to see the 'rushes' (films had to be developed in those days, then cut and edited).

The rushes were superb and the editors were pretty open-mouthed. The camera never wavered, rock-steady, filming out through the Perspex hood as the world twisted and turned around us. And always the next red Gnat in perfect formation, so close one would think to lean out and touch it.

The feature was screened as a special to considerable public and professional acclaim.

That autumn I went back to Broadcasting House and lodged my application for the post of Assistant Diplomatic Correspondent, still yearning to go back abroad. There were boards and interviews. I was twenty-eight and the job normally required someone two decades older.

I met Chris Serpell, the middle-aged Diplomatic Correspondent, whose deputy the job was all about. He seemed formal and distant, staid, and in all things more like one of the Foreign Office mandarins with whom he daily consorted than a journalist.

But, amazingly, they gave me the job, effective from the next February. Foolishly I was elated, for I had no idea what I had stepped into.

There are times in life when you discover what was really going on but too late: when you can say, 'If I had known then what I know now I would have acted completely differently.' Had I known the full level of incompetence of the Commonwealth Relations Office and its sister the Foreign Office, and the level of slavishness the BBC foreign news mini-empire at Broadcasting House would dedicate to both ministries, I would have resigned at once, or never applied for the job in the first place. But awareness came later, too late.

A Taste of Africa

THAT SPRING OF 1967 I joined the foreign news team full of hopes that I would soon be sent abroad again to cover foreign news stories. What I did not know was that my presence on that team was absolutely undesired.

My new boss, the foreign news editor Arthur Hutchinson, had been extremely upset that he had not been seated on the interview board that had given me the post. Had he been, I would never have got it, because he had a protégé of his own that he wished to bring on. As Tom Maltby explained to me months later, from the first my card was marked.

There is a permanent question in office politics: does your face fit? This one emphatically did not. All that was needed was an excuse and this I liberally provided.

To start with my tasks included attending the regular morning briefings at the Foreign Office and the Common-wealth Relations Office. These two ministries in the heart of Whitehall covered all British foreign affairs, the second one obviously concerning itself with the residue of the fast-dissolving empire and its successor the Commonwealth.

It seemed to me the other diplomatic and Commonwealth

correspondents had really gone native, inasmuch as they were as close to mandarins in attitude and posture as the senior civil servants, languid and disdainful, who briefed them. I never recall a penetrating question or a hint of disagreement with what we were being told. The received wisdom was duly and obediently noted and thence reported to the public. But by mid-spring a single issue was dominating all others: the Middle East. Gamal Abdel Nasser of Egypt was steadily preparing for war with Israel.

If the briefings at the two ministries, seated by the grave Chris Serpell, were boring, the growing crisis in the Middle East was absorbing much of the world's attention. Nasser was no friend of Britain nor vice versa. In 1956 we had invaded Egypt via Suez in collusion with the French and the Israelis. It had been a disaster and still rankled in Britain on the centre-right.

Yet in the Foreign Office the anti-Semitism was unmissable. I found this odd. On most issues the senior mandarins reflected a lofty disdain of foreigners, yet made one exception, a preference for Arabs and Islam. This was mirrored in the left-wing media.

In his young manhood, as an impecunious provincial furrier, my father had been treated with great kindness by the fur houses of the East End of London, all run by Jews, many who had fled Hitler. My own views therefore were the other way.

By the time Nasser closed the Straits of Tiran to Israeli and Israel-bound traffic, it became hard to see how war was avoidable. I wanted to go out there on assignment but was pinned to London. In frustration I took my summer leave.

It was on leave that I watched the Six-Day War via the

media. It was a war that shattered an awful lot of misconceptions and frustrated many prejudices. In early June, Israel took on four surrounding Arab armies and three air forces and crushed them all. The air forces of Egypt, Jordan and Syria were destroyed on the ground before they even flew. With unchallenged control of the air above them, the Israeli ground forces raced across Sinai to the Suez Canal, roared east to take the holy city of Jerusalem and almost all land up to the river Jordan, and in the north stormed Syria's Golan Heights.

In Britain the left had been practically salivating at the imminent destruction of the Jewish state and could only watch in slack-jawed amazement. Most of the British people just cheered. The hero of the hour across two continents, Europe and the USA, became the Israeli defence minister, a one-eyed veteran called Moshe Dayan.

There were three pools of influence in the UK that were not so enthused: the left-wing newspapers, the BBC and the Foreign Office. In those environs I was much in a minority when I returned from leave in mid-June. What nobody was paying any attention to at all was a brewing crisis in Nigeria, which pitted the federal dictatorship against its own region of Eastern Nigeria.

It was on 6 July, forty days after the Eastern Region had declared unilateral secession from the federal state, that Nigeria invaded to end the insurrection. That day I was called into the office of Mr Hutchinson's deputy (he was on leave) and asked to go to Nigeria to cover the extremely short-lived campaign.

I protested that I knew nothing of Africa, cared less and did not want the assignment. It was pointed out that everyone else was either still wrapping up in the Middle East or on leave. I capitulated. There was a day of jabs from the resident medical officer and a minutely detailed briefing on what had led to the revolt, what I would find and what would happen next. This came from a man from the West African Service of Bush House, the famed World Service, the official voice of Britain. I recall it even now.

The issues, I was told, were quite simple. The East was the homeland overwhelmingly of the Ibo people who, on the spurious basis of some riots a year earlier and led by the military governor of the region, a self-serving rogue called Col. Emeka Ojukwu, had declared secession from the very fine republic of Nigeria, the jewel in the crown of the British Commonwealth in Africa. Their collective character was long-term troublesome and their claims had no merit.

Even so, they had been unwillingly goaded into secession by Col. Ojukwu, and had unwisely agreed to follow him. The Nigerian head of state, the marvellous Col. Yakubu Gowon, had no choice but to use the federal army to reconquer the East, which was styling itself the Republic of Biafra.

The rebel army was a rabble of cooks and bottle-washers who would be no match for the British-trained Nigerian army. This force would soon march into the rebel enclave, sweeping all before it, topple the upstart colonel and 'restore order'.

I was not wanted in Lagos, the capital 400 miles west of Biafra, constantly referred to only as the 'rebel enclave'. Events out of Lagos would be covered by our veteran West Africa expert Angus McDiarmid. My job was to fly to Paris and thence to Douala in Cameroon, the republic east of Nigeria. Then over the border into Eastern Nigeria and as best I could cross-country to the regional capital Enugu.

It was not wanted that I actually file any report, as communications were cut off from all sides. I would report to the British Deputy High Commissioner there and stick close to him. As the Nigerian army swept south, he and his retinue would retreat south to the coast where we would all be taken off the shore by an arranged vessel and returned to Cameroon. Once I had re-established phone contact from the best hotel, I was to file an 'upsummer' – a complete report on the short-lived revolt.

The operation would take between ten and fourteen days. Then I should fly home. Job done. So I flew to Paris and thence Douala.

I found travelling companions in the form of Sandy Gall of Independent TV News, his cameraman and sound recordists, and we agreed to travel together all the way. The two assignments were rather different.

Sandy had a TV team, I did not. He had to spend one week covering a range of stories as they presented themselves, file nothing, ship no film, just return after one week with whatever he had got. I had to stay until the end.

We arrived in Douala, checked into the Cocotiers Hotel, chartered a small plane and flew to Mamfe, the Cameroon–Nigeria border town. From there a local taxi and a lot of persuasion took us through the border into the 'rebel enclave'. After an exhausting drive we arrived at Enugu and checked into the Progress Hotel, the principal hostelry of this pretty small provincial capital.

It must have been the next day, about 12 July, that I made contact with the British Deputy High Commissioner, Jim Parker. He was a real veteran, an old Africa hand, steeped in knowledge of the country and its eastern region. I recall that I saw him alone. Sandy and his team were out filming what they could get of interest in a town still completely at peace. Jim asked me what I had been told.

I related my briefing to him, almost word for word. He listened grim-faced then put his face in his hands. He knew where the briefing had come from; I did not. The author and source for it all was the British High Commissioner (Ambassador) in Lagos, one Sir David Hunt. I had never even heard of him.

I would meet him eventually, years later and after the war, in the guest suite of a British TV programme. He turned out to be about the nastiest piece of work I have ever come across. An intellectual who had missed out on every plum in the diplomatic service, ended up in West Africa, the trashcan of diplomacy, and seethed with resentment; a crashing snob and a racist who hid his unpleasantness behind a veneer of affability, about as convincing as a four-pound note.

The reason Jim Parker had put his head in his hands became plain as he talked. Every word I had been given was complete and utter garbage. But David Hunt had sold it hook, line and sinker to the Commonwealth Office. Who in turn had passed it to the West Africa Service at Bush House and the foreign news department of the BBC at Broadcasting House. No one dreamed of disputing a word of it.

Jim Parker spent the rest of the morning explaining to me what had really happened and what was happening right then. Which was nothing. Starting on 6 July the Nigerian army, composed entirely of Muslim Hausa tribesmen from the north and numbering about six thousand, had captured the northern

180

border town of Nsukka, which was not defended. Just south of the town they met the first defences, oil barrels filled with concrete. And stopped.

They could have gone round them but they were frightened to enter the rainforest, which they believed was full of evil spirits. They remained there for weeks.

In the deep south a landing party from the Nigerian navy had captured the offshore island of Bonny, which had an oil refinery. But the navy could go no further into the shallow and treacherous Niger Delta and they had no amphibious units.

'So what is happening?' I asked. My briefing said the Nigerian armed forces should be sweeping across the rebel enclave.

'Nothing,' he said cheerfully. 'Welcome to Africa. Let's go for lunch.'

His houseboy had prepared pickles and salad. After that we went to a press briefing at State House, the residence of the regional governor, now of the newly announced head of state, to meet the demon Ojukwu.

The drive enabled us to see a microcosm of the crowds in the streets, consumed with exhilaration at what they saw as their present and continuing freedom at last. They were waving their new half-a-yellow-sun flags and the youths were queuing at the establishment booths to go and fight.

The populace had not yet learned to loathe the BBC and never learned to hate the British so they ran grinning up to the car with the Union Jack pennant on the bonnet, waving and laughing.

Colonel Emeka Ojukwu was not quite as painted to me in London. The son of Nigerian multi-millionaire and Knight of the Empire Sir Louis Ojukwu, he had been sent to a British-run preparatory school in Lagos, then to Epsom College in Surrey. Then to Oxford, where he gained a master of arts degree in history at Lincoln College.

As an ardent federalist he had joined the army because he thought it the only truly pan-national institution and devoid of regional jealousies. He had risen by merit to Lt-Colonel and after the first of the two coups of the previous year, the January one, had been appointed military governor of the East. His native Iboland. He had been in office for fifteen months until the declaration of independence. He was thirty-four.

He explained in measured terms and an Oxford drawl that he had resisted popular clamour from the people for a separation from Nigeria as long as he could before facing a decision he could no longer avoid. He could either resign and leave, or he could agree to lead his people along the path they had chosen. He opted for the latter.

He told all the foreign journalists present – about six apart from Sandy and me – that we were free to rent cars and wander where we wished. His staff would issue a laissez-passer to all, in case of problems at the over-enthusiastic roadblocks.

Back at the Progress Hotel to change, I discovered there were over a score of other expatriates, mostly British, in residence. These were businessmen representing large firms and franchises who had been there for years. Engineers from a number of foreign aid projects and so forth. If I wanted con-firmation of anything Jim Parker would tell me, I would find it in this community, also steeped in local knowledge.

I took tea with Jim Parker back at the Deputy High

Commission and he explained to me where and why the London briefing was wrong on every single point.

It was a chastening seminar to confirm the old adage for foreign correspondents. Never mind what the embassy says: go and ask the old sweats who have been there for years.

End of Career

THE TROUBLE WITH Nigeria was that historically it had never been one country, but two. Some say it still is.

A hundred years before the British arrived, a Muslim warlord called Usman dan Fodio had led his Fulani army out of the Sahara, through the Sahel of semi-desert and scrub and into northern Nigeria to wage war on the Hausa kingdom. His horsemen stopped at the line of the rainforests because their mounts contracted tick-borne diseases and died in the tropical rain. So the Hausa/Fulani settled the whole of the north, almost 60 per cent of what became Nigeria.

About 120 years ago, the British arrived by sea from the south. Sir Frederick Lugard conquered the tribes of the forest and annexed the north. Lady Lugard grandly called the place Nigeria and map-drawers drew a single line round it.

The Muslim north was ruled by sultans and emirs who resisted the British until the white men used their Maxim machine guns to urge a rethink. Missionaries arrived by sea to convert the animists of the rainforests, not to Islam but to Christianity. So, two countries, and for fifty years the British ruled them as two countries.

Northern Nigeria continued on its sleepy way with nominal rule by the British but real rule by the emirs and sultans with British agreement. There was no middle class, education and technology were shunned and the common people were slavishly obedient to their liege lords. This extreme deference was extended to the British civil servants, who loved it.

But in the Christianized south, the two main ethnic groups, the Yorubas of the west and Ibos of the east, became avid for education and technical mastery, learned from the British. One of the two, the Ibos, passionate for knowledge, consumed education with both hands and became the effective motor of the country. And they spread throughout Nigeria, north and south.

In the north, southerners had to live in closed ghettos, but they enabled the British to run the place with a minimum of white faces. The Ibos especially were the drivers, mechanics, switchboard operators, masters of machinery, office staff and junior civil servants. They were also entrepreneurial: they became the traders, shopkeepers, bankers and money-changers.

And they made themselves unpopular. I once heard a British civil servant, in London but ex-northern Nigeria, refer to the Ibos as 'the Jews of Africa', and it was not a compliment. By the Fifties there were over a million Ibos resident in the north. That was when the trouble began – the Fifties.

London decided that Nigeria had to be independent within a decade and it had to be a united Nigeria. Having run the place on the basis of a schooled but controlled mutual antagonism between north and south for so long, that was a tall order. Even taller was the decree that it had to become a democracy, a concept wholly alien to the feudal north.

The emirs and sultans opposed democracy firmly until it was pointed out that as they had the numerical majority they could form a single political party, win the coming election and rule the whole country. Then they agreed, but only on that condition. A party was formed, the election was held and of course the Northern People's Congress won. The army had also been intensively northernized with the infantry entirely Hausa and the southerners taking the 'technical' commissions. Independence was accorded on 1 October 1960 under a northern-dominated federal government.

All this I learned from the old sweats visiting the Progress Hotel, Deputy High Commissioner Jim Parker and books, as the first four weeks of this eventless pseudo-war drifted by. I was still bound by my instruction not to file anything but to wait for the coming federal army conquest of the 'rebel enclave'.

Trouble really began in January 1966 with the first of two coups d'état of that year. It was a very odd one, planned and carried out not by generals as usual but by a cabal of radicalized, educated and left-wing junior officers. These were the days when a portrait poster of Che Guevara was on every student's bedroom wall.

It was later accused of being an Ibo coup. Actually the junior officer plotters were multi-ethnic, but six Ibo officers were the most prominent, because they had attended courses in England where they had become radicalized. When they returned, everything about northern feudal rule posing as democracy offended. So did the institutionalized corruption, the scourge of Africa.

They struck fast and accurately. It was a virtually bloodless coup, but the dozen victims were the national leadership. In a night the federal prime minister, the prime ministers of the north and western regions and several other ministers were assassinated. But the coup plotters did not take over. The army woke up, mobilized and arrested them all. But that done, the government was gone. An army regime was the only alternative. It took over as the plotters were led off to jail. The Chief of General Staff, General Ironsi, took over. By chance (and it was chance) he was also an Ibo, but a traditional, by-the-book stickler. It did not save him. The north seethed in quiet rage.

Ironsi appointed a military governor to each of the federal republic's four regions. A Fulani to the north, a Yoruba to the west, a mid-westerner to the mid-west and Ojukwu to the east.

In July the north struck back and this time it was spectacularly bloody. Hausa soldiers raced through barracks across the country, killing their colleagues of southern ethnicity. Hundreds died that way but that was just the start.

Northern mobs with local encouragement swept into the ghettos and put thousands to the sword. The survivors fled south in waves. The total death toll will never be known; Biafran propaganda later said 30,000 Ibos alone died up there. The British government pooh-poohed it all as several hundreds.

This was the 'storm in a teacup' that had been mentioned to me in the London briefing as the frivolous reason for the East's secession. The expatriates briefing me in Enugu were not racially bigoted but they had watched it all happen and concluded it was by any standards a major pogrom. But the east did not secede from the federal union. That was in July and August 1966. Secession was in late May 1967. It took ten months of blithering incompetence by Lagos to achieve it.

General Ironsi had been assassinated and every Ibo officer and technician had fled east. A group of Hausa/Fulani officers formed the new government but on British advice they appointed a harmless Middle Belt junior colonel as the new head of state. Col. Yakubu Gowon was totally unknown, an office wallah and a token mission-school-educated Christian from a Muslim-majority part of the country. Ethnically he was a Tiv and had done a course at Sandhurst, England. He was friendly, agreeable, polite and not very bright. He was a puppet leader; the real power behind the throne was Col. Murtala Mohammed, who would later topple him.

After August 1966 relations between the pretty traumatized Ibos of the east and the federal government in Lagos deteriorated. In London the mandarins of the Commonwealth office and later the Foreign Office quickly showed a passionate favouritism towards the federal regime, stoked by the resident High Commissioner. British governments do not habitually show such adoration of military dictatorships, but this was an exception that stunned even Jim Parker.

Sir David Hunt quite liked Africans so long as they showed him respectful deference. Col. Gowon apparently did. When the High Commissioner entered his office at Dodan Barracks, he would leap to his feet, slap on his cap and throw up a quivering salute. Just once, as the crisis became deeper and deeper, David Hunt came east to visit Ojukwu in Enugu, and quickly developed a passionate loathing of the Ibo leader.

Emeka Ojukwu did indeed rise as his visitor entered the room but in the manner of one welcoming a guest to one's country home. He did not throw up a salute. It became quickly plain he was the sort of African, meaning black man, the former Greek don Hunt could not stand. Emeka was a British public schoolboy, he was an MA of Oxford, once a first-class wing three-quarter for the college rugby team and almost a Blue. His voice was a relaxed drawl. He showed no deference. Jim Parker, who told me this, was standing a few feet away. Hunt and Ojukwu detested each other on sight, something that was clearly mirrored in my London briefing.

Early in his time as governor of the east, Ojukwu, against all the prevailing wisdom elsewhere, tried to reinstitute a form of democracy. He formed three bodies to advise him; one was the Constituent Assembly, mainly the professional class, doctors, lawyers, graduates. Second was the Council of Chiefs and Elders, vital in an African society where age and experience at clan level are revered. Third, surprising to Western eyes, was the Market Mammies Association.

Jim Parker explained to me that Ibo society is almost a matriarchy. In contrast to the north, women are hugely important and influential. The market was the core of every village and city-zone. The Mammies ran them and knew everything there was to know about the mood on the streets. These were the forces urging Ojukwu to pull Eastern Nigeria out of the Federal Republic.

The public mood was not aggression but fear. Radio broadcasts out of the north threatened that the Hausa were preparing to come south and 'finish the job'. Most Ibos believed these threats, the more so as neither federal nor northern government would close them down.

But the real secession point was eventually compensation. Ojukwu had about 1.8 million refugees, all penniless. They had fled leaving everything behind. At the one single meeting that might have saved the day, at Aburi in Ghana, Gowon had conceded a withholding of federal oil taxes as an income stream to cope with the crisis. After Aburi, Gowon returned to Lagos and, under pressure, reneged on the lot.

British official sources in Lagos and London briefed the British media that Ojukwu had been grossly unfair to Gowon. He had turned up fully briefed and was simply smarter. That sort of behaviour, journalists were told, was obviously unacceptable. After that the path slid downhill to 30 May and formal secession, and on 6 July to war.

And yet there was no war. My first four weeks in Enugu were very solitary. Sandy Gall and his team had flown out via Cameroon after their single week. I had been assigned a cameraman from another agency, Comtel. He just happened to be there on another assignment. In dumb amazement we both sat with other expatriates round the hotel radio listening to the BBC news broadcast out of London but emanating from Lagos. It was quite extraordinary.

In Lagos a discredited former politician called Anthony Enahoro had been charged to set up the Ministry of Information, meaning propaganda. Each day he issued the most weird claims.

According to his morning bulletins, the rebel situation was dire and becoming ever worse. There were anti-Ojukwu riots, brutally put down; the Nigerian army was advancing on all fronts and even now at the outskirts of Enugu.

(We expats were on loungers round the pool, the others staring at me pityingly.)

The reason was simple. Out of Lagos, Angus McDiarmid,

300 miles from the Niger river, was reporting all this as BBC-endorsed fact. Every journalist will know that he may have to report what a dictatorship is saying but must make plain early on that it is the government talking, not him. This is the 'attribution' . . . the words 'according to the Nigerian government'.

To be really fair, add the words 'no independent confirmation could be achieved'. And early on, in the first paragraph. Failing that, the listener will gain the impression the allegations are all true and endorsed by the mighty BBC. The broadcasts out of Lagos that first month had attribution, if at all, in the fourth or even fifth paragraph. It sounded like the BBC itself talking. Sitting listening to it as the expats around me roared with derisive laughter made me frustrated as hell. It was not the bias, it was the sloppiness, which Reuters would not have tolerated for a minute. Then at last I got a message from London.

It released me from my instruction not to file out of Enugu. The ten-day war was three weeks old and nothing had happened. I was asked for a 'matcher' to the dailies out of Lagos.

In journalistic parlance a matcher is both confirmation and endorsement. I was supposed to file that all being said was absolutely true.

The only 'riots' were actually queues of Biafran youth trying to join up. The entire Nigerian army was stuck behind a roadblock on the border. I could not report 'in voice' but at least a telex connection had been established for written messages. So I sent one.

All right, I agree it was probably intemperate. Deep in the

obedient editorial bowels of the Broadcasting House newsroom it did not go down well. What I had actually done was
point a Colt .45 at the forehead of my reporting career with
the BBC and pull the trigger.

It was not out of mischievousness but naiveté. I was trained
by Reuters. I had never covered a controversial story in my
two years with the BBC. I did not realize that when broadcasting for the state, a foreign correspondent must never report
what London does not want to hear.

And that is what I had done. I had told them that my
briefing had been garbage and the reports out of Lagos were
tripe. Then something very peculiar happened. Tiny Biafra
invaded Nigeria.

Ojukwu or one of his staff had noticed that Lagos had
transferred the entire Nigerian army across the river Niger way
up on the northern border. There was a huge bridge at Onitsha
crossing to an arrow-straight road to Lagos. The bridge was
intact, the road undefended. The sheer amateurishness was
breathtaking. So the Biafrans put together a column of
Landrovers and trucks, scraped together their meagre supply
of rifles and Bren guns, and rolled over it, heading west at a
steady cruise. I went with them.

There was no opposition. A platoon of Nigerians at the
western end of the bridge took one look and ran. The column
rolled on across the mid-west state to its capital at Benin City.
This too was abandoned, and that included the British Deputy
High Commissioner (there was one for each federal state), who
hightailed it into the bush. That was how the news got out:
someone in the radio room alerted Lagos, which spun straight
into panic.

It was the success that was the undoing. The Biafrans could not believe their own speed of progress. Instead of refuelling and pressing on for the Carter Bridge, access to Lagos city, they paused for two days.

The next day of motoring brought us over the next border into Western Region, land of the Yorubas, with whom the Biafrans had no quarrel. In several village doorways there were hands waving. The jeep I was in reached the small town of Ore. There had clearly been a clash. Several dozen Nigerian soldiers lay dead round the village square. Wild pigs had been feeding on the soft parts of the faces. Without cheeks or lips, the dead heads stared up in insane greeting. Then I noticed the shoulder-flash insignia. They were General Gowon's personal praetorian guard.

As my colleague from Comtel filmed the scene, I remarked to my escorting officer that if they were using the elite of the elite as a stopgap panic measure, the road must be open and undefended. He nodded but a second panic was setting in. The sheer nerve was receding like an ebbing tide.

Later, much later, it was reported that the British High Commission in Lagos was preparing to shred documents and Gowon's personal aircraft was at Ikeja airport with propellers turning and a flight plan for the north. It was really that close.

It all went wrong, of course, and as usual the flaw was betrayal. Ojukwu had appointed a certain Colonel Banjo to lead the mission but, arriving in Benin, Banjo had contacted Lagos by High Commission radio and tried to cut a deal – for himself. He was later tried and shot for it, but too late.

The column began to retreat, back to and over the Onitsha

Bridge. Then engineers blew it up. It remained uncrossable until the end of the war two years later.

Back in Enugu I noticed the tone of messages out of London had changed again. The early ones begged for every detail of the invasion across the Niger. Once it was known that had failed, I was peremptorily ordered back to London. So I packed up, said goodbye to (by now) General Ojukwu and an army jeep was assigned to take me to the Cameroon crossing point on the eastern border.

Thence with a local Mammy-waggon to Mamfe and another bus south to Douala. Finally in the Cocotiers Hotel I would get a phone connection to London. The instructions were the same. No reports, thank you, just get the next flight home.

I did so, and walked into Broadcasting House to be met with an urgent instruction to talk to no one but to report at once to Arthur Hutchinson. It was a brief interview and to the point. According to him, my reporting must have been biased and I was summarily fired.

But the BBC does not actually fire people; it sends them to a form of internal Siberia, hoping they will resign, serve out their three-month notice and leave quietly. I was out of the foreign news team and reduced back to home reporter. I should report to that department's head, Tom Maltby. I would never travel abroad for the BBC again.

That is a serious charge, but no one could explain why a seasoned foreign correspondent, sent to cover an obscure African war, would lose his mind to the political ambitions of an African tribe he had never heard of. However, the decision was final and there was no appeal.

There was no point in turning to Sir Hugh Carleton-Greene; he was struggling with his own resignation dilemma in the face of the departure of far bigger bananas than I after the imposition of Lord Hill on the whole corporation.

So I wandered along the third-floor corridors until I came to the office of Tom Maltby.

Farewell, Auntie

Tom Maltby was a very decent man and kindly. He had been in the navy during the war, seen combat but never made a fuss about it. He knew exactly what had happened to my BBC career and why. I tried to explain anyway.

I had only reported out of Nigeria what I had seen or, if reported speech, with immediate attribution. Where was the bias? He explained that was missing the entire point.

What I had done, he explained as to an erring nephew, was contradict the High Commission in Lagos, Sir Saville Garner the senior mandarin at the Commonwealth Office (and thus the British government), the BBC World Service and Mr Hutchinson.

But they were all besotted by the original flawed analysis, I protested. Nevertheless, it is the only analysis that is acceptable, he pointed out. Then he added the argument that prevented me resigning straight away.

'It is about duration,' he said. 'If this ten-day or two-week war goes on for, say, six months, they will surely have to reconsider.'

It made sense and he could be right. If the Biafran

insurrection did indeed collapse rapidly, the analysis of the mandarins would have been proved right, if somewhat delayed; and my own voiced predictions that this was no storm in a teacup would have been shown to be mistaken.

To avoid the strained atmosphere of my mooning about in the reporters' room he suggested I be transferred to the Parliamentary Desk down at the House of Commons. The Political Correspondent, Peter Hardiman Scott, had a vacancy for an assistant. So in October 1967 that is where I went.

It was a small and friendly office that over the five months I was there taught me much about the way the country is actually run. It also wiped away an awful lot of benign illusions about the merits of MPs and peers. I was able to avoid the vipers' nest going on up at Broadcasting House as rival coteries vied for power and influence. Then, in February 1968, something happened to change my mind.

In the interim, the Nigeria civil war had not ended or improved. It had got worse. The Lagos government had instituted call-up and hugely increased the size of its army. This was being quietly equipped with torrents of British weaponry, shipped out covertly by the Wilson government, which was assuring one and all that it was neutral.

But the Biafrans had not collapsed. On the contrary. Before secession Ojukwu had moved the entire financial reserves of the Eastern Region beyond the reach of Lagos and was increasing the size and equipment of his own army on the international black market. Biafra had also set up a representation office in London and engaged the services of an agency to handle media communications.

It had also secured the agreement of Spain to use its colony on Fernando Po island as a staging base, and the agreement of Portugal to use offshore São Tomé island for the same purpose. It was no longer cut off. In February Biafra organized a mass-media visit. Just about everyone accepted, with the notable exception of the BBC, which was still filing Nigerian propaganda out of Lagos.

I found the decision so weird that I went to visit Arthur Hutchinson to ask why and to volunteer to return with the rest of the invited British media group to see what was going on. Existing reports indicated that military action was slowly increasing, the federal forces had made a few gains but that casualties, mainly among civilians, were increasing.

It was another short interview. I was told bluntly that I was going nowhere, and as for another BBC man going, he told me verbatim: 'You have to understand, we are not covering this war.'

This struck me as bizarre. Every day the horrors of Vietnam were copiously reported, but that was an American mess. Nigeria was a very British one, apparently to remain clothed in secrecy.

The all-media group duly flew out, stayed a week and returned. I sought out a few whom I knew and asked for their experiences. It was clear the Nigeria–Biafra war was not even looking like achieving a quick resolution and was indeed getting worse. So I decided to take a week of owing leave and go independently.

I thought it wise not to tell anyone, including the Biafran office in Kensington. I just took some of my savings and flew to Lisbon. From what I had learned, the covert arms flights were leaving from there and the shipper was a sort of aviation mercenary called Hank Wharton, an American and an amusing rogue whom I traced to his hotel in the Portuguese capital.

He was very laid back when I explained that I could not pay him but said he had a four-prop Constellation leaving in the morning and I could hitch a ride. There were no seats in the clapped-out old airliner so I perched on a crate of mortars in the back.

It was a long droning flight, to which I would become much accustomed, the only diversions being trips up to the flight deck to talk with the crew and seek yet another cup of coffee.

Wharton had absolutely no over-fly rights because the members of the Organisation of African Unity all sided with Lagos, being all military or civilian dictatorships. So we flew out at sea with the Atlantic through the right-hand portholes and the smudge of the African coast to the left.

There was a refuelling stop at Portuguese Guinea, also gripped by an independence war. Coming in to land, low and slow over the jungle, some bright spark from Amílcar Cabral's nationalist fighters fired up at the Constellation. The bullet came through the floor, missed the crate of mortars by two inches, went between my parted thighs and out through the ceiling. Welcome to Africa.

On the tarmac the crew examined the holes, pronounced that there was no harm done and we would refuel and fly on. It got a bit draughty in the back after that. In the middle of the night, with no lights showing, we drifted into the old Eastern Nigeria's only airfield at Port Harcourt. I was immediately arrested.

I explained to a highly educated major, who had been an accountant until he enlisted, what I was doing there and why. He contacted Enugu and was told to put me in a jeep for the capital. Once there I was taken to State House to see General Ojukwu, who greeted me with huge amusement. When I explained I had come alone to see for myself, he mused that he had played host to a score of British journalists so one more would make no difference. He assigned me a jeep with an army driver, a billet in the old Progress Hotel and said I could go anywhere and see anything I wanted. He would put me on a Wharton plane on Friday for London.

Within three days it was clear this war was not going to end any time soon. The popular mood was that Nigeria would realize the futility of continuing fighting with the close-down of its revenue-producing oilfields, all now inside Biafra, and respond to Ojukwu's standing proposal of ceasefire and a second peace conference.

He had offered to share the oil and was quietly negotiating with Shell-BP, the main concessionaire. France under de Gaulle, never slow to exploit a British disadvantage, was making covert gestures of support and weapons were arriving in a steady stream.

For the record there were no starving children visible at that time. They would appear later, and the ghastly images of them, splashed across the world's media, would transform everything.

On the Friday I left for London, confident of flying from Lisbon to the UK on the Sunday, ready to reappear at work on the Monday, the end of my leave. Then things went wrong. The first stage was to São Tomé island and there Hank Wharton's plane broke down. I could not contact London to say I would be late back; I just had to kick my heels until we flew on Monday. I was in London on Wednesday morning. A call to a friend inside the BBC indicated all hell was let loose.

When I reached my flat it had been broken into. It was a pretty hammy job. The lock was only a Yale, which could have been opened with a credit card or an artist's palette knife. The two goons had stove in a door panel to reach the lock from inside. My neighbours told me there had been two of them, from the BBC, and they said they had been 'worried' about me, the inference being that I might have committed self-harm under the pressure of career-stress.

But my body would have been pretty obvious. These guys had gone through everything. I knew I had left no traces of where I had been. But it was pretty clear that, once again, the party was over.

I packed a grip, left a note abandoning the lease with a friendly neighbour destined for the landlord, and decamped to spend two days and nights on the sofa of a friend.

When a reporter is told by his employer to publish something he knows to be a pack of lies, there are only three things he can do. The first is to look to his security, his salary, his pension pot, and do what he is told.

The second is to sit in the corner blubbing his heart out at the unfairness of it all. The third is to raise a rigid middle finger at the lot of them and walk out. I sat down and wrote a long letter of resignation. It was to Tom Maltby.

I thanked him for his consideration towards me but informed him that in my view the Nigerian war was going to be a major story with considerable length and many casualties. In view of the BBC's policy of non-coverage (except from a Lagos hotel), I was going to cover the story myself as a freelance.

I signed off and posted the letter late on Friday, aware it would not be opened and read until Monday morning. On the Friday-night plane I was back in Lisbon, confronting a bewildered Hank Wharton and asking for another hitch to the war zone. By Sunday night I was in Port Harcourt under arrest again and on Monday morning, about the time Tom Maltby was opening his mail, I was shown into the office of an even more bewildered Emeka Ojukwu.

The practice of embedding war reporters into military units was unknown back then so the question of paying my way arose. I said I wanted to stay but had no funds and no employer behind me.

Ojukwu offered me half a tin-roofed Nissen hut, food from State House kitchens, a Volkswagen Beetle and a petrol allowance. Plus access to the communications company he had engaged to get news despatches from Biafra to Geneva and thence to the world. After that I could go anywhere, see anything and report anything.

I made plain I would not report what his own propaganda bureau wanted, but only what I saw with my own eyes or learned from reliable sources. But what I wrote would be fair.

'That's all I want,' he said. 'Fair. After that the story will tell itself.'

So our deal was struck. I was a freelance with no clients. All I had was a story that deserved to be told and the opposition of a British Establishment that seemed determined no one should hear about it.

And somewhere, deep in the bush, the children began to wither and die, but no one knew.

Biafra had been in lock-down since the start of the

secession ten months earlier. That meant all borders were closed and the blockade included food. The native Ibos grew their own cassava and yams in ample quantities. Pounded cassava root and pounded yams made the staple diet and never ran out. But both are totally carbohydrate.

It is a fact that an adult needs one gram of pure protein per day to stay healthy. A growing child needs five.

The native population had always raised a few chickens and some small pigs for their eggs and meat. Other than these there was no protein source and, unperceived, the hens and pigs had been consumed.

The traditional protein supplement had always been fish; not river-caught fish but enormous quantities of Norwegian-imported dried cod called stockfish. These rock-hard sticks of cod went into the family stewpot, became rehydrated and served as the family protein ration. No stockfish had entered the surrounded and blockaded enclave for nine months. The meat/milk sources were gone. The national diet was now almost 100 per cent starch.

In the deep bush mothers noticed their babies' limbs were withering to sticks. Heads with glazed eyes lolled on weakened neck muscles. Bellies swelled to great drums but full only of air. Thinking their children were hungry, the mothers of the bush fed their offspring more carbohydrates. It would not be until May that they would come out to show their babies to the missionaries who would know what they were looking at.

My first two months were almost idle. There was little movement on any of the fronts. I had some savings left and remembered a long-standing offer from a friend to be his guest on a visit to Israel. So I took him up.

Living History

ISRAEL IN THE spring of 1968 was still infused by a spirit of bemused euphoria, deriving from its smashing victory of the Six-Day War.

The size of its territory had virtually doubled, more so if one includes the barren wilderness of the Sinai Peninsula, long since conceded back to Egypt. The old, confused borders left over from the 1948 war had been swept away. The Nablus Salient was gone. The city of Jerusalem had been conquered and the holy places, forbidden to Jews by the Mandelbaum Gate, were open for worship.

Diggers were still revealing foot after foot of the long-buried Wailing Wall, the last remaining section of the old Temple of Solomon. There was a countrywide mood of slightly intoxicated optimism.

But the country that had always contained some Palestinian Arabs had now absorbed half a million more and the problems of the future were still too far ahead to contemplate, had anyone wished, which they did not.

Some have deemed this mood to be the conqueror's arrogance; I choose to accept it was the euphoria of a

Dr Pangloss and his belief that 'all's for the best in the best of all possible worlds'. There seemed no problem, including that of a negotiated and lasting peace, that could not be achieved. Seen from forty-five years later, it was the product not of gloating but of a slightly touching naiveté.

I determined to see as much as possible of the land during my stay and with the help of my London-based friend had set up a few points of contact. Starting at the Dan Hotel, Tel Aviv, I headed south out of town for Beersheva and the Negev desert. There was a man living in almost complete isolation in the Negev writing his memoirs, who had agreed to give me a few moments of his valuable time.

There is only one way to see the real Israel and that is to travel everywhere by the Egged buses, so I took one from the Tel Aviv terminal to Beersheva and changed for the connection to Eilat. They may not be fast and they stop everywhere but they are cheap and my funds were meagre.

Out of Beersheva we passed the nuclear research facility at Dimona, birthplace of Israel's nuclear weapons array and mockingly referred to as a 'jeans factory'. Then it was the desert.

During National Service my hitched-lift Hastings from Lyneham to Malta had refuelled at the RAF airbase of El Adem in Libya. Otherwise I had never seen the real desert, let alone motored through it. Later I would see many more but they are all the same. They just seem to go on and on, a wasteland of dun-brown sand and gravel. Only the Bedouin choose to live in them.

After hours bumping along we came round the curve of a hill and far ahead and below was a brilliant patch of green, like a pool table dumped in the middle of nowhere. The green was the irrigated crops of the moshav or collection of smallholdings I had come to visit. The bus stopped at the gate, I descended, it broke wind noisily and headed on to Eilat.

Inside the compound I was pointed to a residence that was little more than a Quonset hut standing alone. Outside was a single giant Israeli paratrooper, apparently the only security. He examined my passport, turned and knocked. A middle-aged housekeeper answered, also looked at the passport and beckoned me in. 'Twenty minutes,' she snapped in English, evidently housekeeper and dragon-guardian. She knocked on a study door and showed me in. Behind a desk cluttered with papers a tiny man beneath a snow-white candyfloss cloud of hair rose and smiled. I was meeting David Ben-Gurion, once one of many but now regarded, also by many, as the founding father of Israel.

He explained in flawless English that I created a perfect excuse to break from his labours at his memoirs. We sat in opposing chairs and he looked expectant. I wondered how many interviews to journalists he had given; thousands, probably, many famous, and now to a complete unknown.

I calculated that old men can often recall with total clarity what they did in their youth, while having completely forgotten whom they had dinner with last week. I know the feeling too well now. It seemed to me he must have been badgered many times for details of the Six-Day War, even though it was Levi Eshkol who was premier at the time.

'When you landed on the shore of Israel for the first time in 1906, sir, what was it like back then?'

He stared for several seconds then came alive as if jolted by an electric charge. Then he started to talk, eyes closed, recalling those very first early days. He was not a statesman back then, he was a penniless immigrant from a poor Jewish shtetl in Russian Poland.

He and his companions had berthed at the Arab port of Jaffa but they were not welcome and could get no lodgings, so they trekked north and camped among the sand dunes. They spoke Russian and Yiddish, not modern Hebrew, which had not been invented.

They were camped in a range of low sandhills and it was spring. The Hebrew for 'hill' is *tel* and for 'spring' *aviv*.

It took six days on a donkey to travel from the coast of this Turkish province to Jerusalem, which he did with a petition for land to the Ottoman governor. Ten years later he was there when the Ottoman empire fell. He saw General Allenby of the conquering British army enter Jerusalem.

He told me how the general had abandoned his horse and entered on foot in deference to the holiest shrine of three religions. Somewhere out to the east Lawrence, at the head of the Arab Revolt, was moving towards his own treasure. Damascus.

Over the years he had seen it all: both world wars, the Mandate between them, the rise of Zionism, the utterance of the Balfour Declaration, the creation on a Franco–British map of Lebanon, Syria, Jordan and Iraq. He had seen the dictators and the monarchs come and go, rise and fall, as the Jews pursued their single goal of, one day, a nation of their own. He had not only seen it all, he had been at the epicentre. He had met the generals and the giants, Roosevelt and Churchill.

Several times the dragon popped her head round the door

to object that it was time for his nap, but he waved her away. What struck me was his tolerance. He had fought all his life for his dream yet he seemed to hate no one, not even Al-Husseini, Grand Mufti of Jerusalem, who so admired Adolf Hitler and wanted every Jew on earth dead. He had huge forbearance for the Palestinian Arabs, whose language he spoke perfectly. The only people he had no time for were the fanatics of the Irgun and the Stern Gang. At their mention he sneered and shook his white-clouded head.

The British, for so long the unwilling army of occupation, he liked, even though he had helped form the Haganah, the Palmach and the Mossad to outwit and out-manoeuvre them.

I could have filled ten notebooks, but I just sat and listened to an old man who was sixty years of living history and who had seen it all. Finally tired, he indicated that he needed his sleep. I went to fetch the dragon, who glared at me and escorted him to his sleeping quarters. At the door he turned and said:

'Goodbye, young man. I hope you have been interested. And stay lucky.'

I had indeed. Fascinated. I was shown out and walked to the gate. It was dusk. An Egged bus came by. I waved, it stopped and took me on to Eilat as darkness fell. David Ben-Gurion died six years later at the age of eighty-seven. He was one of the greatest men I ever met.

Eilat

As late as 1945 what is now the huge port and vacation resort of Eilat hardly existed. It was a motley collection of shacks with orange-crate furniture, clinging to the water's edge opposite the bigger Jordanian port of Aqaba, captured by Lawrence in 1917.

The early settlers and pioneers must have been tough as boots. There was nothing there but they began to build and to plant. Among the earliest to arrive were Dr and Mrs Fay Morris from Manchester. He had flown with the RAF in the war, qualified as a doctor and emigrated with his young wife. By 1968 both were pillars of the community but lived modestly in a house they had built themselves.

The previous summer the Israelis had swept across Sinai as General Israel Tal and his elderly British tanks pushed Nasser's forces back to the Suez Canal. That three-day conquest, although fought along the northern rim of Sinai, brought the entire triangular peninsula under Israeli control. And that included the Sinai Bedouin, to whom Dr Morris had been appointed official medical officer. The Egyptians, who had always treated the Bedou contemptuously, had never accorded them a doctor.

Because Sinai is girt on the west by the Suez Canal, which runs down to become the Red Sea, and on the east by the Gulf of Eilat and the Gulf of Aqaba, which also run down to become the Red Sea, and along the north by the Mediterranean, it is virtually an island. And the Bedouin seldom cross water.

From their desert wilderness the Bedouin have watched the Romans, the Phoenicians, the Greeks and the armies of Islam cross and re-cross their land, in conquest or defeat. Later came the Crusaders, Napoleon's legions, Allenby's British Tommies and the Israelis.

The Bedouin have witnessed them all over the centuries. The marching and the fighting were mainly along the northern rim, up by the Mediterranean. The hinterland was always theirs. And their policy was always the same: withdraw into their deserts of sand and rocks, do not interfere, do not take sides, watch and survive. After July 1967, the Israelis were the first people to treat them decently.

Army engineers built a fresh-water pipe from Eilat, through El Arish and right across to Suez. They installed taps and troughs every couple of miles. And the water was free, in a land where water is life.

At first the Bedouin thought there must be a trap, but the taps were unguarded and slowly they began to come by night, refill their camels, their bellies and their goatskin bags. Then first contact with Arabic-speaking officers was made. They were offered medication for their many ailments and infections. That was where Dr Morris came in. He set up clinics at specific oases and slowly his patients appeared.

Many of the sufferers were female and the miseries were

mainly gynaecological. It was out of the question for him to examine a Bedou woman, not because he was Jewish but because he was male. So an army nurse would go into the tent, shout through the flap what she had found and he would shout back the treatment.

The Bedouin replied in kind. You never see the Bedouin unless they allow you to, but they see everything. Each time a group of Egyptian commandos landed on the Sinai shore, the nearest Israeli army post would be alerted. Duly ambushed, the Egyptians would be disarmed and sent back, but never killed. It was almost a formality.

Through Dr Morris's offices I was allowed to accompany an Israeli army group in a command car on a two-day tour of Sinai. It was wild and bleak, a mighty ocean of football-sized boulders that would break most suspensions, interspersed with patches not of fine sand but of red-hot gravel. At two oases we took coffee with Bedouin while the women crouched out of sight inside the camel-hair tents.

Today it is so different. Right down the eastern coast is a chain of scuba-diving holiday resorts from Taba Heights to Ras Mohammed. There are tourist visits to the ancient monastery of Santa Caterina, right in the centre of the desert, marking the spot where Moses is believed to have been given the tablets with the Ten Commandments. In 1968 the monks had hardly seen an outsider for years.

Finally back in Eilat I repaired to the beach bar of Rafi Nelson for a very cooling dip in the gulf and a long, cold beer. Among those at the bar was one Yitzhak 'Ike' Ahronowitz, who spoke perfect English because he had studied in America. He had also been captain of the *Exodus*, the refugee ship turned back from the Palestinian coast by the British Royal Navy in 1947. He was still only in his mid-forties.

I had been too young to recall 1947, but I knew it had been a powerfully emotional incident and had generated Leon Uris's explicitly anti-British novel and the film that followed in 1960, which I had seen. I asked him if he shared Mr Uris's feelings. He thought it over.

'Well, your navy officers were obeying their orders. And they were bastard orders.' He grinned and raised his beer in mock-toast. 'So you were bastards, but at least you were polite bastards.'

A few days later I wished goodbye to the Morrises and took a bus north to Jerusalem.

Jerusalem

I WILL DEFY ANYONE to visit Jerusalem for the first time and not be fascinated by that maze of ancient streets and shrines revered by the world's three greatest religions.

Since the departure of the British and the inconclusive outcome of the 1948 post-independence war, the Old Quarter of East Jerusalem had been closed to the Jews while available to Muslims and Christians. Now it was open to all.

I played the tourist, staying at a humble boarding house, wandering the streets and alleys where fifty generations of worshippers and warriors had been before me. From the Via Dolorosa to the hill of Golgotha, from the Dome of the Rock to the Mosque of Al-Aqsa, to the Wailing Wall and all that was left of the Temple of Solomon after the total sacking by the Romans, I just wandered and gawped. After three days I was invited to take tea at the King David Hotel.

I had heard of it. Once the headquarters both of the British Mandate government and the army HQ, it was one of the more modern landmarks of the city, and though the damage of the bombing of 1946 was largely repaired, the scars were still visible. My reading before arriving had taught me the bare outlines.

On 22 July 1946 agents of the ultra-Zionist Irgun organization had eluded the pretty sketchy security measures and driven a van into the underground stores-delivery area. From the van, milk churns packed with 350 kilograms of explosive had been unloaded and scattered round the basement and night club.

When they went off, ninety-one were killed and forty-six injured, mostly civilians. If the army HQ at one end of the building was the target, the bombers placed the device at the other end, hence the civilian casualties.

Twenty-eight British died, including thirteen soldiers, but they were well outnumbered by forty-one Arabs and seventeen Palestinian Jews. I mention this only because of what happened to me later that week.

For years controversy raged as to whether a telephoned warning had ever been made, or if made received, and if received disregarded. But the bombing was denounced by David Ben-Gurion and the Haganah, both yearning for the British Mandate to end and independence to arrive. In their view the British were going to leave anyway, as soon as the newly born United Nations in New York made up its mind.

Mr Ben-Gurion had just told me in Sde Boker, his desert retreat, that the real struggle would come after independence when the Arabs launched themselves at the new Israeli state to snuff it out. To that end the Mossad LeAliyah Bet, the purchasing agency outside the country, and Haganah inside the Mandate were trying to smuggle in both fighters and weapons under the noses of the British, who might choose to look the other way or not. Thus the King David bombing, which poisoned relations, was regarded by the calmer heads as completely counter-productive.

I was taking tea with friends on the upper terrace when I was invited over to be introduced to someone. I found myself facing the black eyepatch of General Moshe Dayan, defence minister and architect of Israeli tactics for the Six-Day War. We talked for half an hour.

I had always presumed he lost that eye to a bullet but he explained to me how it happened. Before the Second World War he had been on patrol with the British Zionist Orde Wingate, who designed and taught the principle of guerrilla warfare in that part of the world.

Wingate was a strange one, a Christian with an encyclopaedic knowledge of the Old Testament and a conviction that God Himself had given the Holy Land to the Jews. Hence the Zionism. His skills in guerrilla warfare were such that Churchill later plucked him from the Middle East to form and lead the Chindits behind the Japanese lines in Burma.

On that patrol Moshe Dayan had been staring at an Arab position through field glasses when a stray bullet hit the other end of the lens. It was the eyepiece that was rammed back into the socket, blinding him.

I had one last interview set up via my contacts. I wanted to talk to Ezer Weizman, the founder of the Israeli Air Force and another revered figure after the IAF's performance during the war of 1967. By then he was transport minister and I turned up as agreed the next day at the ministry.

He came bursting out, late, in a tearing hurry and having completely forgotten about our interview. The only way of achieving it was to do it on the drive back to Tel Aviv, but he did not intend to drive; he wanted to fly and the airfield was only minutes away.

'Do you mind flying?' he asked. I knew he had once flown British Hurricanes with the RAF in Egypt during the Second World War, so I mentioned that I also had my RAF wings. He stared, then grinned.

'Right, you can be my co-pilot,' he said, and barked an order at the driver. His ministry attendant looked horrified.

I presumed he would be flying in a multi-seat staff aircraft but his chosen transport was a very small high-wing monoplane of the Cessna/Piper variety, although Israeli-made. We were strapped in, he did the pre-flight checks and took off. Almost immediately the rising thermals from the Judean desert caught us and the aeroplane began to rock and twist in the upcurrents.

The interview would have to be conducted through face masks above the roar of the engine. He climbed to about 5,000 feet and set course for Sde Dov, the military airport outside Tel Aviv. So I asked him how he had established the now mighty IAF.

He explained that as independence approached back in 1947 he had been charged to find and buy some serviceable fighter planes. The Mossad LeAliyah Bet traced a few to Yugoslavia, then recently liberated from German occupation and under the rule of the former guerrilla Marshal Tito.

Tito may have been a Communist but it did not matter. He needed the foreign currency and the Haganah was anti-imperialist. The deal was done. There were four of them, abandoned by the Germans, still in maker's grease, stored in their original crates. An Israeli team went north to assemble them. He and his three other pilots followed. Rather strangely, they were four young Jewish fliers at the controls of four Messerschmitt 109s in full Nazi insignia.

Thus they flew south, refuelled secretly in Turkey and arrived over Tel Aviv on the day of independence and of the launch of the Arab war to snuff out Israel. They arrived, virtually flying on vapour, to be told a squadron of Egyptian Air Force fighters was coming north over Ashkelon. There was no time to land and refuel. They turned south, to find King Farouk's British-built Hurricanes coming towards them. Thus the first dogfight over Israel was between Egyptians in Hurricanes and Jews in Messerschmitts.

Up to this point Ezer Weizman had been gesticulating copiously but now he took both hands off the control column and raised them, fingers spread, to demonstrate how he had led the attack, with Benny Katz from South Africa as his wingman.

The monoplane promptly flicked over and the Judean desert went to the top of the windscreen. He didn't seem to mind. As we began to dive upside down I thought it wise to drop my notepad and pencil and grab the joystick. When she was back on an even keel and heading for the coast, I suggested he resume control. But he just shrugged and went on, with more hand gestures, explaining how they had scattered the Hurricanes, which turned back to Egypt and landed at what is now Ben Gurion airport but then was a grass strip.

He took over again as we came to land, shut the engine down, jumped out, gave me a cheery wave and shot off in his ministerial car. The ground crew let me examine his personal black Spitfire, a superb model, then I took an Egged bus from the main gate of the airbase back to downtown Tel Aviv.

Confession

M Y LAST NIGHT in Tel Aviv on that visit was spent at a pub down an alley going past the Dan Hotel towards the sea. It was owned and run by a very feisty lady, a Romanian redhead, also called Freddie.

There was a crowd round the bar that I was invited to join, including I think Moshe Dayan's daughter Yael and her husband, a former tank commander called Dov Zion. In deference to my ignorance of Hebrew they very politely switched to English and the conversation moved to where I had been and what I had seen. That included the King David Hotel.

Every one of them had been involved in some way in the independence struggle twenty years earlier and half at least had been in the Haganah or the Palmach. As the British had then been the occupiers I expected some hostility, but there was none.

There were anecdotes about smuggling consignments of small arms under melon cargoes past British roadblocks, and all were at pains to tell me that the British were divided into two types, so far as they were concerned.

The other-rank soldiers, many of them Paras, had nothing

against Jews at all, having often been brought up with them in the streets of London, Birmingham and Manchester. The soldiers had been fighting the Germans for four years before being posted to Palestine; some had seen the horrors of the concentration camps and all just wanted to go back home to their wives and families.

They spoke neither Arabic nor Hebrew and the Palestinians certainly spoke no English. So if there was any conversation it was between the Diaspora Jews and the Tommies. It was friendly enough. Among the former guerrillas round the bar were several who narrated how consignments of Haganah weapons went past the roadblocks on a nudge and a wink, the melons undisturbed.

The anti-Semitic attitude came hot and strong from the Foreign Office, the civil servants and senior officer corps, who rarely disguised their preference for the Arabs. I had heard it said before that more desert sand flows through the British Foreign Office than Lawrence ever saw.

But what really surprised me was that their real dislike was not for the British but for their own extremists, the Irgun and the Stern Gang. I could not detect one with a good word to say for them. The collective attitude seemed to be that the back-shooting of British Tommies by the extremists simply made the real job, preparing for the survival war of 1948, even harder.

But at the back of the group was one who stared at me constantly until it became quite uncomfortable. Finally, as drinks were being replenished, I felt a tug at my sleeve and it was the staring one.

'I must have a word with you,' he said. Close up, I realized he was not hostile but pleading.

'Not here,' he said and drew me away to the far corner of the bar.

'I have to speak to you. I have waited twenty years. I have a confession to make.'

Normally when a journalist hears someone wants to make a confession his heart sinks. It is usually about some shoplifting years ago or failure to report a spaceship landing in the garden last night. One looks round for an escape route. In this case there was none.

'Why me?' I asked.

'Because you are British,' he said, 'and you are a Gentile.'

I could not see the connection but I nodded anyway. I would just have to listen to what he had to say. He took a deep breath.

'I was in the Irgun back then. I drove the truck into the King David Hotel.'

There was silence between us. The murmur round the bar was a distant backdrop. He was still staring at me, small, wiry, intense, with black unblinking eyes. Still pleading. I did not know what to say.

'That's it?'

'No, not all. I want you to believe me. I walked out of the basement and went to a café, a French one, right opposite. I used the public phone. I rang the King David exchange and asked to be put through to military HQ. I spoke to a junior officer. I told him there was a bomb.'

'And?'

'He did not believe me. He said it was impossible. Then he put the phone down. Twenty minutes later it went off. But I tried. Please believe me, I really tried.'

Whether there would have been time to evacuate that enormous hotel in twenty minutes was a very moot point.

'All right,' I said. 'I believe you.'

'Thank you.'

'One question from me,' I said. 'Why do you not tell them over there?' I nodded towards the warriors round the bar.

'They would kill me,' he said. He might have been right too.

I left Israel the next day. Back to London, to Ashford to see my folks. Then back to the rainforests. Back to the killing fields of Africa.

Of Mice and Moles

MOST OF THE British media have an ongoing problem with the various organs of the British intelligence community, typified by a seeming inability to work out which is which.

There are three main organs. The least-mentioned is, ironically, the biggest. This is GCHQ or Government Communications Headquarters, situated in a vast doughnut-shaped complex outside the country town of Cheltenham. Its task is mainly SIGINT or signals intelligence.

Basically, it listens. It intercepts and eavesdrops on Britain's enemies and opponents and sometimes even her friends on a worldwide basis. In a quixotic throwback to the days of empire, it has out-stations in various parts of the world which even the American National Security Agency, immensely bigger and more generously funded, finds very useful. As a result there is a constant sharing and interflow of 'product' between the two.

It is this unceasing information-swap, the invisible but crucial collaboration between the two countries' information-gathering and security agencies, that constitute the much-mocked 'special relationship' and that includes a mutual trust and fellowship between the Special Forces also. It has nothing whatever to do with notional and often passing friendships between politicians.

Alongside GCHQ is the Security Service or MI5. Long ago its mailing address was PO Box 500, London, so it is sometimes mockingly referred to as Box 500. Its task is in-country security against foreign espionage, foreign and domestic terrorism and home-grown treachery. It maintains just a few postings overseas to liaise with other friendly security agencies.

The one regarded as the more glamorous agency is the Secret Intelligence Service, usually referred to by a title it renounced years ago: MI6. There is often confusion between the Secret Service and the Security Service, let alone the swapping of their numbers and thus their functions. But everyone remotely concerned is universally described by those on the outside with another misnomer, that of 'spy'.

The true spy is almost certainly a foreigner employed deep inside the clandestine fabric of his own country who is prepared to abstract his country's covert information and hand it over to his real employers. The go-between is called an 'asset' and the full-time employee who runs him is his 'handler'.

There is the relatively new nomenclature of 'spook' but I never ever heard the word 'spy' used within that world. Only the papers and TV ever use it, usually wrongly.

That apart, MI5 is based at Thames House, on the north bank of the river Thames in London, a few hundred yards from Parliament, and the SIS at Vauxhall Cross on the south bank almost a mile upstream, after moving from the shabby old Century House in the Elephant and Castle district.

The task of SIS is foreign information-gathering and its presence is worldwide, with a 'station' somewhere in almost all British embassies and sometimes consulates. Basically, it seeks to discover and forewarn. Politicians are wont to sneer when in opposition but drool with pleasure when, in office, they are taken to a quiet room to have explained to them what is really going on rather than what they thought was going on.

Politicians congenitally loathe to be taken by surprise, which is where the forewarning comes in, but forewarning depends on knowing what the bad people are planning, intending or have in mind. As that is rarely given away, it has to be discovered clandestinely. Hence the espionage.

This broadly devolves into three categories: electronic intelligence or ELINT, the scouring of the surface of the world with look-down cameras, mounted either in satellites, drones or warplanes; signals intelligence, SIGINT, intercepting everything the bad people say to each other even when they think they have absolute privacy; and HUMINT, or human intelligence-gathering.

Britain has never been able to compete with the vast budgets of the USA, and has no space programme, but it brings to the table a worthwhile contribution in HUMINT. Infiltrating an agent into the heart of a tricky situation can produce more product than all the 'gizmos' could ever see or hear. It is the speciality of the SIS.

As for the terms, those inside the SIS called it 'the Office'; those outside use the phrase 'the Firm', and the staffers of the Firm are 'the Friends'. Not to be confused with the CIA, which is 'the Agency' or 'the Company', and its staff who are 'the Cousins'.

Considering the 60-million-plus population of the UK

and the size of its Gross National Product, it has always had a smaller SIS than almost any other developed nation in the world, and thus cheaper. The British taxpayer is far from short-changed. There is a quixotic reason for this.

Unlike all other agencies, the Firm has always been able to rely on a widespread, ad hoc army of volunteers prepared to help out if asked nicely. They come from a vast array of professions which cause them to travel a bit. They may agree while on a foreign visit for business purposes to pick up a package, deliver a letter to a hole in a tree, make a payment or just keep their eyes and ears open and undergo a cheerful debriefing when they get home. It appears a bit weird but it seems to work.

This is because the best 'cover' in the world is no cover at all but the truth. Thus if Mr Farnsbarns really is going to a trade fair to sell his paper clips, he might just slip into a phone booth, remove a letter from the pages of the telephone directory and bring it home in an invisible slit in a specially prepared brief-case. That is where the economics come in; it is not done for money but just to help 'the old country'. Very few nations can match that.

There are times in your life when you meet someone and in short order decide he is a thoroughly decent fellow and you can trust him. If you are ever deceived in this later, it is like a hot dagger.

In late 1968, on a brief home visit from Biafra to firm up some correspondent contracts with various London papers, I met a member of the Firm called Ronnie. He sought me out rather than the reverse and made no bones about what he was, and we hit it off.

He was an orientalist with good Mandarin but to his bewilderment had been made head of the Africa desk. He admitted he knew little about Africa and less about what was really going on inside Biafra. I think we spent about twenty hours over several days while I explained how bad things were as it became plain the children were now dying of starvation like flies. Had I not trusted his word I would never have agreed to what came next.

The Commonwealth Relations Office (the CRO) had amalgamated with the Foreign Office to become the FCO. Both the former secretary of state for the CRO and his deputy the minister of state had resigned, one after the other. The former, a deeply devout Scottish Presbyterian, George Thompson, despite the official reason given, simply could not in all conscience continue to preside over a policy he found disgusting and immoral. His deputy, George Thomas, was a religious Welsh Methodist and shared precisely the same opinion.

(The latter went on to become Speaker of the House of Commons and retired as Lord Tonypandy, a thoroughly honourable and respected politician, not least for his stand over Biafra.)

But the FCO was in the hands of the appalling Michael Stewart, a complete creature of his Civil Service mandarins. They, headed by Lord Greenhill, had absorbed, lock, stock and barrel, the policy of the CRO, itself based on the flawed appraisal of Sir David Hunt, still en poste as British High Commissioner in Lagos and pushing the pro-Nigeria, crush-Biafra policy line with every despatch.

But there was a debate beginning after fifteen months of

the Nigeria–Biafra war, and made more intense by the torrent of hideous pictures showing Biafran babies reduced to barely alive skeletons.

The public marches of protest were starting, notable figures were protesting; the debate might be at a very high level and in complete secrecy, but the FCO was fighting a rearguard action for the minds of the vacillating Harold Wilson government.

Technically the SIS comes under the FCO but is entitled to disagree in certain circumstances, specifically if it has factual information rather than mere opinion. Ronnie's problem was he had no specific eyes-on information from the heart of Biafra to offset the assurances coming through from Lagos to the effect that the horrors were grossly exaggerated and the war would in any case be over in very short order – the song that had now been sung for fifteen months of a two-week war.

I did what I did, not in order to do down the Biafrans – far from it. I did it to try to influence the Whitehall argument that continued intermittently for the next fifteen months until the final crushing of Biafra with a million dead children.

The argument was between:

'Prime Minister, this cannot be allowed to go on. The human cost is simply too high. We should reconsider our policy. We should use all our influence to urge a ceasefire, a peace conference and a political solution.'

And:

'Prime Minister, I can assure you the media reports are as usual sensationalist and grossly exaggerated. We have infor-mation the rebel regime is very close to collapse. The sooner it does, the sooner we can get columns of relief food into the rebel territory. Meanwhile we urge you to stick with the hitherto agreed policy and even increase the support for the Federal Government.'

Neither Ronnie nor I could know in October 1968 how long there was to go nor how many more were to die. But the argument for a ceasefire lost because of two reasons: the vanity factor and the cowardice factor.

It is said that if a tigress sees her cubs endangered she will fight with deranged passion to defend them. But her dedication pales into submission compared with the fury with which senior civil servants, and most notably of the Foreign Office, will defend the fiction that they cannot have made a mistake.

The cowardice applied as usual to the politicians, Wilson and Stewart. Basically it was: 'Prime Minister, if you concede to the "reconsider" argument you would have to admit that for fifteen months your government has made a mistake. How then do you reply to the media question: "How can you explain to the public the quarter-million children dead so far?"' At that point the response from Wilson and Stewart was: 'Very well, do what you feel you must. But hurry.'

So the military, advisory, diplomatic and propaganda help to the Lagos dictatorship quietly increased. Ronnie convinced me that the Firm might be able to win the argument if it could rebut the charge of media exaggeration with eyes-on evidence that the situation was as reported or worse.

But to do that he needed an asset deep inside the Biafran enclave, what he termed 'someone in on the ground'. When I left for the return to the rainforest, he had one.

The job was threefold. To report, through the various

newspapers and magazines who had accepted me as a 'stringer' (local correspondent on a non-staff basis), the military war as it crawled on its way. To use the same outlets to portray the humanitarian situation, the disaster among the children dying of kwashiorkor (protein deficiency) and the church-based efforts to keep them alive with an air bridge of illicit mercy flights bringing in relief food donated by literally the whole world.

In this there were at least a dozen other journalists, sometimes twenty, who came and went; there were delegations of parliamentarians, senators, emissaries from various concerned groups, who simply felt they had to see and report back.

In Europe and North America the issue, based on the reports, the still and moving pictures, became massive, linking left and right, young and old, in marches and protests. There were times when Harold Wilson appeared almost under siege and twice, I learned later, the 'reconsider' policy was almost adopted. Had the opposition Conservative Party lent its weight, the change of policy might have gone through and the dying of the children ended, but Edward Heath, the Tory leader, shared with the FCO his European Union obsession and he was their man.

The third task was to keep Ronnie informed of things that could not, for various reasons, emerge in the media. Just once, after nine months, things became sticky when a rumour spread that I was working for London. Had the suspicion developed, my situation might have become thoroughly tiresome. I discovered the source was the ex-Legionnaire German mercenary Rolf Steiner, with whom I had never been on the best of terms.

There was nothing for it but to have a word in the right ear. Two nights later, yelling and screaming, not a happy camper, with his hands roped behind him, Steiner was bundled on to a plane for Libreville and never returned.

A Media Explosion

IT SHOULD NEVER be forgotten that the Nigeria–Biafra war fell into two quite different periods and the transition from one to the other lasted no more than a fortnight.

For the first year, from July 1967 to June 1968, it was just an ordinary African war, plodding its incompetent way across the landscape. The Nigerians, with their standing army of 8,000 infantry in the summer of '67, had presumed they would sweep through the secessionist province as of right. The Biafrans believed that Lagos would wage war for a few months and then, realizing it was hopeless, give up. Neither happened.

After the short-lived debacle of the Biafran invasion of the mid-west across the Niger, Nigeria introduced compulsory conscription, forcing into uniform tens of thousands of unwilling young men. This huge expansion required weapons from rifles to artillery, armoured cars, staggering quantities of ammunition to replace that which was largely fired into the treetops, and training. That was where the British Establishment came in. Behind a mendacious screen of 'neutrality', the Wilson government poured in the equipment, without which the war could not have proceeded. That was what the Biafrans had not foreseen.

The Whitehall-sourced propaganda stumbled from lie to lie but for the first year the media paid little attention because eastern Nigeria was obscure, far away and of minimal reader interest. The first lie was that London would only 'fulfil existing contracts' but these were soon swamped by the expansion of the Nigerian army and shipload after shipload were needed.

Payment was not the problem; there were always the oil royalties and Nigeria's credit was good. It came down to the licences. Impelled by urgings from the High Commission in Lagos, these were granted without demur.

Another early lie was that no weapons at all were being shipped from Britain to fuel the war. The key word was 'from', not 'by'. In fact, the supplies were coming from British stocks at the immense NATO weapons park outside Brussels, and thus technically from Belgium. They were then replaced by shipments from Britain to Belgium.

Slowly both the enlargement and the supplies had their effect. The Nigerian army crawled across the territory, village by village and town by town. The capital Enugu was taken, to be replaced by the town of Umuahia. Port Harcourt fell and its airport was lost. With Enugu airport also gone, a new one was created at Uli from a stretch of road two miles long. This became the only entry and exit point, with clapped-out old cargo planes coming in from the offshore islands of Fernando Po (Spanish) and São Tomé (Portuguese.)

The transformation started deceptively in May 1968 when the missionaries noticed worried mothers from the deep bush bringing emaciated children for examination.

The missionaries were a network right across the country, mainly the fathers of the Holy Ghost and the nuns of the Holy

Rosary, both from Dublin. These ran the churches with, attached to them, a school and a dispensary. There were some Protestant missionaries but the great majority were Catholics. The Ibos were overwhelmingly Catholic, and Islam had never penetrated south of the savannah land.

The priests and nuns knew exactly what they were looking at: kwashiorkor, extreme protein deficiency. The total shut-off of protein-rich foodstuffs was finally having its effect. No one had foreseen this because no one had thought the war would last that long. Without the Wilson government intervention it would not have done. But the appearance of kwashiorkor transformed an incompetent bush war into a massive humanitarian tragedy the like of which neither Africa, nor Europe, nor North America had ever seen. But they were about to.

The priests appealed in Ireland for funds and a few suitcases of medications came in. But no one took any notice. The media visit of February, which the BBC had ostracized, had been and gone before the signs were evident. I had arrived back after Israel some time in May. In June two British newspapers sent a team of one reporter and one photographer each. They were the *Daily Express* and the now-defunct *Daily Sketch*.

Due to the action of Stewart Steven, the foreign editor, I had been retained by the *Daily Express*, so my job was to escort Walter Partington and David Cairns. The visit started with the usual formalities: a briefing on the military situation and then a visit to a couple of fronts where there was some combat going on.

Walter, who had arrived with a half-case of whisky and several cartons of priceless cigarettes, declined to move from the allotted bungalow where he sat consuming his supplies and sharing with no one. David Cairns and I went off to the fronts with army escorts. When we got back Walter was a bit too indulged to be able to write copy so I wrote and transmitted all his despatches myself, but in his name.

(Rather amusingly, when he got home he filed the lot for the International Reporter of the Year award – and won.)

Then we found the starving children at a Catholic mission house. David Cairns and his colleague from the *Sketch* took hundreds of pictures, stored the rolls in light-proof capsules and took them home. Back then, we could transmit words by telex, but not photos.

I never saw the editions of the *Express* and *Sketch* that appeared the following week but the effect was dramatic. Today we have all seen pictures of starving children from Africa and Asia but in 1968 no one in the West had ever seen anything like it.

This was the catalyst the situation required. It changed everything, turning a low-intensity, low-interest African war into the greatest humanitarian cause of the decade.

Back in Britain, later Europe and then the USA, ordinary citizens just expressed their horror, protested and donated. Out of this was created the most extraordinary mercy mission the world has ever seen, a nightly air bridge from the offshore islands to the ultra-basic Uli airstrip in the heart of the rainforest.

From Denmark a Protestant minister, Vigo Mollerup, recruited pilots from all the Scandinavian airlines to give up their vacations to fly freight planes carrying baby-milk concentrates through the night to Uli. That was called Nord Church Air. What they carried was contributed by the World

Council of Churches (Protestant) and Caritas (the international Rome-based Catholic charity). The Pope ordered Monsignor Carlo Bayer, a Silesian, to raid the funds of Caritas and mount the Catholic contribution.

Also in the mix was the ICRC (International Committee of the Red Cross) under the Swiss Karl Jaggi. And what was really extraordinary was that the whole thing was illegal. In law those life-saving planes were invading Nigerian air space against the wishes of the Lagos-based military junta, which acquired MiG fighters and pilots from the communist bloc to try to shoot them down. That was why the relief planes had to fly at night and land in darkness. It had never happened before and it has never happened since.

By late autumn the air bridge, collectively called Joint Church Aid, or mockingly Jesus Christ Airlines, was up and running, or rather flying, and it continued to the end. The three main agencies, WCC, Caritas and ICRC, all put the number of children who died at about a million and the number saved from death at a similar figure.

By the end the network of feeding centres sprawled across the still-defiant enclave, where the children lay waiting for death or a bowl of protein-rich milk, had an estimated transient population of half a million. The burial parties would often put a hundred children from one centre into their mass grave in a single day.

And the media came, in hundreds, with their reporters and their cameras, along with hundreds of volunteers who just wanted to help in whatever way they could. Many had to be refused passage – there were just too many.

And the British government of Harold Wilson and the

Foreign Office? It stuck doggedly to the old discredited policy, doubling up the supplies, advice and propaganda aid to the Nigerian junta. The press office of the FCO stooped to quite incredible levels of mendacity to fulfil its brief.

One canard seriously proposed to the attendant press in London was that there were really no starving children in the 'rebel enclave' save for a group kept deliberately as living skeletons for display purposes. Whenever a mission of visiting VIPs was touring the villages, these emaciated wretches would be trucked ahead of them so they were always there to greet the visitors. It was an ex-public-school product with an old-school tie and a degree who offered that little gem to the media.

On another occasion the war hero Group Captain Leonard Cheshire VC was asked to go to visit, be shown around Nigeria only and return to peddle the official line. He duly went to Nigeria but then refused not to go to Biafra. What he saw on the second visit so shocked him that he came back and denounced the official policy. He was immediately smeared as a gullible fool.

The smearing of every journalist who expressed disgust at what was going on as either a mercenary, arms dealer or Ojukwu propagandist was pretty standard, even though a million pictures are rather hard to dispute.

No massive humanitarian tragedy, save those inflicted by Nature herself, is possible without two kinds of contributor. Hitler could never have accomplished the Holocaust that he did if he had relied only on the uniformed sadists of the SS. Behind them had to stand another army of organizers, administrators and bureaucrats – the enablers.

Someone had to constantly supply the uniforms and the boots, the guns and the ammunition, the wages, the rations and the barbed wire. Someone had to oversee the supply of instruments of torture and of gas pellets. These people never pulled a trigger or turned on a gas chamber. But they enabled it to happen. It is the difference between the doer and the desk-doer.

Starting with a biased and flawed analysis by Sir David Hunt, adopted by the Commonwealth Relations Office, taken over and intensified by the Foreign Office, cravenly endorsed by Harold Wilson and Michael Stewart, I remain convinced to this day that what happened could not have happened without the wholesale and covert contribution of the Wilson government.

Nor was it necessary to protect some vital British interest, and what interest merits a million dead children? Britain could have used its huge influence with Lagos to militate for a cease-fire, a peace conference and a political solution. It chose not to despite repeated opportunities, pursuing Hunt's conviction that Biafra must be crushed no matter what the cost, but without ever explaining why.

That is why I believe that this coterie of vain mandarins and cowardly politicians stained the honour of my country for ever and I will never forgive them.

A Useful Certificate

THE PLAN WAS to march many miles through the Nigerian lines to blow up a bridge which formed a major supply route to one of their most advanced salients into Ibo territory.

To be frank, there were no 'lines' in the sense of fortified trenches across the landscape. The media liked to draw lines on maps by linking Nigerian advance points, villages which they had reached and where there was a Nigerian army presence. But in that rainforest there were myriad narrow tracks known only to guides from the nearby villages along which it was possible to march through the 'lines' and into the bush hinterland behind. To reach the target bridge, such was the plan.

The mission was to comprise three mercenaries and twenty of the best-trained Biafran 'commandos', along with a couple of local guides who knew the tracks in the bush. I elected to go along, suspecting a good journalistic story.

On the first night we were halfway there. We camped because even the guides would not march at night. It was not just dark in the forest, it was pitch black. So we camped and built a small fire. After a pretty basic dinner, the group settled down to sleep, as ever consumed by mosquitoes and amazed at how noisy the jungle is at night.

There was Taffy, the South African with the Welsh name; Johnny, the Rhodesian with a South African name; Armand, a Parisian with a Corsican name; and me, an Englishman with a Scottish name. And the Biafrans who were all Ibos. Out of the darkness Taffy suddenly spoke.

'I'm prepared to bet I am the only person round this camp fire who can prove he's sane.'

We all lay there slowly working out that the only way you can prove you are sane is if you have a certificate to say so. And the only way you can be issued with such a certificate is on release from a lunatic asylum.

I lay there thinking: I am miles from bloody anywhere. If I disappear tonight no one will ever know what happened to me, or even ask. I could simply vanish. So I am lying next to a giant, who is armed to the teeth and joking that he is half-mad. I stayed awake.

There are moments when the question 'What the hell am I doing here?' simply will not go away. The next day Johnny, the explosives wizard, blew the bridge and we marched back through the bush into the Biafran heartland. I made a point of marching behind Taffy in case he had forgotten about his certificate.

Mr Sissons, I Presume

THE PLAN WAS TO motor by Land Rover to the last known Biafran position then march on to a point far down the Aba-to-Owerri road and mount an ambush. I agreed to go along even though this would be an all-Biafran affair with no white mercenaries involved.

I was always quite chary of going with an all-Ibo patrol because if things went seriously pear-shaped they could simply vaporize into their native rainforest whereas I would be lost within ten yards and quite likely to walk into a Nigerian army unit, mistaking one for the other. The faces were the same, the uniforms similar and the forest bewildering.

But everything went smoothly. We knew Aba had fallen and was a new Nigerian strong point. Owerri was still being contested. The road might carry Nigerian convoys of troops and supplies; hence the night ambush. It never occurred to me that some fool on the Nigerian side might send up a party of visiting journalists.

So the commando officer picked his spot on a grassy bank above the road and we settled down to wait. After an hour there was the low rumble of engines coming up from the south, then the wash of dimmed headlights.

Back in Biafra children were starving. This photo was taken by David Cairns in
June 1968, one of the first seen in English newspapers. The effect was dramatic.

By June 1968 I was back in Biafra. I travelled by boat (**top left**) with Walter Partington, in front, and David Cairns of the *Daily Express*, who took this picture. I am in the back behind Bruce Loudon, a stringer for the *Daily Telegraph*. David took many photos of the escalating war, among them this one of me looking on while an elderly Ibo draws in the dirt (**top right**), and this picture of an unexploded British-made shell, supplied to the Nigerians. So much for denials from London. In September 1968 the *Nigerian Observer* even went so far as to report that I had joined the Biafran army (**right**).

THE NIGERIAN
OBSERVER

Vol. 1. No. 104.   THURSDAY, SEPTEMBER 26, 1968.

BBC MAN JOINS REBELS

REBEI DECII NOW C

MR. Fredrick Forsythe former BBC correspondent and commentator on Nigerian affairs who was based in Lagos for many months has now joined the rebel army as a major. This information was

IN a matter of DAYS the rebels will hav

top
REGISTRATION
capital of the F
Catholic School,
announced in Lag
The announce
vernment has pro
rest houses in the

As more photographs appeared in the British press of the famine in Biafra (*left and below*), the real state of affairs was becoming apparent. A protest rally was held at Speaker's Corner in August 1968 calling the BBC and the Wilson government to account (*bottom*).

Family matters.

My parents (*left*), a constant source of support and encouragement, at their cottage in Willesborough, near Ashford.

Carrie, Stuart and me at home in Ireland in 1979 (*below*). Shane came along the same year (*bottom*).

They soon grew up: here we are bagging game in South Africa, and later scuba-diving in the Gulf of Oman.

Sandy and I collect my gong, awarded for charity work, October 1997 (*right*).

The Day of the Jackal was written on my portable typewriter in thirty-five days in January 1970 (**left**), published the next year, and two years later made into a film directed by Fred Zinnemann, starring the relatively unknown Edward Fox (**below left**). It was the back jacket of the German edition (**below**) that blew my cover when I was doing research for *The Dogs of War*.

Next came *The Odessa File* (**left**): I used the story of the true-life Nazi war criminal Eduard Roschmann (**below**); the release of the film in 1974 led to his arrest by the Argentinian police. He escaped and died in Paraguay three years later.

The French edition of *The Dogs of War* (**left**) was used as a handbook by French mercenaries when they attacked the Comoros islands. They succeeded in taking them over!

Michael Caine starred in the film of my 1984 novel, *The Fourth Protocol*. We had some convivial times together (**below**).

Research is important: in 2009 I went to Guinea-Bissau to research cocaine trafficking for *The Cobra* (**bottom**).

Back to the beginning. In a Spitfire, flying high over the Weald, just like they did in 1940.

We were invisible in the long grass and under the trees but the road, with no tree cover, was visible by moon and stars. The leading Nigerian Land Rover stopped several bullets and drove itself straight into the rain ditch, blocking the road for the convoy and preventing escape forwards. The lorries behind panicked, stopped and began to shed the dim forms of the men inside them. The Biafrans kept firing and the Nigerians started shouting and screaming.

Then above the noise I heard a single voice shouting in perfectly accented English: 'I've been hit, oh my God, I've been hit.' That was the first indication there were any Europeans down on the road.

Peering into the gloom I discerned the shouting figure on the road and the voice made plain it was a fellow countryman. Next to me a Biafran soldier also spotted the target and raised his FAL rifle to complete the job. Journalistic rivalry may occasionally become tense, but never that bad. I reached out, eased his barrel upward and his shot went off through the tree-tops. He turned and I could see the whites of his eyes glaring at me. Then the ambush commander blew his whistle – the signal to shimmy backwards off the bank, into the forest and run like hell.

The Englishman on the road had taken a bullet in the thigh. Months later I learned that he was Independent Television star Peter Sissons, who was evacuated, flown home and made a full recovery.

Years later, at a fancy dress charity ball of all things, and being somewhat in my cups, I let it slip. He and his wife were there. Peter took the news with appropriate dignity but it was his wife who gave me a big wet kiss.

Worth a Large One

A DOZEN YEARS AFTER the Biafra war I found myself in a London bar with a long-term veteran of the SAS regiment. Out of the blue he remarked: 'You owe me a large one.'

If someone like that tells you he is owed a drink, do not argue. Just go to the bar and buy him a double. So I did. When he had taken a deep draught I asked him why.

'Because,' he said, 'I once had your head in the cross-hairs of my scope sight, and I didn't pull the trigger.'

I reckoned that merited an entire bottle. It also confirmed something I had long suspected. The Special Air Service specializes (among many other things) in deep penetration into target territory, information-gathering and withdrawal unseen. Rumours had long persisted that part of London's extensive help to Lagos had been the presence of our Special Forces. Political denial had always been a bit too shrill.

There was certainly no such presence until 1968. My only time west of the Niger had been as a BBC correspondent with the Biafran invasion across the Onitsha Bridge the previous year. After my return in 1968 I had always been inside the Biafran enclave. The only time my contentedly sipping bar friend could have seen me was through a screen of trees deep inside Biafra.

So much for official denials.

Bits of Metal

O F ALL THE bits of metal that have been thrown in my direction the nastiest are mortars. This is because they are silent. The only thing you hear from a falling mortar bomb is a soft, feathery whisper just before it impacts. Usually not even long enough to dive for cover.

If the ground on which it falls is soft or swampy, as sometimes happened in Biafra, the bomb might embed itself at the moment of impact, spending much of its explosive force and its sheets of shrapnel in the surrounding mud.

But if it falls on hard ground it detonates with an earsplitting crack. That is not the problem; the problem is that the casing transforms into a rain of many hundreds of fragments of razor-sharp metal that spray outwards from knee-high to well over the head, and in a 360-degree circle from the explosion. Anyone caught in that hail of shrapnel will probably be torn apart and killed or at least crippled.

That is why I came to loathe them – the silence. The Nigerians, unlike the Biafrans, had artillery with shells, constantly resupplied by London despite the lies. But they were comfortingly inaccurate as gunners, and an incoming shell makes an audible whoosh like a subway train entering a station. Just enough time to go face-down in the dirt and hope the blast will go over your back.

Machine guns are not funny but the Nigerians simply put the gun on to full-automatic, using the entire magazine in one blast, usually aiming high and taking the tops off innumerable innocent trees. Time enough to hit the dirt or dive into the friendly rain ditch and get below ground level.

When it came to rifles, the Nigerians used the NATO-issue SLR or self-loading rifle. These also they put on to 'automatic' fire setting and went through the magazine in seconds. When you saw the branches above your head start to shred, you hit the dirt and would probably stay alive. That apart, the half-trained (if that) compulsory recruits had trouble hitting a barn door at ten paces. Literally hundreds of millions of bullets went through the treetops.

The Biafrans had far more limited supplies, coming in by planeload rather than shipload, but the mercenaries trying to teach ammo-conservancy had an impossible task. In Africa, 'spray the landscape' seems to be the only infantry tactic.

Among the Biafrans the two most feared weapons were the Saladin armoured car and the Ferret scout car, both London-supplied. The Saladin had one cannon, which the crew did not know how to use, and each had a heavy machine gun, which was really nasty. But you could also hear them coming, the growl of the Ferret and the whine of the Saladin usually giving you time to get out of the way. Unfortunately if the Biafrans heard the Saladin-whine coming their way they would just run for it, and down went another defended village.

At a certain point Nigeria acquired an air arm: Ilyushin

twin-jet bombers and MiG-17 jet fighters, both flown by mercenaries, Egyptians or East Germans. The Biafrans had no anti-air forces though that did not stop them wasting ammunition by blazing upwards whenever they saw one. The Nigerians had no pilots at all because the only ones they had ever had were Ibos. So the Ilyushins and MiGs could fly low, pick their targets and bomb or strafe them. But they never changed the course of the war. I was only once caught by a MiG.

I happened to be on a long straight laterite road with grass fields on either side, so no tree cover. The MiG appeared to my right, visible through the driver's side window of my Volkswagen Beetle. (Nigeria then drove on the left of the road.) I had seen him but he had also seen me, and he was flying in the same direction at about 3,000 feet.

Through the windscreen I watched him drop the port wing and haul the fighter through 180 degrees, diving to level out just above the road. I slammed on the brakes, baled out and went into the rain ditch just as he opened up.

He came down the road with his cannon ripping small fountains out of the laterite surface, roared overhead and was gone, making only one pass. He could not have been much good. Despite ploughing up the road he missed the Beetle completely. When he was a dot on the horizon heading for the Niger and home, I was able to start up the VW and crawl through the potholes and thus get back to my bungalow in Umuahia town.

But the one who came nearest to sending me to a new and apparently better place was the mortarman outside Onitsha. I had been visiting the front line south of the riverside city by the bridgehead, but it meant a long hike back across a bare and exposed hillside to where I had parked my car deep in a grove of trees. I was a third of the way across the flank of the hill when someone across the river must have seen me, presumably with field glasses. It was probably the white face that irritated him because he really let fly.

I heard that soft whisper and went flat. It was a ranging shot and landed over a hundred yards away. No damage but also no cover. I looked around for a friendly rain ditch and spotted one twenty yards to one side. I made it just in time as the second one landed.

Rain ditches make good cover but the locals tend to use them as latrines. In the rainy season the waste matter is washed away but this was in the dry months, so a rain ditch is not recommended for a crawling holiday. Still, it is better than getting shredded. I lay and counted the seconds. Seven. Then the third landed. Closer, but above my head.

I jumped out and began to jog, counting the seconds and hoping my new friend was going to be short on imagination.

He was. At six seconds I went back into the ditch and at seven the next one came down. This was not a 60-millimetre party planner but an 81-millimetre 'company' mortar. Very nasty.

I hoped he was watching the fall of his shot, then dropping his next effort down the tube. Travel time for the bomb, exactly seven seconds. I have never liked jogging and this jog least of all. Up-run-dive-bang. Then I made it to the point where the hillside curved away from the river. Two more runs and I would be out of sight.

Hoping he could see me, I turned and gave him a rigid

middle finger. Then I was out of sight. There were three more but they became wider and wider, until I could reach my car and drive home. And that is why I hate mortars.

Of More Mice – and Mercs

THE EXPERIENCE OF foreign white mercenaries was for the Biafrans extremely patchy. Both sides used them, but the idea that they were invincible game-changers, a reputation deriving from the Congolese wars a few years earlier, proved to be a myth.

For the Biafrans the first intervention came from France, then ruled by Charles de Gaulle. His principal 'fixer' in Africa, Jacques Foccart, responsible for a wide range of skulduggery in the ex-French empire and elsewhere, arranged for about forty mainly French 'mercs' to be recruited by ex-Legion icon Roger Faulques and sent down to show how warfare should be done. They cost Biafra a fortune in its scarce hard-currency reserves.

They duly arrived and were assigned to the Calabar sector, where Nigerian and Biafran troopers were locked in a struggle for the riverine city. On their way there, driving without forward scouts, they ran into an ambush and lost several men. Retreating in disarray, their next stop was the airport where they demanded to go back home. General Ojukwu in disgust just let them go.

But seven opted to stay and were joined by three non-French who came later. They were a mixed bunch. Two were deluded fantasists, two had a taste for killing and one enjoyed cruelty. Some of the French group stayed because they were wanted in France for various offences. Finally there were ex-soldiers from national armies who had simply failed to adapt to civilian life.

There were also three mercenary pilots who flew in Biafra's short-lived air force until they were shot down or crashed their aircraft and left. Three of the land-based mercs died in combat. Of those who fought as soldiers, Giorgio Norbiato, whom I never met, was an Italian and the first to die. He was killed fighting in the river Imo area as the Nigerians advanced out of the creeks towards Aba.

Mark Goossens was a former Belgian paratrooper, another huge man. He died with a bullet through the liver during a forlorn attempt to recapture Onitsha city.

The third to die was a Britisher, Steve Neeley, whom I found thoroughly unpleasant. He drove around with a bone-white skull on the bonnet of his Land Rover. It was the head of a dead Nigerian which he had boiled fleshless and mounted above the radiator cap with steel wires.

He disappeared in the Abakaliki sector and it was later rumoured one of his own men might have done the job. They attested he was dead but the body was never found.

Those who survived included 'Tiny' or 'Petit Bill' Billois, a French giant weighing in at around 350lbs. He died later in a light-aircraft crash in France, years after the war. Always at his side was his cousin Michel, who was so self-effacing he was hardly noticed and that included when he left. And Rolf

Steiner, who had been appointed their commander and called himself colonel. He was ex-Deutsches Jungvolk (a sort of Hitler youth), ex-Foreign Legion, invalided out of Dien Bien Phu, Vietnam, just in time, and one of the Faulques group who elected to stay on. He postured and paraded around in his confiscated American limousine, his staff car, but I never recall him going into combat. He spoke only French and German, so I did a fair amount of interpreting. That made him a good source of information but I never took to him.

Then there was Taffy Williams, already mentioned.

The only three I could like were Alec, a Scot who survived, returned to the UK, married and qualified as a truck driver; the Rhodesian Johnny Erasmus, the explosives king, ex-Rhodesian army; and Armand from Paris. Armand was lanky, swarthy with the black hair and eyes of his Corsican ancestors. He spoke rarely but observed the world with an ironic half-grin.

Armand had only gone to Biafra because the chief of the Brigade Criminelle of the Paris police had advised him in the friendliest way that he should leave Paris for a while to avoid an embarrassing arrest. There were no hard feelings, the spirit being that we all have to make a living. So he had joined the group being organized by Jacques Foccart, the French government's Mr Dirty Tricks for Africa, to be led by ex-Legion legend Roger Faulques. When the French contingent ran for home after a week, Armand stayed on, and indeed to the end.

I discovered that he had actually sought out the Irish missionaries and monthly handed over his pay to buy more food for the children. He also told me, when I learned of it, that he would be immensely displeased if word got out. One did not lightly displease Armand so I kept quiet.

Finally, there was the mythical Major Atkinson, in the form of this writer, thus nicknamed by Ojukwu himself. One day in the autumn of 1968 I turned up at a Biafran advance head-quarters intending to go up to the front line to see if there was a journalistic story worth covering. Seeing me in the usual pale safari jacket, the brigade commander objected.

His case was perfectly sound. It was well known the Nigerian army was quite paranoid about white mercenaries and had never heard of a war correspondent. To show up in a leaf-green forest environment with a white face and a pale jacket was asking for trouble. One glance through the trees and the entire zone would be drenched in automatic fire. Apart from anything else it was unfair on the Biafran soldiers who might be close by.

He insisted I change into a camouflage jacket and ordered one of his staff officers to lend me his spare. It happened to have the half-a-yellow-sun emblem of Biafra on each sleeve and a major's crowns on each shoulder. In order not to waste the day I put it on and went into the front.

That apart, I had taken to carrying a French automatic in a holster at the waist. This was because I'd had described to me in detail what the Hausa soldiers would do to a white mercenary if he were taken alive. So my borrowed pistol had one slug in it – for me, if worst ever came to worst.

On the way back I ran into a group of British Press, also being refused access to the front line and not happy about it. One of them recognized me and that was that. On their return to London the Foreign Office press desk seized upon it with alacrity. Too late to protest that I always changed out of the 'cammo' jacket when not at the front, and that the pistol remained locked in the glove compartment of the Volkswagen.

As for the real mercenaries, I think they are mostly dead now, though when this book comes out I might be in for a couple of surprises.

Memories

THERE IS NOTHING noble about war. The adjective may apply to those who have to fight in them in defence of cause or country. But war itself is cruel and brutal. Things happen in it that coarsen the senses and scar the memory. And the most vicious of all conflicts is the civil war.

Of the thousand memories I bore back from the two years I spent trying to convey the realities of Biafra to the readers of Britain, Europe and the USA, the most abiding is that of the dying children.

They died in the villages, by the roadsides and, alongside those who survived on the relief food, in the feeding centres. These were almost wholly established round the missions – church, school, dispensary and a field the size of a football pitch where they lay in the grass, on rush mats or the laps of their mothers, who held them close, watching them wither and slip away, and wondering why.

As the effects of kwashiorkor intensified, the dark brown curly hair diminished to a ginger fuzz. The eyes lost focus but appeared immense in the wizened face. The weakness of departed muscle made them listless until, unable to move at all, they passed away and a figure in a cassock came to intone a last blessing and take them to the pit.

The bellies ballooned but only with air; the lower limbs were drenched with faeces; the heads lolled on vanished muscles. And always the low moan as they cried in pain. And one image above all, on the grass field outside the window of my hut.

I was tapping away at my typewriter with the window wide open. It was late summer 1969 and the air was balmy. I almost missed the low sound above the clatter of the keys. Then I heard it and went to the window.

She was standing on the grass outside, a scrap of a girl of seven or eight, stick-thin, in a flimsy cotton shift stained with dirt. In her left hand she held the hand of her baby brother, stark naked, listless eyes, bulbous belly. She stared up at me and I down at her.

She raised her right hand to her mouth and made the universal sign that means: I am hungry, please give me food. Then she held her hand up towards the window and her lips moved with no sound. I looked down at the tiny pink-palmed hand, but I had no food.

My food came twice daily from the cooking compound behind the cluster of Nissen huts where the few visiting whites lived. But that night I would dine with Kurt Jaggi of the Red Cross, good nutritious food imported from Switzerland. But not for three hours. The kitchens were closed and locked and there was no way either child could take solid food. Until dinner I would exist on king-size cigarettes. But you cannot eat cigarettes; there is no nutriment in a Bic lighter.

Foolishly I tried to explain. I'm sorry, really sorry, but I have no food. I had no Ibo, she no English, but it did not matter. She understood. Slowly her outstretched arm sank back to her side. She did not spit, she did not shout. She just nodded in silent understanding. The white man in the window would do nothing for her or her brother.

In a long life I have never seen such resignation, such towering dignity, as in that wasted form as she turned away, all last hope gone. Together the two little forms walked away across the field to the tree line. In the forest she would find a shady tree, sit at its foot and wait to die. And she would hold on to her kid brother, like a good sister, all the way.

I watched them until the trees took them, then sat at my table, put my head on my hands and cried until the despatch was damp.

That was the last time I wept for the children of Biafra. Since then others have written documentaries about what happened in those last eighteen months of the thirty months of the 'ten-day war' predicted out of Lagos. But no investigative writer has ever undertaken to expose *why* it happened and who exactly enabled it to happen. For the Whitehall Establishment the subject is closed. It is taboo.

Flight Out

IT WAS TWO nights before Christmas 1969 and clear that the last embattled enclave of the Biafran revolt was finally crumbling. The Ibos were simply exhausted to the point their soldiers could hardly stand. In the manner of Africans when all hope is lost, they simply 'went for bush'. Meaning, they just vaporized into the rainforest and returned, without weapon or uniform, to their native villages.

The Nigerian army could have taken the remnant of the enclave that night but they continued their snail-like progress for another fortnight until the formal surrender on 15 January. I had no way of knowing it would be that slow and found myself at Uli airstrip to see Emeka Ojukwu leave for years of exile.

His supporter President Houphouët-Boigny of the Ivory Coast had sent his personal jet for him but that was a very crowded flight with no room for hitchhikers. Also on the airstrip that night was another plane, wholly unexpected and unheralded.

It was a very old and pretty clapped-out Douglas DC-4, a four-propellers job that seemed to have an awful lot of air miles under its belt. The pilot and, as it turned out, owner was a South African whom I met surrounded by Irish nuns. His story was bizarre.

His name was Jan van der Merwe and he had never met Ojukwu. But he had seen him on television and been impressed. Without any invitation and at considerable risk, he had flown in from Libreville, Gabon, to see if he needed a flight out to safety.

I was surprised that an Afrikaner, almost certainly a keen supporter of apartheid, should decide to take such a risk to help a failed black man whom he had never met. But I had noticed Ojukwu sometimes had that effect on people.

Van der Merwe's offer was politely rejected on the grounds that the Biafra leader already had transport, but the nuns had ideas of their own. They were in charge of two or three lorryloads of children and babies so emaciated that if they did not get professional care without delay they would also surely die. So the South African agreed reluctantly to take them on board instead. The nuns began to carry them one by one up the gangway to the dark interior of the freighter. There were no beds or seats, so they laid them on the floor and came back down for more.

Eventually there were three planes left on what had once been the busiest nocturnal airport in Africa, the Douglas and two official jets from the Ivory Coast and the Red Cross. I later described all this, just the way it was, in the first few pages of my novel *The Dogs of War*.

I gratefully accepted a king-size filter from Jan and asked if he had a co-pilot. He had not; he had flown alone. Up on the flight deck the right-hand seat was free. It was mine if I wanted it. I did.

The Nigerians had been kind enough to put a price on my head, rumoured at 5,000 naira; not a fortune but more than enough for a poor Hausa soldier to claim it eagerly. And the terms were dead or alive, so survival seemed unlikely. The third-from-last plane out was a better bet than trying to hide among the missionaries. My knowledge of the Creed was a bit shaky.

When the loading was finished, Jan and I climbed to the flight deck and he started the engines, one by one. It was pitch dark and the airport lights were off when we taxied out to the far end, turned round and faced down the runway. After a pause, waiting for runway lights which never came on, Jan just pushed the four throttles open and we took off in darkness, apart from the low glimmer of the stars. There were Nigerian jets up there somewhere and had they seen us it would have been 'game over'.

The first problem began out over the Niger delta. Jan wanted to get clear of the landmass before turning for Gabon so he took the shortest route to the sea, due south. The last of the mangroves of the delta were dropping behind us when the port outer failed. It coughed several times and cut out. Jan closed down the fuel lines to it and the moon came out. We could see the propeller blades rigid and motionless in the moonlight. He carefully turned east for Gabon. We were hugely overloaded and flying on three.

I rose, walked back and looked through the door from the flight deck to the hold. The babies lay in their blankets wall to wall, the nuns trying to minister to them by dimmed torches, surviving somehow amid the stench of vomit and diarrhoea. I closed the door and returned to the right-hand seat. Over the Gulf of Guinea the starboard outer began to cough and splutter. If it packed in we were all dead. Jan coaxed and nursed it to stay turning.

He began to sing hymns, in Afrikaans of course. I just sat in the right-hand seat, staring out at the moon on the water coming closer and closer as we dropped towards it. Far away on the forward horizon was a dim line of lights. Libreville airport.

The French colonists had built their airport right on the sea. The DC-4, wheels dangling, came over the sand dunes with a few feet to spare. As the tarmac appeared the spluttering engine gave up the ghost and stopped. The old crate dropped with a noisy clunk on to the runway and ran to a halt.

Red Cross ambulances appeared for the Biafran children and the Catholic church for the nuns. Jan van der Merwe and I sat on the flight deck wondering why we were still alive. He was muttering the old Dutch prayers of thanksgiving; I listened to the ticking of the engine blocks cooling in the tropical night.

We adjourned to the airport crew room and I met an officer from the officers' mess of the Foreign Legion. I said goodbye and thank you to Jan and went across to the mess for food and a bath as a guest of the Legion, simply because they were avid for news. A bit of influence was brought to bear and I secured a free flight back to Paris on the morning Air Afrique plane. From there my last remaining funds got me home to Kent via Beauvais and Lydd. Thence a hitchhike to my parents' retirement cottage at Willesborough outside Ashford. They were quite surprised to see me, but at least we had Christmas together.

They were elderly so New Year's Eve was quiet and I

returned to London on New Year's Day. My situation was pretty dire.

I had no flat but a mate let me doss on the sofa. I had no savings left but my father loaned me a few hundred pounds to get by. I certainly had no job and no prospects of ever getting one for a long time.

In my absence, I had been comprehensively smeared from the usual official quarters. I was not the only one. The late Winston Churchill, grandson of the war leader, had also visited Biafra representing *The Times*, had written of his horror at what he had seen and been denounced as a professional publicist for 'the rebels'. And there were others. From the pro-Establishment organs of the media the gloating was unrestrained.

The situation was so miserable that I decided to do something that even then was seen as crazy by all I knew. I thought I might get myself out of this mess by writing a novel.

As a recourse it was lunatic. I did not know how to write a novel, let alone secure its publication. I knew nothing of publishing or the finances of book-writing. I thought you could take a manuscript to a publisher and, if he liked it, he would buy it for a single sum like a pound of butter. I had no agent and knew nothing of royalties, or the years-long delay before they actually arrived.

But I did have a story – or I thought I did. I cast my mind back to the Paris years and my conviction then that the OAS was not going to succeed in assassinating Charles de Gaulle with their own volunteers being hunted high and low by the far more professional counter-intelligence forces that Paris could bring to bear. Unless they brought in a professional from outside.

On 2 January 1970, I sat down at the kitchen table in my borrowed flat with my trusty old portable typewriter, with its bullet scar across the tin cover, rolled in the first sheet of paper and began to type.

Charles de Gaulle was still alive, in retirement at Colombey-les-deux-Eglises. He died on 9 November that year. I was told later that no one had ever postulated the murder of a living statesman since Geoffrey Household's *Rogue Male*, about an attempt to kill Adolf Hitler. But that gunman never went through with it.

I was also told no one had ever had an entire novel with an anonymous hero, or featured real politicians and police officers in a fictional manhunt. And no one had attempted such an obsession for technical accuracy. In other words, it was all madness. Still, when you have nothing else to do and nowhere else to go, you might as well get on with it.

I wrote for thirty-five days from when my friend went off to work until her return after dark; that is to say, all through January, seven days a week, and the first two weeks of February. Then I typed the last line of the last page.

I rolled the first page back into the machine and stared at it. I had called it THE JACKAL. That seemed a bit bare and might be taken for a nature documentary set in Africa. So in front of the title I typed THE DAY OF. If I say it myself, not a single word has been changed since.

I was still very broke but I had a manuscript. The remaining problem was that I had not a clue what to do with it.

An Unwanted Manuscript

FOR THE WHOLE of the spring and summer of 1970 I hawked the manuscript of *The Day of the Jackal* round the publishing houses of London, choosing my targets from *Willings Press Guide*. It actually went to four; three rejected it outright and I withdrew it from the fourth. But along the road at least I learned what was wrong – apart from the fact that it might be a rotten novel.

The unsolicited manuscript is the bane of the publisher's life. They arrive by the trolleyload: typed (in those days), hand-written, illegible, ungrammatical, unreasonable. There used to be a tradition in which on Monday mornings they were distributed among the junior readers for first assessment.

The junior reader was often a student or very recent arrival in-house and a long way down the pecking order. His or her job was to read it and provide a brief synopsis with judgement, and that was what would go up to the next level of assessment. But no one high up the food chain would dream of reading anything other than an established author or possibly a very famous person who had put pen to paper.

The horror stories were the legends of publishing. Most

authors, hailed as mega-bestsellers, had had their first manuscript rejected over and over again; and it still goes on because
no one has the faintest idea who will be the next Ken Follett
or John Grisham or J.K. Rowling.

Among authors the nightmare stories that go the rounds
concern the year-long struggle to find anyone to publish their
masterpiece. Among publishers the horror tales are about those
who turned down *Harry Potter* because who cares about a
schoolboy wizard with a wand? And usually it is only the first
chapter that is read anyway.

The Day of the Jackal had a major problem here because the
first chapter is ridiculous. It purported to outline plans for
the killing of a former French president who was very much
alive, and everyone knew it. So the junior readers' judgements
probably said: 'We know the climax already, the plan fails.'
Manuscript returned.

Two of my rejections were simple printed forms. One was
kind enough to write a letter. I wish I had retained and framed
it, but I threw it away. It said the very idea would have 'no
reader interest'. Then I had yet another lucky break.

I was at a party and was introduced just socially to someone
called Harold Harris. I had no idea who he was. Towards the
end of the party someone mentioned that he was the editorial
director of Hutchinson, a major publisher.

I had already decided my solution might be to write a
three-page synopsis of the plot, pointing out that the point of
the story was not the death of de Gaulle, which clearly did not
happen, but the manhunt as the assassin came closer and closer,
eluding the huge machine ranged against him.

The following day, a Friday in September, I am afraid I

ambushed Mr Harris quite blatantly. I turned up at Hutchinson's office in Great Portland Street and faced the usual screen of secretaries in place to keep unwanted wannabes away from the Presence behind the big door.

But I explained we were close friends and my call was social. I was allowed in. Harold Harris was puzzled until I pointed out we had met socially the previous evening. His perfect manners caused him not to summon the burly commissionaire but to ask what he could do for me. I replied: 'I have a manuscript of a novel.'

His eyes glazed over in horror but I had got this far so I plunged on.

'I know you have no time, so I will not take it up, Mr Harris. Well, maybe five minutes, tops.'

With this I advanced to his desk and placed the brief synopsis upon it.

'All I ask is that you glance at this and, if you think it is worthless, then chuck me out.'

Looking as if root canal surgery would be more welcome, he started to read. He finished the three pages and started again. He read it three times.

'Where is the manuscript now?' he asked.

I told him with which publisher it had lain for eight weeks. He stared pointedly at the ceiling.

'It is quite out of the question for a publisher to read a manuscript while a copy resides with another publisher,' he told me.

Asking him not to move, which he had no intention of doing, I was out of the office and down the stairs. I could not afford taxis, but I hailed one anyway and drove to the other publisher. It was the lunch hour. I could raise only the hall porter with my demand for my manuscript back and he found a junior secretary on her sandwich break who retrieved my paper parcel from the reject pile and gave it back to me with a pitying smile. I returned to Great Portland Street and handed it over.

He read the whole thing over the weekend and rang on Monday morning.

'If you can be here at four this afternoon, with your agent, we can discuss a contract,' he said.

I had no agent, but I was there anyway. With my ignorance of publishing, royalties and contracts he could have skinned me alive. But he was an old-fashioned gentleman and gave me a fair document with an advance of £500. Then he said:

'I am toying with the idea of offering you a three-novel contract. Do you have any other ideas?'

The thing about journalists is that they lie well. It comes from practice. It is also why they have great empathy with, or antagonism for, politicians and senior civil servants. Common territory.

'Mr Harris, I am brimming with ideas,' I told him.

'Two synopses, one page each. By Friday noon,' he suggested.

Back on the street I had a major problem. The story about the Jackal was supposed to be a one-off, something to tide me through a bad patch. I had not the slightest intention of becoming a novelist. So I tried to analyse the story that had been accepted and to recall what I knew about from personal experience and could use as background. I came up with two conclusions.

The Day of the Jackal was a manhunt story and I knew a lot about Germany. While in East Berlin I had heard about a mysterious organization of former Nazis who helped, protected and warned each other in order never to have to face West German judicial hunters and answer for their crimes. It was called ODESSA but I had thought it was part of the relentless East German propaganda against the Bonn government.

Perhaps not. Ten years earlier the Israeli Mossad had hunted down Adolf Eichmann, living under a pseudonym outside Buenos Aires. Perhaps another hunt-down of a disappeared mass-murderer?

And I knew about Africa and white mercenaries hired to fight in jungle wars. Perhaps a return to the rainforests, not to another civil war but to a mercenary-led coup d'état?

I wrote both down, as required, on a single sheet of A4 paper and presented them to Harold Harris on that Friday. He skimmed through them and decided without a second's hesitation.

'Nazis first, mercenaries second. And I want the first manuscript by December next year.'

I did not know at the time that he was Jewish, lapsed but from an orthodox parentage. Nor that in April 1945 he had been a young German-speaking officer in British army intelligence. Nor that he had been summoned across Schleswig-Holstein to interrogate a mysterious but suspicious prisoner. He had not arrived in his jeep when the prisoner bit on a cyanide capsule and killed himself. The man was Heinrich Himmler.

I had one last problem before signing the three-novel contract. Apart from the coming £500 I was still broke.

'There will be living costs and research and travelling and lodgings,' I said. 'Could I have something to tide me through?'

He scrawled on a sheet of paper and gave it to me.

'Take this to accounts,' he said. 'Good luck and stay in touch. Oh, and get an agent. I recommend Diana Baring.'

The piece of paper I clutched was quite an act of faith. It was an authority to draw £6,000 against future royalties. In 1970 that was rather a lot of money.

Back on the street again I started to think. Who the hell knows about Nazis? Then I recalled a book called *The Scourge of the Swastika* which I had read years earlier. It was by Lord Russell of Liverpool, who had been a senior British prosecutor at the Nuremberg trials of the Forties. I would have to track him down and see if he could help.

Before then I had yet another lucky break. I had met a man called John Mallinson who prided himself on being an agent, albeit without clients. I did not look him up but coincidentally we met again at the flat of a friend. I told him what had happened in Great Portland Street. He became quite excited.

'What about the film rights?' he asked. I had not a clue. He scoured the Hutchinson contract. 'They're still yours. Appoint me as your film agent and I'll find a buyer.'

By November he had done exactly that. The film deal was with Romulus Films of Park Lane, headed by John Woolf. But his right-hand man in all things was John Rosenberg and it was with him that we dealt. The offer was £17,500 plus a small percentage of net profits, or £20,000 outright sale in perpetuity.

Most people are good at some things and useless at others. I am pathetic at money. I had never seen £20,000 so I took it.

I have no idea how many millions the film has made over the years. I can only excuse myself with the thought that I had no idea the book would sell over a hundred copies or the film would ever be made. Even the way it was made was a fluke.

That winter the Hollywood giant Fred Zinnemann flew over to discuss a project with John Woolf. It was to film a successful play called *Abelard and Heloise*. There had always been a problem. The film could not be made while the play was on stage anywhere. That December it closed in England and was not staging anywhere else.

The day before Zinnemann arrived, it was decided the play would reopen in a British provincial city. The Hollywood director's trip was fruitless after all. Desperately embarrassed, John Woolf was apologizing in his office, knowing his guest had to face a rainy London weekend with nothing to read. Frantically, he reached for something John Rosenberg had placed on his desk.

'We have just bought this,' he said. Mr Zinnemann took it and left. He was back on Monday. 'This is my next movie,' he told a delighted Romulus Films.

I knew none of all this until later. Looking back, it was not really *The Day of the Jackal*, the one-off to clear my debts, that changed my life. It was Harold Harris and his three-novel contract. It just occurred to me that if I could make a good living dashing off this nonsense, why get my head blown off in an African rain ditch?

But the more immediate problem was trying to find Lord Russell of Liverpool and ask him about underground Nazis. And I had the problem of what to call them. I needed two titles. In German ODESSA stood for Organization of Former

Members of the SS. As far as the world was concerned Odessa was a city in the Ukraine or a town in Texas. Well, here was a third one. *The Odessa File.*

For the mercenaries I recalled a quote from Shakespeare. 'Cry havoc, and let slip the dogs of war.' I had heard someone had used 'Cry Havoc' but not 'The Dogs of War'. So I filched it from the bard.

The ODESSA

Lord Russell of Liverpool had retired to a small cottage at Dinard, a town on the French coast facing the Atlantic, and that was where I found him. I had no introduction so I just turned up and knocked. When I explained what I needed he was helpfulness itself.

Though he was a mine of information about the war and the Nuremburg trials, these had been twenty years earlier. I sought details about secret pro-Nazi elements still in existence in 1971. He referred me to the wellspring of Nazi-hunting, the Vienna-based researcher Simon Wiesenthal. With a letter of introduction I headed south to Austria.

Like David Ben-Gurion, Simon Wiesenthal began by conceding he could spare me twenty minutes of his time but when I explained what I sought became so enthusiastic that we spent days poring over his records. The germ of my idea was not for a Nazi fugitive who had fled to South America but one who had changed his name and disappeared right in the heart of Germany, but with help from equally covert friends. The response of Herr Wiesenthal was that the right choice might be difficult, not because there were so few but that there were thousands of them.

It seemed there were two mutual-help brotherhoods still very much active in the Germany of 1971. There was the *Kameradschaft* or Comradeship, and the ODESSA, which was in no way fictional.

'What I seek,' I explained, 'is to invent a mass-murderer of the Nazi era who, like so many, had stripped off his uniform at the very end, adopted another persona and disappeared into post-war German society, returning to office, influence and respectability under another name. Like a concentration camp commander.'

He beamed and gestured to a shelf of files behind his desk.

'Why invent one? I have a dozen real ones.'

We pored through the files and settled on Eduard Roschmann, former camp commander at Riga, Latvia, and known as the Butcher of Riga. He had been a real monster, but one among many.

And I learned of that amazing day in the spring of 1945 when a single US army jeep, driving north through Bavaria with just four soldiers on board, had seen plumes of smoke rising from the courtyard of a medieval castle.

Driving unchallenged over the drawbridge they had dis-covered a dozen SS men in overalls tending a bonfire. They arrested the lot and hosed out the fire. Experts came up from General Patton's headquarters to discover that what was being burned was the entire SS personnel archive. Only 2 or 3 per cent had been consumed by the flames. The rest was now lodged under American care in West Berlin. That included the entire file on Captain (Hauptsturmführer) Eduard Roschmann of Riga, an Austrian-born fanatic now high on the 'wanted' list. Slowly, my story was coming together, but there was less and less to invent; it was beyond fiction but it was all true.

The real irony was that I could say anything I wanted about this monster. Wherever he was, he was hardly likely to come out of hiding to sue.

Finally Simon Wiesenthal pointed me back north to Germany with a huge volume of information and even more warnings. I thought his conviction that West German officialdom was comprehensively penetrated by a generation steeped in either participation in, or sympathy for, what had happened between 1933 and 1945 might be just paranoia, but it was nothing of the sort. It all came down to the issue of 'which generation'.

A fanatical Nazi aged twenty-five at the end of the war would have been born around 1920. He would have been steeped in Nazi education from age thirteen onwards and almost certainly a member of the Hitler Youth from that age. He could well have been a mass-murderer by twenty-five.

By the time of my research he would have been fifty-one or -two; that is, at the prime of life and a high-ranker in any of a hundred official positions. Nor would I receive obstruction only from wanted criminals. Behind them was the even larger army of guilty desk-doers, the bureaucrats without whose organizational flair the Holocaust could never have happened.

This was the generation that now ran Germany, blossoming in its Economic Miracle. After 1949, the founding under Allied aegis of the new Federal Republic of (West) Germany, the Chancellor was the undeniably anti-Nazi Konrad Adenauer. But he had a terrible quandary to resolve.

Nazi Party members were so pandemic that had he banned them all the country would have been ungovernable. So he cut his Faustian pact. Delving into the past when considering appointment or promotions was neither practical nor desirable. According to Simon Wiesenthal, every branch of the public function was impregnated with bureaucrats who had never pulled a trigger but had helped those who did. Research, he said, was not a question of open hostility but of closed doors. Police officers who volunteered to join the Nazi-hunting commissions quite simply terminated their own careers. They became outcasts. And he turned out to be right.

He also pointed me towards clandestine groups who still really believed in the coming of the Fourth Reich one day and whose meetings I could attend with my fluent German. So I did. The more I delved into the murk of pre-1945 Nazism and its post-1945 admirers, the more I came to the view that in all the history of the human race there has never been a creed so foul. It had not a single redeeming feature, appealing only to the nastiest corners of the human soul.

But it was all hidden, back then. The participant generation never spoke of it and the young generation was profoundly ignorant and indeed deeply puzzled by foreign hostility when they met it.

Despite their professed loathing of Fascism and Nazism, the Communists of the East, behind the Iron Curtain, offered no help or cooperation whatsoever.

Thus all investigation of the crimes committed east of the Iron Curtain during the Nazi time was allocated to different State Attorney offices spread across West Germany. Riga came under the State Attorneyship of Hamburg. I started there and met a blank wall of closed doors. I was puzzled. Surely they were lawyers? I rang Simon Wiesenthal. He roared with laughter.

'Yes, of course they are lawyers. But whose lawyers?'

I realized many must have been or still were in the Comradeship. But slowly I made contact with either younger men, untainted because they were too young, or anti-Nazis who had lived through it and survived unsullied. They talked, but quietly, furtively, in darkened beer-bars, once convinced I was just a British investigative reporter. And slowly the story came together that in 1972 appeared under the title *The Odessa File*.

Starting in Hamburg I drifted back south again until I returned to Austria, from which my villain Roschmann had come. In an antique shop I found an old Jew who had been in Riga under Roschmann and had survived, even the Death March west as the Russians advanced. His wife assured me her husband had never spoken of it and never would. But she was wrong.

The old man was courtesy itself and offered me tea. We sat as I explained the plotline of the story I had in mind. I do not know why but he began to correct me. It was not like that, he said, it was like that. Darkness fell. As his wide-eyed wife brought relay after relay of tea, he talked for twenty hours. In the book, the testimony of Salomon Tauber is the one recounted to me, detail by detail, by candlelight in a Viennese antique shop. I just moved Herr Tauber to Hamburg.

For a hero I needed a young investigator of the new generation to inherit the diary of the dead Tauber and do something about it. So I invented Peter Miller, and his investigative trail almost exactly matches my own during that summer of 1971.

I returned to the UK in June for the launch of *The Day of*

the Jackal. It was a very quiet affair. No one had heard of the title or the author. It had not been reviewed. Hutchinson had begun with an audacious 5,000 copies, raised to 8,000 as the book buyers of the major stores slowly increased their orders. The PR lady for the launch was Cindy Winkleman, now the stepmother of British TV star Claudia.

Then I went back to Germany to tie up the last details. I wrote *The Odessa File* that autumn and presented it to Harold Harris as promised before Christmas. Slowly *Jackal* was climbing the charts and the second novel had a better media reception. Hollywood succumbed to the wiles of my new agent Diana Baring and bought the film rights.

The movie, when it came out in 1974 starring Jon Voight as Peter Miller and Maximilian Schell as the villainous Roschmann, led eventually to the quixotic twist in this tale.

In 1975 in a fleapit cinema on the coast south of Buenos Aires, an Argentinian was watching the Spanish-language version when it occurred to him that Eduard Roschmann, who had reverted to his real name, so convinced was he of his safety, was living down the street. So he denounced him.

Argentina was in one of its brief windows of democratic government under President Isabel Perón, widow of the old tyrant Juan Perón, and, seeking to do the right thing, had Roschmann arrested. West Germany slapped in a request for extradition.

Before the legal formalities had been completed between the West German embassy and the Ministry of Justice, Roschmann, on bail thanks to a local magistrate, lost his nerve. He ran north for the sanctuary of the pro-Nazi dictator

Stroessner of Paraguay. He reached the border and waited for the ferry across the river Paraguay to safety.

Right in the middle of the river he had a massive heart attack. Witnesses said he was dead before he hit the floor, or in this case the deck. What followed must have come from a very flaky comedy show.

On the Paraguayan bank the terminal master refused to accept the body on the grounds it belonged to Argentina. The captain insisted the dead man had paid full fare for his crossing and the cadaver belonged to Paraguay. The ferry schedule insisted the boat depart so the body went back to Argentina, still lying on the foredeck.

It went back and forth four times, becoming ever more smelly under the tropical sun. Then two detectives arrived from Vienna to identify it. Thanks to the American jeep in Bavaria in 1945, they had fingerprints and dental records from the Roschmann file in the SS personnel archives. They asked for the body to be unloaded at last and the Paraguayans conceded.

Proof positive was established and the clincher was the two missing toes, amputated when Roschmann fled the British through the border snows in 1947. With the ferry refusing to have the corpse back, the Paraguayans buried it in a gravel bank just back from the water's edge.

So today the bones of the Butcher of Riga lie in an unmarked grave in a gravel bank beside the river Paraguay. It took a bit of time but eventually, thanks to the movie, job done.

Dogs of War

JUST AS MY years in France had convinced me the OAS was not going to succeed in toppling Charles de Gaulle, my years in Africa taught me something else.

This was that in the immediate aftermath of the colonial era there were several independent republics on the continent so small, so chaotic, so badly governed and defended that they could be toppled and taken over by a small group of professional soldiers with the right weaponry and a few dozen loyal levies. Thinking to write my third novel and set it in Africa, I notionally selected three.

Top of the list was Equatorial Guinea, an island republic off the coast of Nigeria. It had once been Spain's only African colony, linked to an enclave on the mainland called Río Muni. For a while, under Spain, it had been a stopover for Biafra-bound food flights by the International Red Cross. Independence came in 1968 and it plunged into chaos and terror.

The ruler was Francisco Macías Nguema, a Fang from Río Muni. He was probably mad and certainly savagely cruel. He transferred his government to the island, then called Fernando Po, now renamed Bioko. He had a small army of Fangs which terrorized the indigenous Bubi people. His cruelties soon became legendary. But behind the screen of terror, he was immensely weak.

His bodyguard/army was hung with weapons, but he was so paranoid that they had no bullets because he could not trust them. Had he fallen, no one would have come to his aid. His fellow Fangs were hundreds of miles away, the Bubi loathed him and the very few diplomats and aid workers left despised him.

He lived in the barracks of the former Spanish gendarmerie, converted into his fortress, on top of the national armoury and the national treasury, which he had confiscated. If that one building fell, so did the republic.

Researching all this was no problem. There was no need for me to risk going there, so I did not. But I was able to talk to a score of former inhabitants, mainly Spanish, who gleefully explained how he could be toppled by a small attacking force. One remarked: 'To knock off a bank is merely crude. To knock off an entire republic has a certain style.'

With control of a republic comes membership of the United Nations, international loans, arrest-free diplomatic passports and various other Christmas treats. There was even an exiled rival in Madrid who could be installed on the presidential throne as a puppet successor.

There need only be five rules. Strike hard, strike fast and strike by night. Come unexpected and come by sea. Parenthetically the eventual book was imitated twice. In 1975 the French mercenary Bob Denard attacked and took over the Comoros islands at the top of the Mozambique Channel.

He was acting with the knowledge, assistance and on behalf

of the French government. Amusingly, as his French mercenaries came up the beach in the pre-dawn darkness, they all carried a paperback edition of *Les Chiens de Guerre* (*The Dogs of War* in French) so that they could constantly find out what they were supposed to do next. Denard succeeded because he came by sea.

In 1981 South African mercenary Mike Hoare tried the same trick on the Seychelles, but he failed because he came by air.

For my own story I soon had all in place – the men, the ship, the target – but lacked vital knowledge. The weapons. Where in Europe could a clandestine mercenary operation secure its weapons? The cover story would be a plausible private-sector operation involving deep-sea diving for oil exploration and upon invitation.

But the African levies to be picked up en route, one of the sub-plots, would need submachine carbines and plenty of ammunition. The half-dozen mercs would need a heavy machine gun, RPGs (then called bazookas), grenades, 60mm mortar flares and explosive charges. All that would also require practice and rehearsal time, hence the long slow cruise on a small merchantman out at sea.

But where to get all this stuff? Back then I could not call on informational help from the authorities. To find out I would have to penetrate the world of the black-market arms dealers and see it from the inside, and I was not prepared to attempt a thriller with such vital areas unexplained.

My contacts advised me the heart of the black-market arms world was in Hamburg and its kingpin was a certain Otto X who posed as a respectable businessman – but then, they all do.

So to Hamburg I went with another advance from Hutchinson, who were very happy with the sales of the first two.

I thought it unwise to use my own name so I took that of the pilot who flew me out of Biafra and declared I was Frederik van der Merwe, a South African. I even had papers to prove it, prepared by the forger who had taught me about false passports in *The Day of the Jackal*. Mr van der Merwe was the youthful assistant of a South African multi-millionaire wishing to assist Jonas Savimbi in the Angolan civil war. And thus I managed to get into the inner councils of Herr Otto X.

There I learned about End User Certificates, the documents purporting to come from a reputable sovereign government entitled to purchase defence equipment for its legitimate purposes. For a fee, Otto X could obtain false ones on the right headed paper and signed by a 'purchased' African diplomat assigned to an embassy somewhere in Europe. It was all going swimmingly until something happened that I had not foreseen.

One morning Herr Otto X was in his limousine when it stopped at a red light next to a bookshop which that day was launching the German version of *Der Schakal* (*The Day of the Jackal*.) There was a display in the window but one copy had fallen over and on the rear cover was a picture of the author.

Herr Otto X found himself staring at Mynheer van der Merwe and suffered a complete sense-of-humour failure. Fortunately I had an unknown and unsuspected friend at court. I was in my hotel room opposite the main station when the phone rang. There were no introductions. A voice spoke, clearly British, with the clipped tones of education.

'Freddie, get out of Hamburg now. And I mean now. They are coming for you.'

Like my father in 1938 I did a runner. I grabbed passport and a fistful of money, left the luggage and went down the stairs, past the receptionist and across the station square. I did not bother with the ticket office but went straight for the trains. There was one just beginning to move, doors closed but one window wide open.

I went through it on a forward roll and landed on the lap of a plump German businessman, who also lacked the gift of humour. I was still apologizing when the conductor appeared to check tickets. No ticket.

I explained I had just had time to catch the train which was gathering speed through the suburbs and asked to pay in cash.

'Where are you going?' he asked.

'Well, where are *you* going?' I replied.

'Amsterdam,' he said.

'What a coincidence. A single to Amsterdam, in economy.'

'You are in first,' he said, 'you'll have to move.' So I got my ticket, apologized again and went to find a harder seat.

My father's younger brother was living and working for a British company in Scheveningen at the time. He managed to get me a passage on a merchantman out of Flushing for England.

Back in my London flat I gathered my research papers around me, sat down and wrote *The Dogs of War*, presenting the manuscript to Harold Harris just before the deadline.

I wondered about the voice on the phone that had saved my bacon in Hamburg. The only explanation that made sense was that also in the circle around Herr Otto X was another infiltrator from the body I knew as the Firm, checking on behalf of my government on possible arms sales to the IRA. But I never found out who he was and so far as I know never met him.

The spring of 1973 was restful. I had completed my three-novel contract, had no ideas for a fourth and was just beginning to see some serious money coming in. Then I dropped by at John Mallinson's flat for a drink and someone else, on her way home from a modelling assignment, also came by. She was an auburn-haired girl whose legs seemed to go on for ever. Carrie and I married in Gibraltar that August.

And a letter came from David Deutsch, the producer appointed by John Woolf to make the film of *Jackal*. It had filmed in London and was then shooting all the French scenes in Paris. Would I like to come over for a visit and meet the star, Edward Fox? Of course I would.

I knew the face because months earlier during pre-production Fred Zinnemann had asked me to his office for a consultation. With his old-world Viennese courtesy he explained there was a problem with the casting.

The Hollywood studio who would distribute the movie wanted a known star. Michael Caine had been interested, ditto Roger Moore. Charlton Heston had begged for it. But Zinnemann wanted a man who, though an excellent actor, was still little-known enough to vanish in the crowd, as the Jackal was supposed to do.

In his Mount Street office the director solemnly placed six photos before me, all postcard size. They were all of handsome young men, blond, staring at the camera.

'Which, for you, is the Jackal?' he asked. I scanned them

all and placed my finger on the bottom right-hand photo. 'That one.'

'I am so glad. I have just signed him. His name is Edward Fox.'

The other five were male models. Edward had already gained his spurs as Lord Trimingham in Joseph Losey's *The Go-Between*. But internationally he was still relatively unknown. *The Jackal* was going to change that.

An Unusual Dinner

FRED ZINNEMANN WAS a brilliant director but it was as if he were two men. Off the set he was old-world courtesy personified, but on the set he was a miniature dictator. Perhaps he had to be to get the films made; there are some very large egos in film-making.

He was staying at the Hotel Westminster in the Rue de Berri, just off the Champs-Elysées, with Edward Fox very much under his wing and control. He did not really want his new young star going off into town at night, lest he was late for the early starts that were necessary to get out to the studio and into make-up.

I arrived at the hotel on time and he introduced me to Edward. Dinner was friendly but slightly formal and ended rather early for the city of lights. I suspected Edward might have been up for a more adventurous evening.

As we were crossing the lobby towards the door and out of earshot of Mr Zinnemann I asked if he had actually ever met a contract hitman. He said he had not.

'Would you like to?' I asked.

'Well, as I am supposed to be playing one, it might be interesting,' he said.

I told him that at eight the next evening there would be a taxi parked across the street with me in it. He should just cross the road and jump in.

It was quite a long shot but I was lucky. I hoped Armand would be in town and when I contacted his doting sister she said he was indeed and she would tell him to call me at my hotel. He rang just before midnight and I told him what I had in mind. He seemed amused but would not come to the 8th Arrondissement, setting up a 'meet' in the heart of the red-light district at a café-bar I had never heard of.

Of the six mercenaries who had stayed on in Biafra after the bulk of the French-supplied contingent ran into an ambush and then the airport to evacuate themselves, as I said, I really only liked three: Alec the Scot, Johnny the Rhodesian and Armand the Parisian.

Armand had never really been a gangster in Paris because he never joined a gang. But he occasionally acted as settler of accounts between the gangs of the Paris underworld. The city police had no objection to the place being cleaned up a bit, which was why they mostly left him alone.

On one occasion Madame Claude, proprietress of the corps of the best call girls in Europe, felt she was being followed, possibly with intent to kidnap. She too consulted the chief of detectives, who recommended she engage Armand to look after her.

A week later her driver again noticed the lights of the stalker car in his mirror. Armand, sitting beside him, asked him to pull over and stop. The car behind did the same. Armand got out and strolled back to have a word. There was a brief conversation through the side window of the car behind. It hung a U-turn in the middle of the boulevard and drove off. That was the end of that.

Although he was much younger than her, Mme Claude developed a huge crush on him, made more so by his polite disinclination to take advantage. So she offered him the choice of her school of extremely pricey ladies – on the house, so to speak. But he preferred, as he put it, to roll his own, so he left her employ.

The bistro he had stipulated was down a side street and as the taxi entered it we noted that both pavements were lined with streetwalkers. We got out and as I paid the driver we received a chorus of the usual salutations.

'*Alors, Blondie, je t'emmène? Tu veux monter, non?*'

Edward, who had been to Harrow, of course did not understand a word but the sense was clear enough. It was a warm night, their dresses were minimal and their bosoms jacked up to resemble party balloons. I settled up with the taxi and ushered him inside.

There was a bar, then a bead curtain and the dining area behind it. We penetrated the curtain and joined Armand at the table in the far corner where he was toying with a citron pressé. (He did not drink alcohol.)

Introductions made, we had a civilized dinner. Armand spoke no English and Edward schoolboy French, which is to say very little indeed. I interpreted. With his innate manners Edward asked no really embarrassing questions so there were no tense moments, until the end.

And that was not the fault of any of us. Word had spread to the bar area and thence to the street that there was a film star dining inside. The French are film-crazy and the idea of a real film star a few yards away was to the streetwalkers as a large fly to a salmon. They invaded the dining area, shoving their figures at us both until they realized that only Edward was in films. Then they were making him some very bawdy suggestions.

The future Jackal was pink as a traffic light, the underworld executioner was laughing his head off and I was trying to get the head waiter so that I could settle up and escape. Then Armand was gone, out the back via the kitchens, and I have not seen him since. The bar owner summoned a cab by phone and I was able to deliver Edward back to the Westminster and Fred Zinnemann pretty much intact.

Forty years later, at a garden lunch party at my home, I told the anecdote to a merry audience to explain how we met. Edward was there with his wife, Joanna David, who had never heard it. I ended by saying that in forty years I had never told him what it was the girls were saying to him. He leaned across the table.

'No,' he said. 'You never did. What was it?'

'They were offering you freebies. Whatever you wanted. On the house. And in their world that is a very serious compliment indeed.'

He thought it over.

'I don't suppose there is any point in going back?'

As we are both well into our seventies, I very much doubt it.

Perfect Joy

IF YOU WERE to ask ten people for their definition of perfect joy, you might well get ten definitions or a few less than that. Pretty high in the choices would be that moment when a father gazes down at his newborn child, the tiny face puckered in outrage at having been expelled from a safe, warm womb into a world of troubles. Of these it knows nothing and from them must be protected, which is where the lovelorn father comes in.

There will be other choices, including palm-fringed lagoons or a hole-in-one while winning the US Open. Reject all of these, for I know what is perfect joy because I have seen it.

The call when it came in summer 1973 was, as always, terribly diffident. Could we possibly get together for a chat? Of course we could. They did not want me to come to Century House in case someone saw me. And a lunch booth in a restaurant, however expensive and discreet, can always be bugged by a waiter working for the other side.

So it was a safe house, in reality an apartment in a block, scanned daily and certainly before every use. It was so discreet that I have forgotten where it was, save only it was in Mayfair,

London. There were three of them and they were not from the Africa Desk but concerned with operations in East Germany, so I did not know them. But they knew me, or at least the contents of my file.

'There is no question of trying to pass for a German, so no refresher course. Just a question of a British tourist slipping inside and bringing something out.'

I still reckoned the voice on the phone that got me out of Hamburg just in time was that of a Friend, someone from the Firm, and one good turn deserves another. Besides, it all seemed so simple.

There was an asset, a Russian colonel, working for us deep inside East Germany and he had a package that we needed brought out. No, not in East Berlin but based outside Dresden. He could not get further than a meet in Dresden. It began to be not quite so simple. Dresden was a long way in.

The proposed plan had been minutely studied long before the safe house meeting and appeared to have the fewest flaws. It would have to be by car because the package, which in deference to Alfred Hitchcock I always called the McGuffin, would have to be concealed far from prying hands and eyes on the way out. Besides, there was another package for the asset which had to go in. So, a swap. One in and one out.

They knew I had a car, at that time a Triumph Vitesse, drophead convertible. Could they borrow it for a day or so? Of course.

I had to leave the Triumph outside my apartment with the keys under the floor mat. I never saw who took it or returned it. No need to. It just vanished and reappeared, but slightly different.

The battery in the Vitesse was in the engine bay. It sat on a tray beside the left-hand engine wall. Two metal clips prevented it moving and a thick rubber pad prevented vibrations. The pad had been removed, slit open and a cavity created.

To get at the cavity one had to use a spanner to release the positive and negative leads, then undo the two retaining clips. Lift the battery out and place it to one side. Peel the rubber pad open and there was the fat wad of papers destined for the asset, and the cavity in which his reports (whatever they were I would never know) would ride out of the workers' paradise.

I spent a day by the kerbside in the warm summer sun practising until I had it all down to less than thirty seconds. And there was more.

The 'cover' was a visit to the Albertinum Museum, East Germany's cultural jewel, amazingly untouched by the Anglo-American bombing of February 1945 which had flattened most of the city. Graeco-Roman treasures were my new enthusiasm and there were books to study as if for an exam. Finally, it seemed I was ready to roll.

It was a long drive across France and West Germany to the East German border, but under the Four Power Agreement my British passport entitled me on to the autobahn running across East Germany to the enclave of West Berlin. Once there I avoided all contacts made during my time ten years earlier.

But there was a travel agency permitted by the East German authorities to be the conduit for visas for genuine Western tourists, whom the Politburo was keen to entice into East Germany for the foreign currency they brought.

My handler, Philip (a pseudonym, of course), certainly did

not wish to be photographed sitting beside me in the passenger seat when the Triumph entered East Germany, so he had flown in to Tempelhof, the airport that serviced West Berlin only. He waited in a different hotel until the visa came through. The agency took its fee and gave me my passport back. Philip secured the final OK from London, meaning the asset was ready, and I was cleared to roll through Checkpoint Charlie the following morning.

There were several conditions for the visa. A minimum sum in Deutschmarks had to be changed into worthless East Marks and this was duly done. On the East German autobahn south, there were specific filling stations where I was allowed to refuel. I had no doubt that if the Stasi were not going to tail me all the way, there would be checkpoints along the route at which the dark blue Triumph with British number plates would be 'clocked' and noted.

And there was just one hotel in Dresden where I was expected and where a reservation had been made.

I had not seen Checkpoint Charlie for ten years but it was much the same. Foreigners queued as usual by the checking sheds while mirrors on wheels were run under the chassis to scan for contraband.

The usual 'bonnet up' and 'boot open' orders, the usual nervous obedience, the usual tourist attempts to be light-hearted, the usual grim unsmiling response. The border guard assigned to me looked around the engine bay but touched nothing. The battery pad had passed its first test.

My small valise had been emptied and searched inside the shed and, that apart, the boot contained nothing so I was allowed to replace it and slam the lid shut. Then the final curt wave towards East Berlin, the barrier rising and the roll into Redland.

I had memorized the route through the southern outskirts of East Berlin towards the Dresden autobahn. Of course there was the second border check – the one to get you out of East Berlin and into rural East Germany. This I recognized: it was the one through which the Magdeburg Stasi had escorted me after the RB66 incident in the pine forest ten years back. I hoped Captain Holland's leg had mended.

Then it was the open road, south into Saxony province and the city of Dresden, which I had never seen. The hotel was clearly marked on my street map and I was installed by mid-afternoon.

The car park was underground and this was before the all-seeing CCTV cameras. There seemed to be no one watching, though I had no doubt my room was bugged, telephone ditto, and that it would be searched while I was at dinner. So I left the McGuffin under the battery pad until the morning.

There was no point in going out to wander the streets. My brass-buttoned blazer yelled 'Englishman' to any drab-dressed East German, so I stayed in and studied the two books I had brought with me on the Albertinum Museum and its many ancient treasures. I hoped these would be noted by the hotel staff and that if they reported, which they almost certainly would, it would be to say the Brit was simply obsessed by Roman antiquities.

Not entirely unnaturally, I slept lightly and woke early. The meet was for two o'clock in a certain aisle between display cabinets inside the museum. I breakfasted at eight and checked out at nine, paying cash (no credit cards back then). But I left my valise with the concierge and was assured my car could remain in the garage until I needed it. I was not told what else would happen – that my case would be searched again. Good, there was nothing in it.

At half past nine I ducked down into the garage, waited until another hotel guest drove out, clipped open the bonnet, removed the McGuffin, slipped it into my blazer pocket, replaced the battery, reconnected it and closed up. Then it was a leisurely walk with textbooks under the arm to the museum. At five to two I was in the aisle between the cabinets, engrossed in shards of pottery.

There were others there. Couples, threesomes, the inevitable guided groups of schoolchildren. I had my picture book open, comparing the photographs with the real artefacts behind the glass, occasionally looking out for a single man with a dark red tie and black stripes. A few seconds after two he turned into my aisle.

Germans usually do not have Slavic features; this one did. And the tie. I saw his glance settle upon my own: dark blue with white polka dots. No one else remotely like either of us. Then a wandering curator in uniform. Sometimes the simplest way is the best way.

'*Entschuldigung* (excuse me), where is the men's room?'

He was politeness itself and pointed out the sign *Herren* above a door at the end of the gallery. No eye contact with 'Chummy' standing ten feet away. He should know the 'meet' would be in the toilet. So I wandered away towards it, entered, relieved myself and was washing my hands when he entered. Apart from us it was empty and all the stall doors were open. He too began to wash his hands. So two noisy streams of water. His turn. In German.

'Excuse me, did we not meet in Potsdam?'

My reply.

'Yes, I was there last April.'

Enough. No one else was talking this garbage in Dresden that morning. I nodded to two adjacent stalls. He took one, I took the other. Under the cubicle partition came a fat package of paper. I took mine and slid it the other way.

I defy anyone to resist the small worm of anxiety in the pit of the stomach at that moment. Is Chummy the real Chummy or was the real asset picked up a week ago and broken in the interrogation cellar to reveal all the places and ID codes of the coming 'meet'?

Is the place about to be invaded by screaming hordes of goons with drawn pistols, handcuffs, clouts about the head? Even the silence seems menacing. But the biggest fear of all is not that you have run out of trade-craft or luck, but that far away back home some bastard has betrayed you. 'They' knew all along, they were waiting for you, mocking all your precautions. That is why Dante put the traitor in the final circle of Hell.

Nothing happened. Chummy left the booth and I heard the outer door slam shut. I have never seen him since. I hope he is all right. There were still eighteen years of USSR to go, and the KGB had a very nasty procedure for traitors.

I also left the booth but had another hand-wash to kill time. When I left I bumped into another man coming in, but he was just a visitor. We nodded, passed and I strolled out, still clutching my textbooks. There were a few more hours to kill until dusk, for I wanted to motor in darkness.

The visa expired at midnight and the way to the West was

not via East Berlin but south to the Saale River Crossing Point, one of the few tourist-approved crossing points. South of Saale, in the town of Bayreuth, Philip would be waiting.

Back at the hotel I collected my valise with assurances of having had a wonderful time in Dresden and copious compliments on the superb Albertinum Museum. Then down to the car park. But there was a large conference party checking in. Too many people. If I was seen waist-deep in my own engine bay, there might be offers of help, the last thing I needed. I kept the McGuffin in my breast pocket, got into the Triumph, which was already attracting curious glances, and drove out. Darkness was descending. I took the signs pointing to the Gera Kreuz, the major autobahn junction where the highway turned south to the Bavarian border.

It was pitch dark when I saw the layby in the headlights and, as I had hoped, the road by night was almost empty. I eased to the right, slid up the shallow ramp until the pine trees enveloped me and stopped. Lights out. Wait, have a cigarette. Relax. Nearly there.

There was a small spanner in the glove compartment. Not enough to arouse suspicion but vital for the nuts on the battery leads. I got out, opened the bonnet and used my spanner to ease the first nut, the one on the negative battery lead. There was no need for a torch, the sickle moon was enough. At that moment the layby was flooded with a harsh white light.

Another car had cruised up the ramp behind me, its headlights undipped. I slipped the spanner into my trouser pocket and straightened up. The car behind was a Wartburg saloon and by its own lights I could see its livery: green and cream, the insignia of the Volkspolizei, the People's Police, the VoPos. There were four of them climbing out.

They had clearly by then recognized the Triumph and the number plates as British. The reason they had come off the autobahn made itself plain when one of them faced the woods and unzipped his fly. A comfort break but that bursting bladder might prove to be their lucky night.

The senior of them was a top NCO, what I took to be the Unteroffizier. The other two examined the Triumph curiously while their colleague urinated. The NCO held out his hand.

'*Ausweis, bitte*.' The 'please' was good news, still polite. I dropped into Bertie Wooster mode – the hapless, helpless, harmless English tourist, completely lost and very dim. Halting German, awful accent.

The NCO examined the passport page by page by the light of a torch from his pocket. He saw the East German visa.

'Why are you stopped here?'

'It just stopped, Officer. I don't know why. Just motoring along and it starts to cough, then cut out. I had just enough speed to get here before it stopped.'

The Germans are probably the best engineers in the world but they know it and love to be told it. Even East German engineering was good enough for its degrees to be acknowledged in the West. So I laid the flattery on with a trowel.

'I cannot understand engines, Officer. So I do not know what to look for. And I have no torch. You Germans are so brilliant at this . . . I don't suppose you could have a look?'

The senior NCO thought it over. Then he snapped an order at the one who had finished his ablutions and buttoned up his fly. In that crew he seemed to be the mechanic.

'*Guck mal,*' he said, gesturing towards the engine bay. 'Have a look.'

The urinator took the torch and went into the engine bay. Inside my breast pocket the fat pack of papers was beginning to feel like a tombstone, which it could turn out to be if I was ordered to empty all pockets.

Then there was a shout of triumph and the engineer straightened up. He was holding up in his right hand the disconnected battery lead, illuminated in the torch beam.

'*Hat sich gelöst,*' he shouted. 'It just shook itself off.'

Then it was all grins of pleasure. Point proved. Germans are better. I was handing round Rothmans, much appreciated. The disconnected lead was replaced and I was bidden to try the starter. It kicked at once into life. Bertie Wooster was beside himself with amazement and gratitude. Bonnet down and locked. Salutes all round. Please, Mein Herr, on your way.

An hour further on I did it again and this time was not disturbed. At half past eleven I rolled into the arc lights and customs sheds at the Saale Crossing.

And there it was thorough. Boot, engine bay, high-powered flashlights into every crevice. Upholstery patted for hidden lumps, mirrors and lights rolled underneath.

Inside the custom shed, pocket and body search. I was the only crosser; I had their undivided attention and I suppose they were bored. Excess cash handed over, passport taken to a back room, muffled sounds of phone calls. Eventually, with expressions of disappointment on their faces, the curt nod. Proceed. Valise back in boot, climb in, start up. Roll.

Back then the East Germans had a trick. Their border point was a quarter of a mile inside East Germany. After the lifting of what looked like the last pole there was a long slow cruise at only ten kilometres per hour down the last stretch. It was bordered both sides by chain-link fence. Unclimbable. And watch towers with machine guns. Easy to hear the roared bull-horn command *Halt. Stehenbleiben.* Halt, stay where you are.

Finally, at the end, another barrier. Behind it the West Germans were watching, hidden behind their own lights, field glasses on the approaching car and the East German controls further back. No shout, front bumper approaching the barrier, which finally jerks into action.

Perfect joy? Oh yes. Perfect joy is the sight of a red-and-white-striped pole rising into the Bavarian night as the rear-view mirror fills with the wash of headlights.

I was very late into Bayreuth and found Philip at the only place in town still open for coffee, the railway café. He seemed distraught. He thought he had lost me. I was touched. So I gave him the McGuffin, went to the hotel and slept like a log.

The next day I filled the tank and drove back across Bavaria, over the Rhine, through France to the Channel port of Calais. Thence the first ferry of the day for Dover and, standing on the forepeak, the chance to see once again the great white cliffs coming through the morning mist.

Friends and Opponents

THERE ARE FEW experiences that appear so harmless but turn out to be so exhausting as the round-the-world promotion tour.

At first blush it sounds varied and interesting. Just twelve cities in twenty-four days with a couple of 'rest' weekends in the middle and first class all the way. Why not? The reason why not is that after six or seven days the effect of rapidly changing time zones, strange beds, constant airports and the draining dawn-to-dusk interviews are starting to drag at the nerve ends, exacerbating the inevitable jetlag.

I only did one such and that was in 1978 to promote the fourth novel, *The Devil's Alternative*. Just Toronto, Vancouver, Hong Kong, Brisbane, Sydney, Auckland, Perth, Johannesburg, Cape Town, Frankfurt and back to London. It was all new to me and exotic. Years later just two stopovers stand out – Hong Kong and Mauritius, which was a weekend break between Perth and Jo'burg.

By the time the airliner touched down at the small and crowded Kai Tak airport in Hong Kong I was only a third into my journey and still pretty fresh. The Peninsula Hotel had sent a car and I had to admit I had never ever been looked after like this.

I had just been bowed into my suite on the tenth floor of the Peninsula when the phone rang. It was 'Johnny', the Firm's Head of Station for the colony and several out-stations besides.

'Are you on for dinner tonight?'

'Er, yes.'

'Splendid. I'll pick you up. Far end of the front car park, eight o'clock, red car.' Then he was gone.

The Peninsula in those days had not one but a fleet of chocolate-coloured Rolls-Royces for its guests. At eight I was on the front steps peering through the regiment of Rollers when I saw a flash of a red car right at the back. It turned out to be the most clapped-out Jowett Javelin I had ever seen, with Johnny beaming at the wheel. The Jowett car company has long ago passed into history, and quite right too.

Johnny clearly knew his Hong Kong intimately but I was lost within seconds of entering the narrow alleys of the Walled City. Finally even the Javelin could go no further, so it was parked by the kerb and we walked.

The thought occurred to me that if the British taxpayer, accustomed to seeing James Bond in his Aston Martin, could see this rolling scrapyard, he would realize he was not actually being overcharged by Her Majesty's overseas intelligence arm.

Johnny strode knowledgeably down alley after alley until we came to a door studded with heads of big black nails. He knocked. A small panel opened. There was a rapid exchange in Chinese, though whether Mandarin, Hakka or Cantonese I could not tell. Then the door creaked open and we were inside.

That was when I realized that my host for dinner was an honoured guest.

The restaurant was not large, perhaps fifteen tables, and entirely populated by Chinese diners. Not a single 'round-eye' in sight. I was not surprised; they could not have found the place.

The serving staff appeared to be two young men, alike enough to be brothers (which they were), and both strapping six-footers with black buzz-cut hair. Out of the kitchen came the proprietor and chef, evidently the father, also over six feet with iron-grey buzz cut. He greeted Johnny as a friend.

There were no menus. Johnny ordered for us both and what he asked for met with beaming approval. When we were alone I asked:

'They are pretty big for Chinese.'

'They are Manchu,' said Johnny. 'They grow big up there.'

'And the language?'

'Mandarin.'

The meal was beyond excellent, probably the best I have ever had. I commented on the warmth with which he had been greeted.

'Well, they are colleagues in a way.'

'Working for London?'

'Good Lord no, they are Beijing's intelligence branch down here.'

I was getting a bit confused.

'I thought they were the enemy.'

'Good heavens no, the Russians are the enemy. The KGB. Beijing can't stand them so they keep us up to speed on everything the Sovs get up to, and they always know first.'

Now the old perceptions were really spinning.

'So we get along with the Chinese although we are supposed to be on different sides?'

'Absolutely. Except for the Nationalists, the residue of the old Kuomintang. They are a pain in the arse.'

'I thought the Nationalists were anti-Beijing.'

'They are. That's why they are a pain. They have a colony several bays along the coast. They scrimp and save until they have enough to buy some illegal guns, then they set off in a sampan or two to invade Mainland China.'

'What happens to them?'

'Oh, I tip off my friend here,' he nodded towards the kitchen, 'and the idiots are intercepted as they land.'

'Aren't they executed?'

'Oh no, we have an arrangement. They just disarm them and send them back. Then they have to scrimp and save for another year to buy some more guns, then it happens again. Look, the People's Liberation Army could take this place before breakfast if they wanted. We are very much guests here.

'A peaceable Hong Kong suits both sides. For Beijing it is a valuable income stream and a meeting point where we can talk unobserved. Their new man Deng Xiaoping is more of a pragmatist than a dogmatist. For us it is a trading centre and a listening post. Anything that threatens to disturb that cosy relationship is a menace. That includes the Kuomintang for us and the KGB for them. All we have to do is keep Beijing sweet and the Russkies inside their box.'

As he settled up and we were bowed out of the door I realized that I had just learned over superb chow mein that what the Western newspaper-reading public had been told for years was complete bunkum.

The car was untouched, though in many alleys of the world it would have been stripped. But no one had laid a finger on it. They wouldn't dare.

The next day the RAF unit tucked away behind Kai Tak gave me a ride round the colony in one of their helicopters. I think it was a Skeeter, but anyway it was extremely small, just a Perspex bubble under a noisy fan. The cabin had no doors so on the steep banks one was held only by the straps from plunging two thousand feet to the ground.

From this vantage point one could see the Gurkhas patrolling the heather hills of the New Territories looking for the refugees who came over in a constant stream seeking a new life away from Communism. But the colony was far too small. So they were picked up, escorted to a camp on Lantau Island (now the new airport) and then sent back.

There was another cosy agreement so that they were not punished – just told not to do it again and resettled a long way away. That evening I was asked to address the Hong Kong Foreign Correspondents' Club. I did so completely sober, to be congratulated as the previous guest, comedian Dave Allen, had fallen face-forward into the soup.

The last day Jardine Matheson asked me to fire the ceremonial Midday Gun, and then it was off to Kai Tak for the flight to Brisbane.

After Australia and New Zealand and the same interview questions another hundred times my flight west from Perth passed right over the island of Mauritius. Hutchinson, my publishers, who were paying for this tour, suggested that as there was nothing for me in Jo'burg until the Monday, I take a rest-break on this lovely resort island. I was lodged at the Saint

Geran Hotel, still one of my world favourites to this day, thirty-five years later.

While there for only sixty hours I fell in love – twice. There was a dive shop and a resort course. A few hours of instruction in the pool permitted two real scuba dives over the nearby reefs. And I was smitten by the silence and the beauty of this underwater world. I have been diving ever since.

And there was a game-fishing boat, the *Chico*, which was booked. But one of the pair who had reserved it cried off and the general manager, Paul Jones, who remains a friend to this day, was looking for a stand-in. As a boy in Kent I had fished for bream and rudd in the Hythe Canal, but this was different. Eight hours on the vast and rolling Indian Ocean with lines streamed for marlin, sailfish, kingfish, wahoo, tuna and bonito.

I forget what we caught, but it was over a dozen without the marlin or sailfish, and when we tied up at the dock in the late afternoon I was smitten again. I later based a story, 'The Emperor', on that day at sea. Then it was a car to the airport and the flight to Jo'burg. I was decanted at Heathrow ten days later feeling like a wrung-out dishcloth.

But since then I have dived the reefs from Lizard Island, Queensland, west to the corals of the Baja Peninsula on the Sea of Cortez; swum with shark and manta ray among the atolls of the Maldives and the Amirantes; hooked marlin, sailfish and amberjack (always returned to the ocean) and wahoo and kings (for the dinner table).

My only drugs are silence and solitude and, in an increasingly noisy, frantic and crowded world, on or under the sea is where I find them.

Five Years in Ireland

THERE WAS NOT the slightest reason why Irish politician Charles Haughey and I would get on, but we did. To his political enemies he was relentless and vengeful for any slight or ill-turn. When relaxed over a dinner table I found him an amusing rogue. And he was certainly a rogue.

As a passionate republican he had little time for the English or anything British, but seemed to make an exception for me, perhaps because he realized I had quickly seen through him.

My wife and I had left the UK for Spain in January 1974 to escape the electoral victory of the Labour Party under Harold Wilson and the tax policies of Denis Healey, who raised income tax to an eye-watering 83 per cent when he came to office as Chancellor of the Exchequer in April. The year in Spain was to avoid the possibility of most of the earnings from the first three novels disappearing, perhaps never to be repeated. But it was never intended that we should settle in Spain. It was the statutory 'year of absence'.

By Christmas 1974 we were in Dublin (outside mainland UK and therefore outside the tax net) looking for a house to buy and settled in the village of Enniskerry, Co. Wicklow, just south of the city. Years earlier, when his party Fianna Fáil had been in office and he was finance minister, it was Charlie Haughey who had introduced a Finance Act with a little paragraph at the bottom that hardly anyone noticed. It made all creative artists, including writers, exempt from income tax.

I must have been the only immigrant who did not even know that. (I may have mentioned that I am not very good with money.) When I revealed my ignorance of the law I was met with local amazement and then approbation. At least I had come because I liked the place.

To make friends in Ireland is the easiest thing in the world because they are so friendly to start with. Add to that a terrific sense of humour. In the north the guerrilla campaign of the IRA against the Belfast government and the British armed forces posted there was at its height, but in the south, the Republic of Ireland, all was quiet and immensely sociable. There were tales of Brits who had to leave because they could not take the partygoing, so they took their damaged livers back home.

It was shortly after settling there that my wife and I met Charlie Haughey socially, but through the offices of his long-time girlfriend. It was a relationship that everybody knew about but nobody mentioned, and the entire media practised auto-censorship. Those days are long gone.

The lady gave small, intimate dinner parties round the pine table in her basement kitchen and that was where we could converse with the other Charlie Haughey – shirt-sleeved, affable and humorous. Like Harold King in the Reuters Paris office, he first tried to intimidate and, if that did not work, relaxed and let the Irish charm come through.

I enormously enjoyed my five years in Ireland and recall with affection the innumerable and uproarious dinner parties. Before going to Spain, in an act of pure madness, I had bought a Rolls-Royce. It was far from new and far from top of the price range. It was a classic, which I had restored at a specialist's in London. Once restored I had it re-sprayed from black to white. It had the old-style vertical Greek-temple grille with the winged lady flying above the bonnet. This monster was driven all the way to the Costa Blanca and a year later shipped to Ireland. In both a Spanish village and Enniskerry it was – how shall I put it? – rather noticeable. But I liked it and might have kept it longer but for the trip north to County Antrim to visit my in-laws.

We drove sedately up through Dublin, past the airport at Swords and on to the IRA hotspot of Dundalk. North of that the road was largely empty until we reached the border post and the start of County Armagh, the first of the six counties that make up British-owned Northern Ireland.

The Irish border post was hardly manned at all. The barrier pole was up and a hand behind the glass of a booth beside the road waved us on. At the British control the pole was down so we stopped. Out of the undergrowth came a strange Caliban-type figure.

He was in camouflage fatigues wearing a tam-o'-shanter with a red bobble on top and clutched a submachine carbine. Apparently one of Her Majesty's soldiers but not one I had ever seen before. He scampered up to the driver's side window, peered through and gesticulated that I should wind it down.

It was electric and when it hummed downwards he jumped in surprise and addressed me. I could not understand a word he said but from the accent, which I had heard in Tangier, I knew it must be Glasgow. When I failed to respond to whatever he asked, he became agitated and the barrel of the submachine gun appeared under my nose.

At this point a quite different figure came out of the bushes: very tall, gangly and clearly an officer. He too approached and spoke but in a laid-back drawl.

'Awfully sorry, old chap, he's asking to see your papers.'

The captain took over and scanned my passport. From his flashes I realized these were the Cameronians, who had established a fine reputation when based in Germany as the Poison Dwarfs.

The pair reminded me of the White Russian officer commanding oriental troops outside Magdeburg fifteen years earlier. The captain dismissed the soldier with a stream of the same incomprehensible dialect.

'Are you the writer fellow?' he asked.

'Yes.'

'Good show. Nice car.'

'Thank you.'

'Do you think it is wise to drive it right through Bandit Country?'

(I recognized the media term for South Armagh, which I still had to cross.)

'Perhaps you should,' he continued. 'Anyway, on you go. And take care.'

With this encouraging farewell I let in the clutch and the white beast purred forward into County Armagh and its silent and hostile hedges. A week later it was the same going back to the south – a very quiet drive both outside the car and inside.

After that I sold the Rolls and bought a nice anonymous Austin Montego estate.

About that time the Cosgrave government fell and Fianna Fáil came back to office, with Charlie Haughey appointed minister of health under prime minister Jack Lynch, with whom he feuded until he finally toppled his own premier and took over in 1979.

Hardly had he got the top slot when Ireland received Pope John Paul II on a state visit. Over the pine kitchen table Charlie put to me a pretty odd request. He said he needed a monograph to present to the cabinet on security – he was terrified of an attempt being made on the pontiff while he was in Dublin.

I suggested it was out of the question for His Holiness to be in mortal danger in Dublin of all places and that the British government had a dozen security experts with years of experience. He countered that he would not turn to London but that the Irish Gardaí had no experience of this sort of thing. He needed the techniques that had kept de Gaulle alive. There was nothing for it but to do what he wanted.

I thought back to all de Gaulle's bodyguards had let slip when chatting with the French media in 1962 and put together a paper stressing the difference between close-up protection against the madman and the hazard of the long-range sniper.

I never knew whether he put this paper to Cabinet as his own work, or mine, or that of some anonymous ace known only to him. Probably the last. Anyway, the three-day visit of the Pope went off without a hitch, though I noticed a few snipers from the Irish army perched on the rooftops scanning all the windows opposite.

Both our sons were born in Dublin: Stuart in 1977 and

Shane in 1979. But in the autumn of 1979 my wife developed an all-consuming fear that something might happen to our two babies.

In the case of Ireland in 1979 such a fear was far from illogical. IRA renegades had already kidnapped Dutch businessman Tiede Herrema, rescued unharmed after a nationwide manhunt, and others had more recently visited the Outwood home of my friend the Canadian tycoon Galen Weston. Neither he nor his wife Hilary were in residence but they terrified his personal assistant.

By the early spring the condition was serious. One friend in Dublin remarked to me: 'You're not the most famous man in Ireland, you're not the richest man in Ireland and you're not the only Brit in Ireland. But you're probably the most famous, richest Brit.'

So a kidnap attempt on one of the babies was not a complete fantasy at all. It was time to go, and it was my Irish-born wife who was the more adamant for a departure back to England. It seemed courteous to inform our friend the prime minister. Without explaining why, I asked for an interview at his office in Kildare Street.

He greeted me warmly but somewhat puzzled. When the door was closed I explained that we were leaving and why. He was horrified and asked me to stay. I made clear the decision was made.

He could not offer me Irish citizenship. As the first-born son of a first-born son of a man from Youghal, Co. Cork, I had that right anyway. So he offered to make me a senator of Ireland. Apparently the Senate is part-elected but a few seats can be nominated. I thanked him but declined.

Accepting the reality he led me out of his office and then down the length of the long hall to the street door, his arm round my shoulders. Doors popped ajar as open-mouthed senior civil servants looked out to see their premier draped round a Britisher, never seen before or since.

A few days later I had one last call from him. It was to give me his word that not a single IRA man in the country would dare raise his hand against me or my family. The only way he could have known that was if he had given a flat order to the army council of the IRA. Not many men could do that.

On 7 April 1980, loaded to the roof and with more luggage on the roof rack, the Montego rolled on to the ferry from Dun Laoghaire to Fishguard.

Margaret Thatcher had won the 1979 election and the maximum income tax rate had tumbled from 83 per cent to 60 per cent which, though high, was acceptable. We arrived in London just in time to see on television the interruption of the World Snooker Championship in the final frame as the SAS stormed the terrorist-occupied Iranian Embassy.

Since then I have lived in Surrey, St John's Wood, Hertfordshire and Buckinghamshire. But I have never emigrated and never will.

A Neat Trick

B Y THE SUMMER of 1982 my physical situation had become
extremely comfortable – boringly so. I was on the threshold
of forty-four, eight years married, the father of two growing
boys of three and five, living in a large white house at Tilford,
a village in the county of Surrey, and had realized that I could
apparently make a comfortable living writing novels. No
wonder I was bored.

There is a passage in the John Buchan novel *John McNab*
where the hero is in a similar state and goes to his doctor. This
shrewd man, after a complete examination, advises his patient:
as your doctor I can do nothing for you, but as your friend let
me offer you advice. Go and steal a horse – in a country where
horse-stealing is punished by hanging.

I did not feel the need to go that far but I had to do something more interesting than sitting on the terrace reading the
papers and drinking coffee.

It happens that though I do not suffer from acrophobia –
the panic-stricken fear of heights – I do not really like them. In
an apartment on the thirtieth floor of a skyscraper I would
prefer not to go to the balcony and lean over. In truth I

would prefer to be back inside behind the plate-glass doors.

I had taken off many times and landed each time but never jumped out halfway. Perhaps that was the answer. I asked around for a good parachute club. A friend in the armed forces advised me the best (by which I mean the safest) was the Combined Forces school at Netheravon in Wiltshire. Being paid for by that ultra-generous philanthropist the taxpayer, it had state-of-the-art equipment and had never lost a trainee to the forces of gravity.

I was of course a civilian but the RAF stretched a point and let me in, so on the given date I motored down there. Even that recently things were far less formal than now. There was no medical, just the signing of that amiable document the 'blood chit'. It simply said that I accepted that if I became a tent peg in the middle of a Wiltshire meadow it was entirely my fault and my estate could sue nobody.

The course on which I found myself had thirty to forty volunteers, all drawn from various branches of the army and air force and all in their late teens and early twenties. In other words, they were all young enough to be my offspring. They seemed to have insatiable appetites and were able to consume up to half a dozen big meals a day. They also had terrifying levels of energy.

Perhaps due to my age, a billet was kindly found for me in the officers' mess, which was familiar enough because Netheravon is an air force base. On the first morning I joined the three-day course in the main hangar.

The CO was Major Gerry O'Hara of the Parachute Regiment but the instructors were Flight Sergeant Chris Lamb of the RAF and Corporal Paul Austin of the Royal Marines, both younger than me and slightly puzzled by my inclusion.

We started with classroom explanations of the forces of gravity, wind drift and speeds of descent. Then came lectures on the equipment yet to come. We would be using the Aeroconical 'chute; none of your flying wings or stunt 'chutes, which were for real experts. The Aeroconical was a simple dome of parti-coloured fabric and we would not even have to open it. There would be a static line attached inside the aircraft which would open the 'chute automatically as we jumped. The instructors would be in the aeroplane with us and would affix the static lines for us. Simple enough.

We would be jumping over the airfield from the side door of a Dragon Rapide from about 3,000 feet and descent speed would be about fourteen miles per hour. The remainder of the 'ground time' was dedicated to coping with the thump of impacting with Mother Earth at that speed and coming to no harm. This involved landing and rolling over at the same time.

The rest of Day One and the morning of Day Two were spent in the hangar, leaping from platforms, landing and rolling, until we could do it without feeling more than minimal impact. All this took place between pauses for the inevitable brews of tea, without which the entire British defence structure would collapse. Lunch breaks involved me going back to the mess for a served lunch with the attending stewards while the youngsters repaired to their refectory for yet another massive fry-up. I failed to understand where they were putting it all. The trick came at the end of the second morning.

The two instructors told us that the next morning would see the first jump. It was a lie, just in case of any middle-of-the-night disappearances. After lunch the first of the two Dragon

Rapides landed and we were told to draw parachutes. There was also to be a draw for the dubious position of 'first out, first stick'.

The elderly but still very serviceable biplanes were standing by with propellers ticking over and side doors open as the draw was made. Due to cramped conditions inside, the 'stick' would be sitting on benches down both sides of the interior and would rise to clip on static lines only at the last minute and on command. But the first man out would have to sit in the doorway all the way, only clambering to his feet when tapped on the shoulder by the Jump Master. Then a hat was passed round.

It was full of small scraps of paper, each with a pupil's name on it. With his eyes closed Chris Lamb groped inside and came out with a scrap. When unfolded I was surprised, as the odds were thirty to one, that the name was mine.

Only later, back on the ground with a chance to examine the hat, did I learn they had all got my name on them. The two rogues had calculated that if the old codger did not freeze in the doorway, none of the teenagers would dare do so either. Freezing up and refusing to jump meant immediate RTU – return to unit.

In reverse order of jump, we piled into the Rapide's fuselage, the 'last out' group disappearing towards the tail. I found I had no seat at all. I had to sit in the doorway with legs and feet in the slipstream. We took off and climbed sedately to a point 3,000 feet above the airfield. I began to get the 'skyscraper balcony' syndrome. The fields were postage stamps, the huge hangars thumbnails. I thought longingly of my home in Tilford.

Paul Austin had a word through the cabin door and the engine noise died. The whirling propellers still seemed about a foot away from my face and I wondered if I would not jump into the blades. It was easy to forget that even with engines throttled back there was still a 50mph slipstream out there and gravity would do the rest.

There was a tap on the shoulder and I stood up. A fist with a raised thumb appeared, meaning 'static line attached'. Then the final tap. Deep breath, lean forward and kick. Within a second it was all gone – engine noise, slipstream, aeroplane. Just silence and the soughing of a gentle breeze, the hemisphere of silk above, the harness tight all around the body, the feet dangling over nothing and the postage stamps coming very slowly closer.

Then it became quite restful. Time for a good look around. Spectacular views over many miles of lovely countryside, surely one was not descending at all. But at 14mph the airfield came up at a rush, then a huge thump as the jumpboots hit the turf. Twist, roll, absorb the shock, turf under the backside then the shoulders, roll again and stand, hauling in the billowing silk before it collapsed in an untidy pile. Then pick it all up and start the long walk back to the hangars.

Willing parachute packers took it all away: collapsed 'chute, shrouds (which are not sheets but nylon lines) and canvas harness. Time for a relaxing cigarette, then the Rapide was landing for the second jump.

I strolled over to the discarded hat where I learned that mine was the only name on any of the scraps of paper, then had a few well-chosen words with Chris and Paul. But there had been three no-jumps so the disgraced ones were being led away to change out of overalls and back into uniform. No second chances.

On the second jump I had a small problem. The landing was too heavy. A gust of breeze lifted the 'chute then dropped me from too high up. A low click in the left ankle. On the walk back to the hangars it began to hurt. I was damned if I was going to miss out on my three-jump certificate so I hid the limp until we were back in the Rapide for the third time. At least now I had a bench to sit on.

The third landing was a one-footer, then there was a Tilly (a blue RAF Land Rover) coming to meet me. Someone in the group by the hangars with a pair of binoculars had seen the limp. At the medical bay an RAF doctor cut the boot off with a scalpel. The meat was beginning to overflow the top of the boot and no one was going to try to pull it off for fear of having to cope with a very noisy author.

That exercise cost me a new pair of top-of-the-range jumpboots to replace the ones I had borrowed and ruined. Luckily it was only a sprain, and duly strapped I was able to hobble along to the celebratory piss-up.

My Jaguar saloon had automatic shift so the next morning I could drive home one-footed, using just the right one for all the controls.

I got my certificate, signed by Gerry O'Hara, and it was suggested I should graduate to sky-diving: coming out at 10,000 feet with a pull-your-own D ring and lots of time to plunge back to Mother Earth at 100mph. But on balance I have preferred to stick to skyscrapers and nice fast elevators made by Mr Otis.

But I still have Major O'Hara's piece of paper on the office wall, and fond memories of Netheravon and its cheeky jump instructors.

The Amazing Mister Moon

THERE MUST BE a reason for it but I have never met a man who has confronted the mighty rage of the oceans in a small boat who does not believe in God.

Man spends most of his time running around in crowded cities convincing himself how important he is in the scheme of things. But there are five places where he can confront the reality of his utter insignificance.

Two of these are the great deserts, of sand and gravel or snow and ice. Lost in these he is but a speck of dust on a huge sheet of pure barrenness. Then there are the mountains, also clothed in snow and ice, peaks among which he will vanish to invisibility.

The sky is a huge and lonely place but here at least his lack of importance is short-lived because when his fuel runs out gravity alone will end his solitude. But most fearsome of them all is the towering, pitiless might of the enraged ocean. Because it moves.

When in 1513 Vasco Núñez de Balboa, peering out of the jungle of Darien towards the west, saw a great expanse of blue water, it was calm, sparkling, seemingly friendly. So he called it

El Mar Pacifico, the quiet sea, the peaceful sea, the Pacific. He had no idea what the Pacific could do when it is consumed with rage. The Indian Ocean is the same.

As with them all, it can be flat as a lake, or moved only by a gentle swell, blue under the sun, welcoming, inviting the mariner to share its calm and splendour. Or it can rise in terrifying mountains, lashed by deranged winds, prepared to seize that same mariner, crush his presumptuous craft, swamp him, consume him and consign him in perpetuity to a cold black grave where he will never be seen again. That is why men who sail the oceans hope there must, please, be Something even mightier who will protect them and bring them home to safe haven.

With hindsight, that twenty-twenty vision which we all have but too late, it was unwise to disregard the maps and go game-fishing off the Mauritian coast in 1985.

We had gone as a family, two parents, two small boys, to the Saint Geran Hotel on the east coast. The weather programmes had mentioned a cyclone but a hundred miles north of the island and heading in a straight line east to west. So I decided to go game-fishing.

The resident game-boat *Chico* chugged out of the lagoon just after dawn, my favourite hour, through the usual cut in the reef and out to sea heading east. At the helm was Monsieur Moun, whom everyone called Mister Moon. He was elderly, dark, wrinkled, a Creole who knew his sea and his island and had never been anywhere else nor wanted to.

It was a one-client charter and the wire-man was his son, sharing the afterdeck with me to tend the four big marlin rods, the lines and the lures, and who would help swing the catch aboard. The breeze was light, the swell gentle, the sky blue and the sun hot – a recipe for paradise. We trolled patiently for two hours, always eastward, until Mauritius was a dim smudge on the horizon. It was about noon that the sea calmed even more, down to a flat and slightly oily sheen. Mister Moon spotted the danger sign; I did not, too busy scanning the four lures astern for a hoped-for 'strike'.

I noticed only when his son began staring at his father, perched cross-legged upon his revolving office stool, adapted to a captain's seat behind the wheel. Then I too followed his gaze. Mister Moon was looking straight towards the north. Along the horizon was a very thin dark line, like a bruise between the sky and the water. I realized it might be serious when he uttered a series of orders in Creole to his son, who began to bring in the four lines and the *Chico* swung in a circle and pointed back to the west. The smudge on the horizon, the island of Mauritius, had almost disappeared.

I did not know what had happened to change the mood both of the sea beneath us and on the deck on which I stood. The cyclone had swerved through 90 degrees. It was roaring down from the north.

The *Chico* was not one of those modern techno-wonders with two huge chunks of Japanese technology bolted to the stern, capable of sending a GRP-hulled fishing boat screaming across the sea at 20 knots in choppy water or 30 in flat. It was an elderly work boat of plywood with an internal chugger of an engine. A chugger it might be but Mister Moon moved the throttle to full ahead, max power. The chugger did its best and we increased speed to 10 knots.

The black line on the horizon widened to an inch and the

sea changed from an oily calm, not to a snapping chop (that would come later), but to a rolling swell becoming ever deeper. At the top of the peaks one could see the horizon-smudge, but seemingly no closer. In the troughs the sea was no longer blue but valleys of moving green, becoming deeper and darker. Indian Ocean cyclones take no prisoners.

Mister Moon said nothing and neither did his son. The lad took the rods out of the holders where they usually travel and stowed them in the small forward cuddy cabin. The *Chico* pounded west as best she could and with agonizing slowness the smudge became the principal mountain peak of the island. The northern sky darkened and clouds appeared, not white and fluffy, high against the blue, but dark and hunched like a fighter entering the ring.

There was nothing to do but stand and watch. I tried to converse with Mister Moon in his other native tongue, French, but he was too absorbed to reply. His gaze just flickered from the island to the cyclone, calculating speeds, angles and engine revs. So I walked back to the stern and joined his son.

It may be thought that a Creole, descendant of the native Africans, cannot go pale. Not true. The lad had a sickly pallor. He was badly frightened and we both knew why. The island crept closer as the old engine banged and hammered under its casing. It was clear our lives were going to depend on this old mariner. The island became more distinct but so did the black-clouded fury behind us. Whatever speed it was moving, it was well above 10 knots and we could go no faster. We rose on swell after swell, seeming almost stopped at the peak, then plunged down into the valley and up again.

Somewhere ahead was the coast of Mauritius and the

lagoon from which we had come. Between us was the reef and the gap in the coral through which we had to pass to stay alive. At last we saw it but then my hopes plunged. It was clear I would probably not see my family again.

For the wind had taken the waves and tormented them to a frenzy of white water. This white wall was slamming into the reef where it exploded upwards into a wall 30 feet high. But the roaring crosswind from the north was pulling the wall like a curtain across the entry gap in the coral. The gap had vanished.

If we hit the coral, the *Chico* would be torn to pieces and her three inhabitants with her. Coral may only be made of trillions of polyps, but it is hard as concrete and fanged with teeth that can cut steel. Few vessels that have ever hit a coral reef have not been torn open. I walked up the deck to stand next to Mister Moon, hunched like a brooding cormorant upon his stool.

His eyes were flickering forward to the mountains of his native land, not behind to the menace from the stern.

He was calculating angles from the mountain peaks behind the wall of foam to the dimly visible roof of the hotel. He was trying to work out where, in the liquid insanity ahead of him, lay the 30-yard-wide gap where the coral grudged a free passage to an incoming boat.

I turned to look behind and realized that if he missed it we were dead. There was no possibility of turning away to find another haven down-coast. None either of turning back to sea. Behind us the cyclone had caught up.

There was a gigantic wave, a vertical wall of rolling green, 20, maybe 30 feet high and foaming at the top as the base responded to the shallowing beach beneath, about to break forward and crash down. It was like the Empire State Building on its side, rolling at 40 knots.

I never saw the *Chico* hit the foam wall. One second it was in front of us and death behind, then the whiteness enveloped the boat, tumbling on to the afterdeck and frothing unto the scuppers. The whiteness cleared and there was blue sky ahead and above. Jagged shards of coral flashed past, barely 6 feet from the hull.

The ocean spat the *Chico* like a cork from a champagne bottle into the lagoon and then the Empire State hit the reef to make thunder seem half-hearted. Observers on the shore said later the spray went up 100 feet.

The *Chico* slowed, engine back to cruise revs. Along the shoreline was the clientele of the whole hotel. I could see my wife with her hands over her face and two small boys jumping in the shallows. We tied up at the dock to meet an ashen-faced Activities Manager.

The cyclone locked down the island of Mauritius for forty-eight hours, then it passed through as they all do and a tropical resort island was restored, as they always are. Take-offs were resumed from La Plaisance airport and we flew home to London.

There is no way of rewarding a man like Mister Moon, who wanted no reward at all, but I did my best. I also learned two things that day. If going out to sea, check the weather; and why men who go on the ocean in small boats believe in God.

Back to Zero – Start Again

IT WAS ON a bright sunny morning in the spring of 1990 that I learned that financially I had been completely and utterly ruined.

In 1988 my marriage had sadly but amicably ended. In an uncontested settlement my wife and I had split everything we had into two equal halves. Very shrewdly my wife had taken the large London apartment in which we lived and a block of investment portfolios. The latter she encashed and invested in property which increased hugely in value.

I had taken the balance entirely in managed funds, all invested in a series of carefully chosen portfolios. In the same year I acquired a small farm in Hertfordshire and moved there. In 1989 I met the lady who would become my second wife and to whom I am still married twenty-six years later.

That spring morning I was writing the first chapter of what became *The Deceiver*. There was a knock on the study door. I was irritated because when writing I ask only to be left strictly alone with the typewriter and the coffee. Interruptions are confined to the outbreak of fire or some major crisis. But I replied with a curt, 'What?'

The answer came through the door. So-and-so has collapsed. She named the head of the investment company through which, but not in which, I had invested my life savings. The man was one whom I had known for thirteen years and whom I thought, wrongly as it turned out, I could trust. His name was Roger Levitt.

I misunderstood the word 'collapse' and presumed a heart attack or stroke, which was odd because he was only in his forties. She meant his company had collapsed and he had been arrested.

Even when I learned the truth I was not particularly worried. After all, my investments were nothing other than chosen on his recommendation and I had insisted on fund managers who were utterly reputable, solid and, above all, safe. No spectacular returns, thank you, no matter how inviting the blandishments. It was only when seated with the detectives of the Metropolitan Police City Fraud Squad that the full measure of the swindle was explained to me.

The investments were simply not there. The documents were forged. The savings had been raided, embezzled and spent trying to prop up the great Wizard of Oz-style façade. And I was not the only one. Other victims were banks, insurance houses and all the private clients.

Receivers were appointed but quickly realized the total assets of the collapsed sham would be just enough to cover their own fees. Naturally. The total missing sum from all the victims combined was about £32 million, £20 million to financial institutions and the remainder from private clients.

It was a strange year. The detectives slowly prepared their case for the Crown Prosecution Service and I was amazed to learn how many victims would refuse to testify. It is the vanity factor. Those who pride themselves on their acumen cannot bear to admit they have been taken.

I had no such inhibitions, having always known I was useless in the management of money. So I became the detectives' favourite guest and they explained how it had all been done.

Actually I was not simply penniless but owed an additional million pounds. This was because, seeking to buy the farm, I had suggested I encash some portfolio to buy the place outright. I was persuaded to take out a mortgage instead, as the shrewd management of the million would generate more than a mortgage would cost. It was all bunkum, of course. The necessary portfolios could not be encashed because they were not there. So it was soon clear I was worth zero minus an extra million.

The case ground on at a snail's pace. Eventually in 1993 it came to court. I was not needed as a witness. Thanks to a brilliant defence lawyer, a useless prosecutor and a judge who had never tried a criminal case in his life, the charges were reduced to two small technical offences and the sentence was 180 hours' community service.

The Biafran affair had deprived me of any faith or trust in the senior mandarins of the Civil Service. The trial of 1993 did the same for my belief in the legal system and the judiciary.

Anyway, I had made up my mind that there was only one thing for it. That was, at the age of fifty, to write a series of more novels and make it all back. So I did.

The Passing of Humpy

THERE WERE THREE of us, standing at the stern of the game-fisher *Otter* out of Islamorada, Florida Keys, and we were after amberjack, those big, heavy, deep-bodied giants of the mackerel family who fight like hell.

Both my boys were with me: Stuart the fanatical angler who never took his eyes off the rigs, and the younger Shane who could get bored when nothing struck. The *Otter* was hove-to several miles out into the Gulf Stream, right over a submerged mountaintop called the '409' because it was 409 feet beneath the water, or simply the 'Hump'. It was the school summer holidays of 1991.

It was Shane who first saw the tiny fluttering object off the stern, struggling towards us on exhausted wings, coming from the east. High above the little traveller was a black-backed gull, orange razor beak eager for a kill. Another joined it and they screamed at the sight of the tiny prey beneath them. One by one we ceased watching the rod-tips for the giveaway tremble of a bite far below and watched the struggle.

The little flier was not a seabird at all — there is none that small. It was evidently exhausted and at the end of its strength.

It dipped in tiredness towards the sea, fluttered frantically to rise and struggle on for a few more yards. We watched in silence, yearning for it to win. A few more yards and it could fall on our afterdeck. But tiredness won. It finally sank again and the sea rose to take it.

But it was only a few feet from the transom. Perhaps there was a chance. I grabbed the scoop net from the deck and, above and behind me, watching from his flying bridge, skipper Clyde Upchurch engaged gear and moved back a few feet. I got the mesh beneath the little bird lying motionless on the swell and hoisted it aboard.

I am no ornithologist but I was pretty certain it was a finch out of Africa. It should have been emigrating to Europe but clearly had been blown way off course and out to sea. Disorientated, it must have taken refuge in the rigging of a freighter and thus had crossed the Atlantic, but seemingly weakened without food or water.

There was land behind us, the chain of Florida's islands six miles away, and perhaps the little fellow had sensed this and tried to get there. But it had failed. Above the stern the gulls screamed in outrage at their lost meal and veered away.

Shane took the tiny body in his cupped hands and went back into the cabin. Because of where we were, we named the little stowaway Humpy. And we went on fishing.

Shane prepared a bed of paper tissues and laid the little corpse, as we presumed, upon it in a pool of sunlight on the cabin table. Ten minutes later he gave a yell. The tiny beady eye that had been closed in death was open. Humpy was still alive. Shane appointed himself nurse-in-chief.

He formed the flat bed into a nest of soft tissue paper, took some bottled water and dribbled a few drops on to the beak. It opened and the drops disappeared. Humpy woke up and began to preen. More spring water, more tissues, a slow wipe-off to clear the tacky salt from the plumage. Humpy perked and fluttered.

It was another thirty minutes before he felt able to fly. Shane was catching trapped flies from the cabin windows. I suggested Humpy was a seed-eater as he refused the flies, while a tiny crumb of bread from the packed lunch was finally accepted. Then he spread his wings and flew.

Not far at first. Just off the table, round the cabin and back to the table. As in pilot-training, we called it circuits-and-bumps. He did about a dozen circuits of the cabin, had a rest, more drops of water and then found an open window. Shane yelled in alarm and rushed outside.

Humpy was doing his circuits all right, but round the moored boat. The afternoon wore on, and it was time to go. The charter was almost over and we had to get back to Islamorada. Then it all went wrong.

With lines retrieved and rods stored there was no cause to stay. High aloft, Clyde engaged gear and pushed the throttle forward. The *Otter* leapt to the command and Shane screamed. Humpy was somewhere astern and his salvation was racing away to the west. We all turned and yelled, but Clyde could not hear us above the engine roar.

Stuart ran up the ladder to tap him on the shoulder. The *Otter* stopped in the water but she had surged for at least 200 yards. We all gazed astern, and there he was. Fluttering above the wake, trying to catch up with the only sanctuary for miles around.

We started shouting encouragement . . . and the gull came back. Humpy so nearly made it. He was 10 yards from the stern when the sharp orange beak took him. I noticed a box of lead weights lying open on the deck, seized the largest I could see and flung it at the gull above us.

A hit would have been impossible, but the gull must have seen some dark object coming towards it for it uttered another raucous scream. And dropped the little finch in its beak. The crumpled form fell back to the surface of the ocean again. Clyde backed the *Otter* slowly towards the feathery lump on the water. Again I fished it out.

But this time there was no hope. The gull's beak had crushed the life out of Humpy and no more drops of spring water could bring him round. Shane tried all the way back to the marina, and the salt on the finch's wings was washed away again, but this time by the tears of a little boy.

That evening, in a cigar box lined with moss, beneath the casuarina trees of the Cheeka Lodge Hotel, we buried Humpy in the sand of the New World that he had tried so hard to reach, like so many before him, and very nearly did.

A Very Burning Question

I T WAS A VERY simple query put to me by the Firm in 1992.
The question was: do you by any chance know anyone high
in the South African government? And the answer was yes.

Because of years patrolling southern Africa I had a passing
acquaintanceship with Pretoria's foreign minister Roelof 'Pik'
Botha, even though by then I had not seen him for several
years.

If the profession of foreign correspondent made a very
good cover for a bit of 'enhanced tourism' on behalf of the
Firm, an established author researching his next novel was even
better. It enabled me to go just about anywhere, ask to meet
and converse with just about anyone and pose just about any
question. And all to be explained as research for a novel yet to
be written – or not, for all anyone could prove.

Back in the Seventies the target had been the Rhodesia of
Ian Smith and occasioned several visits to Salisbury, now
renamed Harare. Once again my amiable but witless 'Bertie
Wooster' pose paid dividends. The men at the top were white
supremacists, which is to say racial bigots.

There is no lure that the bigot can't resist like the earnest enquirer who, basically sympathetic and seemingly right-wing, asks that the complexities of the situation be explained to him. As nothing more than a seeker after knowledge I was favoured with many hours of explanation – and classified information – from the likes of Rhodesian foreign and defence minister Peter van der Byl. He was a way-out racist who referred to his domestic staff – all Matabeles because he loathed the Shona – as 'my savages'.

I do not think any of them suspected, as I listened, nodded and smiled, that my views were the reverse of their own. But what they revealed was useful back home.

In the Eighties, with Rhodesia now Zimbabwe, the target was the South Africa of the National Party, the originator and enforcer of apartheid, which was both brutal and tinged with insanity.

I once found myself closeted with General van den Bergh, the head of the Bureau of State Security, the dreaded BOSS, and he insisted on telling me a story to prove not only his legitimacy but his sanctity as well.

'Let me tell you this, Mr Fosdick' – he always called me Fosdick, forefinger waving, eyes alight – 'I was standing once, quite alone, on the High Veldt when a great storm came up. I knew the land was riven with iron ore deposits and lightning strikes would be frequent and dangerous. So I took shelter under a large mwataba tree.

'There was an old kaffir standing nearby, also sheltering. And the storm raged with biblical intensity. The thunderbolts poured out of the sky and the thunder was enough to deafen me. The tree was struck and split down the middle, its core a smoking ruin. The old kaffir was struck and at once electrocuted.

'But the storm passed, Mr Fosdick, and the sky cleared. And I was not touched. And that was when I knew, Mr Fosdick, that the hand of God was upon me.'

I recall thinking that I was alone with the master of one of the most brutal secret police forces in the world and he was mad as a frog.

On another occasion I was invited as dinner guest at the house of Professor Carel Boshoff, head of the Broederbond, the Brotherhood, which was the intellectual and ecclesiastical (Dutch Reformed Church) origin and underpinning of the whole concept of apartheid.

Dinner proceeded with the usual courtesies until, over pudding, he asked me what I thought of the Homelands Policy. This was a particularly pernicious idea whereby the indigenous ethnic groups that made up the black majority would be allocated tracts of barren and often unworkable land and told that this was their true and original 'homeland'.

As such they could then have a token 'government' and thus lose their citizenship of the Republic of South Africa (the RSA) and any rights they might have had in the first place, which were already few enough. I visited one of the 'homelands', Bophuthatswana, the so-called home of the Tswana people. It made the old American Indian reservations look like Shangri-La, although Sol Kerzner built a resort called Sun City on it to bring in a bit of tourist revenue.

Anyway, I was by then heartily tired of expressing views that were the inverse of what I really thought, so I explained exactly what I thought. My half-eaten dessert was removed and I was escorted from the house.

But in the course of all this I met Pik Botha, the only man

among them that I liked. He was practical rather than theoretical, had travelled very widely and seen the outer world. I suspected that despite his position he was a moderating influence on successive presidents and probably privately despised the extremists around him.

By 1992 it was clear to anyone with eyes that the rule of the National Party and apartheid was finally moving to its close. There would soon have to be elections and they would have to be one-man-one-vote, which the African National Congress under its recently released and newly elevated chief Nelson Mandela would win. The white president, the last, was F.W. de Klerk, and Pik Botha was his firm ally and partner in reform.

Nevertheless, there was something 'our political masters', as the Friends put it, urgently wanted to know and the 'received wisdom' (as they also put it) was that an enquiry via our embassy in Pretoria was not the right channel. Too formal, too un-deniable. What was needed was a quiet enquiry in a very private situation.

It was summer in Europe, winter in South Africa, and both parliaments were in recess. Ministers were also taking their holidays. It was known that Pik Botha had two passions: game-fishing and big-game hunting. But the winter seas off the Cape of Good Hope were too rough so it would probably be a game lodge for the foreign minister.

Then it was discovered he would indeed be vacationing for a week on a game lodge in the South African section of the Kalahari desert.

These lodges are situated in the corners of simply enormous game reserves where the natural fauna – mainly antelope – are protected from their natural predators like lion, leopard and crocodile. So they over-breed. The numbers have to be culled to preserve the life-support system. To defray costs, licences are issued and amateur hunters, escorted by professional game wardens, are allowed to track and shoot limited numbers for a fee appropriate to the size of the animal being taken.

Personally, I will take out of circulation either something that is pest or vermin and has to be culled for the preservation of the rest of the ecosystem or something that will definitely reappear on the dining table. Or, like rabbit and wood pigeon, both. But not for fun and not for a wall trophy. But this would have to be an exception. The question was very important.

Of course, there had to be a cover story and it was sitting at home doing schoolwork. My two sons would come with me.

Over the years I had tried to introduce them to as wide a variety of adventurous holidays as possible so that they could perhaps latch upon what really enthused them.

Thus we had been snorkelling and diving in the tropics, skiing and snowboarding in the Alps and Squaw Valley, flying, riding and shooting. The older, Stuart, had decided already; he was a passionate fisherman and has remained so. Shane had no particular preference but had demonstrated on the estates of friends that he was a crack shot, a natural.

The game reserve where Pik Botha would spend part of his vacation in the Kalahari was discovered and bookings made for me and the boys for the same week. So we flew to Jo'burg, thence to Krugersdorp, and thence by light aircraft to a dusty strip in the grounds of the shooting lodge.

It was a very convivial week and Pik Botha was affable when we met again. He was eager to bag himself an eland and spent days tracking them. I thought it wise at least to 'purchase' something for Stuart and Shane. On the second day Stuart bagged his impala and was delighted when the forehead and horns, stripped to whitened bone, was presented for him to hang on his wall.

Shane was lectured lengthily by a warden as to what he should do, listened politely and then from the back of a stationary truck put a bullet through the heart of a blesbuck with a snap shot at 150 paces. The buck was photographed but the real picture was the warden's face. After that he became their mascot.

My opportunity came on the last day but one. A very small party would camp overnight in the wilderness. There was Pik Botha and his 'minder' from Pretoria; the two sons of the owner of the ranch; my two lads and me. Plus two game wardens and several African porters.

After a long day tracking, the porters built a fine fire of brushwood, a barbecue or *braai* provided a meat supper, sleeping bags were unrolled and we settled down to sleep. The atmosphere was intensely relaxed and I thought the moment was ripe. We were all round the dying fire with the four sleeping boys between the foreign minister and me. So I asked quietly:

'Pik, when the rainbow revolution comes and the ANC takes over, what are you going to do with the six atom bombs?'

South Africa had long had atomic bombs, built with Israeli help. Everyone knew, despite the strict secrecy surrounding them. London also knew there were six and they could be carried by the RSA's British-built Buccaneers.

That was not the problem. Nor was the moderate Nelson Mandela. The problem was that the ANC Party had an ultra-hardline wing including several devoted pro–Moscow Communists, and even though the USSR had been disbanded by Mikhail Gorbachev the previous year neither London nor Washington wanted nuclear bombs in the control of the anti-West extremists. It only needed Nelson Mandela to be toppled by an internal coup, as so many African leaders had already been, and . . .

My question hung in the air for a few seconds, then there was a low chuckle from across the embers and a reply in the Afrikaans-inflected voice.

'Freddie, you can go back home and tell your people we are going to destroy the lot.'

So much for an elaborate cover story. The old buzzard knew exactly what I was, who I was asking for and what they wanted to hear. I tried to share the joke.

But, to be fair, they did. Before the de Klerk government handed over power, they destroyed all six. Three of the casings are on display somewhere but that is all. Three of the Buccaneers still fly out of Cape Town airport, but only for tourist rides.

From Maiko to Monks

OVER MANY TRAVELS I have had the chance to attend a variety of religious ceremonies in rites far different from my own Anglican background. These included Russian Orthodox, Roman Catholic, Jewish and Muslim, and in some of the finest cathedrals, synagogues and mosques of those faiths. But my wife, Sandy, has always been fascinated by the Orient and by Buddhism.

In 1995 my Japanese publishers, Kadokawa Shoten, invited me once again to be their guest in Tokyo to promote the latest novel and Sandy came with me. Going all that way, it made a lot of sense to extend the visit after the publicity work to see more of the real Japan.

So when the usual round of interviews and book-signing in Tokyo was over, we took the bullet train west to the former capital of Kyoto. This is a beautiful little city, full of parks, gardens, temples and shrines, both to Buddhism and Shintoism. But Buddhism could wait; there was another aspect I wanted to explore.

With a guide we penetrated the small area known as Guion, the home of the geisha culture. Contrary to a common misconception, the geisha is not simply a prostitute but a highly skilled entertainer dedicated to restoring the exhausted male client with what is best described as relaxation therapy. Bedtime may follow but it is by no means inevitable.

There are only about 120 true professional geisha left, perhaps because they are multi-skilled after years of training, which costs about half a million pounds. The training madame will hope to recoup this, fee by fee, when her charge starts to earn professional commissions.

A geisha can sing, dance, recite poetry, flatter, and play the samisen, a sort of medieval lute with strings plucked only by the fingernails. To listen to and understand her client's possible financial woes, she reads all the commercial pages in the daily papers and keeps abreast of current affairs.

The uniform is the full kimono with obi sash, bouffant jet-black hair (a wig), bright red lips and a bone-white (powdered) face. Many clients will not wish any of it to be removed. In Guion one can see many of these practitioners of the ancient arts, in full regalia, click-clacking along on their wooden sandals, heading for their nightly engagement, eyes cast down in order never to make eye-contact with anyone but the client.

Sandy and I were lucky as we were invited to visit a geisha training school, something a *gaijin* (foreigner) rarely manages to do. It took a password to gain entry through the heavily timbered door.

The geisha usually comes from the most deprived rungs of society, from parents so poor they are content to sell their daughter into a world from which she will never emerge. But not just any girl will suit. A skilled madame, running such an academy, will look for exceptional beauty, grace, a clever mind and a singing voice that, with schooling, will become crystal-pure. The parents are paid and never see their daughter again.

Once absorbed into the geisha world, it is virtually impossible for the young woman to leave it, marry and become a mother, let alone a housewife. She has something about her that can be instantly recognized and will never leave her.

A husband would immediately know and feel shamed. His colleagues would spot it and might be tempted to become lascivious, or at least mocking. Their wives would become instantly hostile. Conventional suburbia is not for the geisha. It is a closed world with a long hard road in and no way out.

Some madames only run agencies of skilled geishas; a few run training schools, such as the one we visited. The trainees are called *maiko*, meaning dancing girl, but they are taught much more than dancing, and that includes knowledge of every detail of the male body and the male psyche, specializing on the erogenous and susceptible points. The only aim is to please the male. The maiko paint only the lower lip as a sign of virginity. The client who will one day take that will be charged a huge premium.

Considering we were in a sort of bordello, the polite proprieties were scrupulously observed. Anything other would have been crude, rude and offensive. Incidentally, when a Japanese girl laughs or giggles, she may not be amused. She may be profoundly embarrassed. Laughter is also a defensive shield.

So we squatted on cushions on the floor and conversed through the interpreter with the madame while her trainees in their 'apprentice' kimonos served small cups of saké. They are taught to seduce with their eyes alone, eyes made large and docile with skilful make-up, and I have to admit they are extremely disconcerting. Sandy kept shooting me warning glances.

Finally it was time to go, with copious and mutual bowing. Years later I know I could never find it again.

There was a visit to a saké factory where, hidden behind the modern machinery of stainless steel vats and hissing steam, is a small, separate enclave where saké is still made by the old processes involving the transformation of the rice into the purest saké possible, all by hand and therefore immensely slowly and carefully. The product is tiny and dedicated only to the use of the Emperor and the royal court. Nevertheless we were permitted a few cups in tiny ceramic thimbles and it really is like no other saké I have ever tasted.

But the pinnacle (literally) of our tour was to proceed towards Osaka and then, just short of the teeming city, to divert to the mountaintop monastery shrine of Koyasan. This peak is so hard to get to that the railway line runs out and the last section is accomplished by funicular.

In fact, unable to read the train signs at Osaka station, we missed the fast connection and found ourselves on the slow train with over thirty stops to our destination. But it proved an advantage: throughout the journey the train laboured from halt to halt with local peasants getting on and off, clutching baskets of eggs, cages of live chickens and ducks, all the paraphernalia of market day in rural Japan. After recovering from the shock of seeing two *gaijin* sitting in their train, the locals chattered and beamed away, even though we understood not a word, an experience very few tourists achieve on the streets of

Tokyo, particularly since only about 15 per cent of the Japanese are rural any more, the huge majority now urbanized.

Koyasan is a monastery of immense age and holiness, with the graveyard where the founders of Shingon Buddhism are laid. It takes paying guests in the form of pilgrims who wish to spend a long weekend living in the style of the medieval monks.

The first stop was to meet the abbot, who greeted us in broad American. No need for an interpreter this time. He had fought with the Japanese imperial navy in the Second World War, been captured and imprisoned in California and stayed there until the Fifties.

The living accommodation was unheated cells and the diet various cold foods but nothing hot. The better news was that one could place an order for warm saké, which we did, in quantities that raised a few eyebrows.

There is a small town grouped round the monastery, which enabled us to wander and see a side of Japan not to be observed in the cities.

At one point I asked the abbot if his own monks confined themselves to the cold vegetarian food that we were being served.

'Good God no,' he said. 'I wouldn't have a congregation at all if I demanded that. No, they just serve you pilgrims then go round to McDonald's.'

It may have been the altitude or the saké or both, but we slept soundly on our futon mats and were up before dawn for the early-morning service in the temple. I'm afraid I made an ass of myself.

Squatting on the heels with the buttocks just off the floor

and the knees under the chin was the required posture, which Sandy could manage with ease. Before we met, she had spent twenty years in the film business, ending with over two years as PA to Elizabeth Taylor. To stay sane in a completely crazy world, she had taken up kundalini yoga. This included retaining her British calm while attending the garden funeral of the Taylor family goldfish with complete Judaic rite presided over by a rabbi. But as for me, after a few minutes, my old knees were on fire.

I had no choice but to let my backside hit the floor and take the weight, and straighten the knees. But that posed another problem. It is very rude to point the soles of the feet at fellow worshippers, so I had to squirm until the soles were pointing at each other and I was squatting like a frog on a lilypad. At the end it took four other pilgrims to help me up.

That apart it was a beautiful service, all in Japanese of course, with copious helpings of joss and incense, bells and chanting. Among the several hundred worshippers, we were the only other *gaijin* present, and therefore objects of some curiosity.

But top of the range in the hilarity stakes was the ritual communal bath. This was absolutely crucial to the worship, the ritual washing of every part of the body. The women went one way, the men the other.

The Japanese regard dunking a dirty body in unmoving water as peculiar. The washing comes first, then the immersion. I was shown where to strip, given a towel to wrap round the waist, and a small booth with showerhead, soap and scrubber. The booth faced away from the open piping-hot water of the pool.

I noted that there were half a dozen middle-aged

businessmen in the pool, just disembodied heads on the surface of the water, staring at me. So I faced the wall, dropping the towel, and scrubbed from chin to feet. Finally I had no choice but to turn round and face the pool.

The six heads were still staring, but not at my face. Two feet further down, and the expressions were of considerable worry. As I turned the six expressions changed; not to horror but to the most profound relief. Someone had clearly told them something about naked Europeans that was completely untrue.

After that it was a farewell to the abbot, then the train (the fast one this time) down the mountain to the railhead, and the bullet train back to Narita airport and home.

A Very Untidy Coup

WITH HINDSIGHT, IT was probably a mistake to go researching cocaine shipments through Guinea-Bissau and I certainly never intended to land in the middle of a coup d'état.

The reason for the visit to this West African hellhole of a place was simple. I had spent months researching a novel which became *The Cobra* and was based on the enormous criminal world behind the cocaine trade. These quests had taken me through Washington and the DEA, London, Vienna, Hamburg (again!), Rotterdam and finally to Bogotá and Cartagena in Colombia, source of most of the white powder.

But there was something missing. In South America I had discovered that much of the cocaine destined for Europe did not take the direct route at all. Ships with very large consignments left the coast of Colombia and Venezuela to steam due east to West Africa and unload their cargoes in the creeks and mangrove swamps of countries where the entire law-and-order infrastructure could be purchased for bribes.

Then the cocaine bales could be broken down to smaller loads and taken north, via the land trains across the Sahara, to enter Europe from the south. Foremost among these African trans-shipment points was Guinea-Bissau.

This is the former Portuguese colony where I had staged through forty years earlier, perched on a crate of mortars, when a bullet came through the floor and went out the ceiling. Since then it had had twenty more years of independence war and twenty of civil war that had left the capital, Bissau City, pretty much gutted. There was (and for all I know still is) a community of Colombian gangsters who have built themselves seaside palaces and oversee the cocaine operations. As the Michelin guide used to say, 'worth a detour'.

The United Kingdom has no embassy there nor even a consulate. Nor does Guinea-Bissau have representation in London. But I traced a consulate in Paris and was duly issued a tourist visa. The only air passage is from Lisbon (the old colonial connection) to São Tomé island with a stopover at Bissau.

Finally, the honorary British vice-consul in Bissau was a very nice Dutchman with a franchise for Japanese off-road SUVs. I had been in email contact with Jan out of London and he kindly agreed to meet me on landing and show me around.

My TAP airliner took off from Lisbon at 8.30 p.m. What I did not know was that hardly had it turned south than in the Guinean army HQ a large bomb went off, blowing the chief of staff into several artistic pieces all over the office. That was the start of the coup.

Later revelations showed that those responsible were probably the Colombians. The timer and trigger mechanisms were assuredly too sophisticated for local assembly. But that was not the view of the army, which wanted revenge and suspected

President Veira. It was all tribal; the bulk of the army are Balanta but the president and his entourage were Papel. There is no love lost. At 33,000 feet I sipped my champagne and tried for a couple of hours' shut-eye before landing at 2 a.m. local time.

On touchdown the aircrew clearly did not want to hang around and did not even shut down the engines before leaving. Those descending were three or four Guineans and me. I entered passport control quite prepared for the long hassle of luggage-search and bribe-contributing that is habitual between touchdown and car park.

Then Jan came bustling through, waving his diplomatic passport, and whisked me out in double-quick time. We made the usual introductions, he grabbed my valise and strode to his SUV. When we were bowling along the high road to the city, I remarked he seemed to be in something of a hurry.

'Look in the rear-view,' he said.

The horizon behind us was awash with oncoming headlights.

'That's the army,' he said, and told me about the army chief six hours earlier. 'They are coming into town from their bases.'

'What do they want?'

'Revenge,' he said, and stepped on the gas. We made it to the centre of the shattered city ahead of the army and he deposited me at the only hotel in town a European would be wise to stay at. Then he left in a hurry to return to his wife and family to lock themselves in. Considering that he knew about the assassination, it was extremely decent of him to have come to the airport at all.

I checked myself in, went to my room and tried to sleep. But to no avail. At 4 a.m. I put on the bedside light, hauled myself upright and read a paperback already started on the aeroplane. At four thirty, about five hundred yards down the street, there was one almighty bang.

There are three reasons for noises that big in an African city in the darkness before dawn. One is the first thunderclap of a tropical storm. The second is a head-to-head crash between two speeding vehicles. The third is a bomb. This was a bomb. I was only later able to piece together the events of the night.

The local authorities − army, navy, port and harbour, customs, police − were all on the Colombian payroll but the pay-offs are not in the local worthless currency but in a 'skim' of the cocaine shipments themselves. It looked as if the chief of staff had been skimming too much, and paid for it. But for the Balanta tribesmen who made up the army, it was the Papel president they wanted. So they left their out-of-town barracks and came to get him.

The poor old booby was fast asleep in his bed. Because the once-grandiose presidential palace, former home of the Portuguese governor, was a ruin, his residence was a low-build hacienda-style complex in a walled garden. The bedroom was on the ground floor.

The army trucks smashed down the gate and someone put a rocket-propelled grenade through the bedroom window. That was the bang. The 71-year-old politician must have been tough. As his bedroom wing collapsed around him he stumbled through the rubble and out into the garden. The soldiers put three bullets through him.

But still he would not die. Then they realized what a foolish mistake they had made. He clearly possessed a juju that kept him immune from death by bullet. But there is one thing that no juju is proof against. They went to the gardener's store, got a machete and chopped him to pieces. Then he died. The soldiers went off into the night to break into a bar or two and celebrate. And Bissau City waited for dawn.

Before that arrived, the rest of the government had vaporized, heading for their indigenous villages where they would be safe. I descended to the dining room and asked for breakfast. Jan appeared an hour later to say the city was quiet apart from patrolling jeeps of army men looking for Papel victims but not interested in whites. So we got into his SUV and drove to his home.

Business would be very slight that day, he opined, so he could drive me out into the area of the creeks and swamps to get an idea where the cocaine cargoes came in and see the Colombians' mansions by the beach. This we did. While we were away, other things happened. At sub-politician level various functionaries closed both the land borders, north and south, and the airport. The tiny republic was sealed off.

In London my wife Sandy, knowing nothing of this, emailed a girlfriend to set up a lunch date. Part of her text read: 'I'm free this week 'cos Freddie is in Guinea-Bissau.'

Someone in Fort Meade, Maryland, or maybe Langley, Virginia, intercepted this and her screen went berserk. Her message disappeared. Things flashed up with the insignia of the Great Seal of the USA warning her not to use her laptop under any circumstances. She had not the faintest idea what she had done. I was later advised it was those two words 'Guinea-Bissau' that did the trick. Word had leaked out. You can close borders nowadays, shut the telephone switchboard and the cable office, but you cannot silence the internet.

Meanwhile, I was in the creeks peering through the undergrowth at the white sculpted mansions of the Colombians. Never one to look a gift horse in the mouth, I figured this coup was too good to ignore, so the passages in *The Cobra* are not simply accurate but autobiographical.

Back at Jan's house I borrowed his communications technology to contact the *Daily Express* in London and offer them the story. To their utter bewilderment, I insisted I wanted a copy-taker on the other end of the line with headphones and a keypad or a typewriter. Of course I was talking to youngsters who had never heard of any of these things. But eventually the lovely Gladys came on the line and I dictated a 1,000-word despatch, old style, the way it used to be.

Dinner that evening was most convivial. Next to me was the Dutch forensic pathologist. Part of the foreign aid from Holland was a state-of-the-art mortuary adjacent to the general hospital. It was well placed because patients tended to enter by the main doors but only exit in a horizontal box straight into the morgue.

The kindly pathologist was in retirement but serving a three-year stint in return for a nice plump pension when he got home. I asked him if he had had a busy day.

'Extremely busy,' he agreed.

'What were you doing?'

'Putting the president back together again,' he said.

According to custom, the dead head of state had to be presented in an open casket, which was not easy because none of the bits recovered from the garden actually fitted. That problem solved, we tucked into our veal escalopes.

After two days I had all my research done and the next day the airport opened. The TAP flight from São Tomé dropped in and picked up the few of us returning to Lisbon. From there I could take a BA flight back to London.

My wife's laptop remained unusable for five days and then suddenly cleared as the mysterious ban-on-use was removed without explanation. But I retain a silly fantasy of the morning conference at Langley when the news came through.

'No, Mr Director, sir, we don't know what is going on inside. The borders are closed, ditto the airport. There's some weird Limey in there who has a bit of a track record on coups in West Africa and he seems to know what is going down. Yes, sir, we have tried to contact him, but to no avail. He doesn't have a laptop and he won't use a cellphone.'

'Oh, well, let's just screw up his wife's lunch dates.'

Peace Hotel and Tracers

THIS TIME, MY wife Sandy was in serious voice and she had a point.

'You are an old fool to be even thinking of going to a place like that,' she said.

'Calm down,' I advised. 'You could be a rich widow.'

'I don't want to be a rich widow,' she replied.

I thought that was rather touching. There are quite a few women on Planet Earth who would do the trade. But that did not solve my problem. I was in the last stages of the research for the last novel I intend to write. It already had a title, *The Kill List*, after a document that really exists and in which are written the names, continuously updated, of all the terrorists the USA intends to 'terminate' without benefit of the habitual formalities.

The usual travels had taken me round the 'official' tour of agencies, ministries, technical establishments, weapons stores and a score of experts in their various fields. That was all in note form. But there is one thing that is too often missing.

As a reader I am disagreeably picky. When reading about a place in someone else's work I cannot avoid a nagging question: has he actually been there? There is a reason.

Reading about a place is one thing, going there is another. A personal visit, it is my long-held view, reveals a whole range of discoveries that is not available from reading research and certainly miles more than is on the internet. The next best, if a personal visit is not feasible, is hours with someone who knows the place intimately.

When I needed to describe Iraq under Saddam Hussein for *The Fist of God*, I was advised that, if I slipped in, the dictator's secret police would take about an hour to work out who I was, what I was doing and that it was not going to be complimentary to the tyrant. The occasional risk is tolerable but suicide is just stupid. So I relied for Iraq on a score of people who had lived, worked and travelled there for years.

But this was going to be different. I had tried academic sources, including the internet, and passages from other fiction writers and it was clear none of them had been near the ravaged city that had to occupy a whole chapter in *The Kill List*. Not many people had been to Mogadishu, notional capital of the permanently-at-war Somalia.

The country appeared to be pirates in the north, Al-Shabaab terrorists in the south and a capital under siege in the middle. And my wife had a point. Seventy-four is getting on a bit for bullet-dodging. One slows up. So we agreed on a compromise. She would not blast it all over the internet in her emails about lunch and I would go in with a bodyguard for the first time ever.

Through a few contacts I got in touch with a specialist agency run by Rob Andrew out of Nairobi. He agreed to lend me Dom, who had escorted whiteys in there before and brought them out again. Dom was British, ex-Special Forces, knew the terrain and was steady as a rock if things got lively.

There was one airline servicing Mogadishu, or 'Mog' as everyone called it. Turkish Airlines ran a flight out of Istanbul, stopover at Djibouti (ex-French Somaliland, still run by the French with a huge American airbase), stopover at Mog and on to Nairobi. Then a turnaround and back. Passengers could get on and off at Mog. Dom agreed to be there to meet me on the tarmac. It was a night flight arriving at dawn. Already blazing hot at 7.30 a.m. and there he was.

He saw me through the formalities of passport control and customs, with the usual gratuities to the unpaid officials, and outside in the shade explained to me the local layout.

Mog has two quite different zones: the inner zone, and the city zone. The former is hemmed by sandbag blast walls, razor wire, guarded gates and an entire garrison of soldiers from AMISOM – the African Union Mission to Somalia. These are almost all Burundians and Ugandans. They are armed to the teeth but have taken casualties that would cause government-toppling scandals in a European country but are shrugged off in Africa.

Colloquially the inner zone is known as the Bancroft Camp, or the Camp. It encloses the entire airport, all the (not many) embassies, the HQ of the African military mission and the living quarters of everyone else who is not Somali. These include mercenaries, bodyguards, technical aides and relief workers – in a word, the whites.

Separate at one end of the single runway is the also walled and highly secretive American embassy with its huge CIA mission, suspected UAV drones and a training school for young Somalis destined, hopefully, to become US agents when they qualify. The point is, no one can pretend to be a Somali who is not a born Somali, so no one can infiltrate 'the bad guys' except a Somali.

Somewhere in the undergrowth there is a British embassy pretending not to be. And right in the heart of the Camp is the cluster of lodgings, bars and mess halls where the non-military, non-diplomatic whites hang out. The hutments are converted steel sea-containers, the bar chairs plastic rejects, the beer supplies constant (the place would be in revolt without them) and the atmosphere raucous. Dom and I spent a few hours there and then, in our rented jeep, headed out of the guarded gate and into town. What I needed, I had explained, was to spend time in the Mog city that my Mossad agent in the novel would be visiting on a covert mission.

Our Somali driver weaved his way through the donkeys, camels and ubiquitous pick-up trucks known as 'technicals' and deep into the heart of Somali Mogadishu. We finally arrived at a side street, up which was a sealed gate. Dom exercised his linguistic magic and it slowly opened to reveal a courtyard into which we drove as the gate closed behind us. We had arrived at the Peace Hotel, charmingly named as it was in a war zone.

The AMISOM troops attempt to hold the outer perimeter of the capital city, while beyond their ring of garrison strong-points the country belongs to Al-Shabaab, who attack fairly regularly. That is where the casualties occur. But many jihadist fanatics are also inside the cordon. That apart, there are the gangs. There are no police – the lifespan would be too short. As Dom explained to me after we checked in:

'It's not so much that they want to kill you, though the fanatics might. The danger is kidnap. Most of these people are living on a dollar a day, if that. With your face you are two million dollars on the hoof. So a snatch is what I am here to prevent.'

Thus reassured, we dumped our luggage in the pretty spartan rooms and headed back out to explore the real Mog. I had just two days, then the Turkish airliner would come in from Nairobi at dawn of the third day to head north to Istanbul – hopefully with me on board.

And the two-day tour was fascinating. We had the jeep with its Somali driver and behind us a second jeep with four Ugandans. They were happy to be earning enough to go home at the end of their contract of service and become wealthy in their villages, with wives and cattle as befitted their new status.

I had noticed that Dom was carrying something metallic under his left armpit and was confident he knew exactly how to use it. The Ugandans had rifles, though I was not quite so confident of their expertise.

Dom took us to the principal mosque, untouched by shot or shell despite twenty years of civil war that had reduced most of the once-handsome Italian-designed colonial city to rubble. We saw just one of the sixteen pitiful refugee camps where the destitute and homeless lived in urine-wet squalor beneath tarpaulins and sacks, and moved on to the old fishing port and the Portuguese quarter.

At one point we found the crossroads where the US helicopter in the film *Black Hawk Down* was grounded and besieged by the fighters of the warlord Aidid. Eighteen Rangers died there so it seemed the decent thing to stand and say the Lord's Prayer for them. Until the growing crowd became rather disagreeable and Dom thought it wise to move on.

That first night we were sitting in the hotel window relishing our camel stew when something red and feathery drifted past the window. I remarked that it seemed odd that someone was celebrating with fireworks. Dom looked at me pityingly and said: 'Tracer.'

Then I recalled that in tracer fire only about one bullet in six or seven is illuminated. The rest you cannot see. Fortunately these rounds were going left to right and not straight at the glass.

Nevertheless I fingered my lucky bullet, worn on a gold chain round my neck. It passed through my hair one day in Biafra and lodged in the doorpost behind me. After the fire-fight, I dug it out, brought it back to London and had it mounted on a chain. Though not particularly superstitious, I adopted the habit of wearing it round my neck if going into any 'rough' environment.

Before bed I tried to shower off but the tap had the strength and capacity of a urinating rabbit so I settled for a bowl and a scrap of towel.

We checked out the next morning, spent part of the day completing our tour of Mog city and withdrew to the ramparts of Bancroft Camp. There at least we could check into a steel container, enjoy a few beers and be free of camel stew. Or it might have been goat, but it was rich and sustaining. We still settled for imported steak.

The next morning Dom saw me back through the airport formalities and on to the Turkish airliner. He later found his way back to his family in Nairobi on a small chartered flight.

When I returned home I had a warm welcome. 'That's it,' said Sandy. 'The next time you pull a stunt like that I'm going to see Fiona.'

She was referring to a mutual friend and the best divorce lawyer in London. But, of course, she doesn't really mean it. Anyway, I agreed that those days really are over, and then a year later . . .

Dream Come True

IT WAS A very small news item and one might have missed it. Down in the heart of the county of Kent, where I came from long ago, is a grass airfield called Lashenden, just outside the pretty town of Headcorn. Lashenden is the home of several clubs, including a branch of the Tiger Club, flying Tiger Moth biplanes, plus a skydiving club and another dedicated to classic aircraft called Aero Legends. The item that caught my eye revealed that Lashenden wished to upgrade all its buildings and facilities and sought donations.

I had an idea and made a call; that was in August 2014. I mentioned the news item to the voice that answered and said I was prepared to be very generous, but there was a condition. The voice replied he doubted it would be possible but he would ask. Four weeks went by. My seventy-sixth birthday came and went. Then the phone rang. Her name was Andrea.

'Are you free tomorrow?' she asked. 'We have one flying in from Duxford.'

I know RAF Duxford; it is the aeronautical end of the Imperial War Museum, a collection of classic and revered warplanes, some still flying. Including a Spitfire. Of course I was available. I had been available for seventy years. So I motored down, parked, checked in and waited. I was issued a flying suit and a cup of coffee. There was a problem. Morning mist hung over the Weald of Kent, but the sun of our Indian summer was burning it off. Up in Cambridgeshire, where Duxford is situated, the fog was worse. Would old Fred's luck still hold? It held. The mist lifted, she took off and headed south, over the Thames and into Kent. She landed just before noon. A Spitfire Mark 9, green-and-brown RAF combat camouflage. And she was beautiful; an icon that had once changed the history of Britain, of Europe and of the world. And she had been adapted with a second cockpit for a single passenger.

She taxied in to the apron near the dispersal huts and closed down. Her pilot, Cliff Spink, a professional who flies classic warplanes for a living, ex-RAF of course, came over and introduced himself. 'Who's first?' he asked. There were two donors awarded a flight. I was ready. He nodded and we walked out into the sun.

She was just as I had remembered her from seventy years ago when, aged five, I was dropped into an open cockpit at Hawkinge field and became mesmerized by the power and the beauty of the Supermarine Spitfire. The long, lean lines, only slightly degraded by the bubble Perspex dome behind the pilot's cockpit; the recognizable-anywhere elliptical wings, the genius of designer R.J. Mitchell. The four-bladed propeller, stark against the Kentish late-summer sky, the same cerulean blue it had been in the summer of 1944. That was when I swore my little boy's oath: that one day I too would fly a Spitfire.

One is older and stiffer than long ago. It took a hefty shove to get me on to the wing and thence I could step into the tiny rear cockpit. Helpful hands belted on the parachute and then the seat straps. A brief lecture on how to bale out if need be. Unhook the seat straps but not the parachute straps as well. Jettison the canopy, stand, turn, dive. Of course. But that is not going to happen.

Cliff climbed up front, his head disappeared out of sight. I used the seat-height adjuster and rose out of the cavern into the bubble dome itself. The Rolls-Royce Merlin engine, all 37 litres of her, coughed once then roared and settled down to a throaty growl. Chocks away. A bit more power. She moved away from dispersal and taxied to take-off. Cliff turned her into the wind and checked with the tower. Clear to take off.

The engine note rose smoothly from low growl to maddened roar and the Spitfire threw herself across the grass field, bumping over the ruts. Then the vibration stopped, the grass drifted downwards, clunk clunk, wheels up, a lurch forward as the impediment vanished. Cliff held her low over the field as the speed built up, then hauled back.

A raging climb into that blue, blue sky. Kent dropping away like a discarded map in a gale. At 3,000 feet Cliff's voice on the intercom: 'You have her.' His hands raised to head height, visible through two layers of Perspex, to prove it. So I gripped the control column and flew her.

Just as I had been led to believe. Ultra-sensitive to the touch, eager, willing, wanting to obey before the order was complete. It had been an awfully long time, but as with the bicycle it never quite leaves you. Diffident at first, confidence growing. Bank, turn, climb, twist, correct. I pulled into a rate-two left-hand turn and looked down.

There was the Weald of Kent as it had been since the Crusaders. A patchwork quilt of woods and fields, manors and meadows, farms and streams, hop oasts and orchards, ancient villages clustered round the cricket green, timbered pubs, Norman churches. The same Weald I had pedalled through as a boy, just as it was in 1940 when Spitfires and Hurricanes hurled themselves at the oncoming Luftwaffe. Enough to make even a cynical old journalist choke up. England, our England.

It was over too soon, but it was done. The seventy-year-old promise was fulfilled and the little boy's dream had come true.

Picture Acknowledgements

Every effort has been made to trace copyright holders, but any who have been overlooked are invited to get in touch with the publishers.

FF: author's collection

Credits read clockwise from top left

Section one

Spitfires of the No 91 Squadron lined up at Hawkinge, Kent, 5 May 1942: courtesy Imperial War Museum/CH5429

Dewald family: *FF*; Hanna Reitsch with Bozo Komac at the German glider championships held at Oerlinghausen, Germany, 31 July 1953: ©TopFoto.co.uk; all RAF photos: *FF*; Tonbridge School from the air and Big School, Tonbridge School: both courtesy Tonbridge School

Frank Keeler: © Archant Ltd; Doon Campbell in the Reuters newsroom, Fleet Street, London, 1950s: Reuters; newsmen at the scene of the attempted assassination of President Charles de

Gaulle, Petit Clamart, 22 August 1962: Keystone-France/ Gamma-Keystone via Getty Images; Kurt Blecha, Press Secretary to the Politburo at a press conference in Berlin, 1 February 1962: Koblenz, Bundesarchiv, Bild 183-90187-0008/ photo Heinz Junge; President de Gaulle's bullet-riddled car, August, 1962: ©1962 Rex Features; East-German border guards at Checkpoint Charlie, Berlin, April 1963: Ullstein via Getty Images; reconstruction of the assassination attempt, August 1962: Patrice Habans/Paris Match via Getty Images

Lt Col. Yabuku Gowan holding a press conference, August 1966: Priya Ramrakha/The LIFE Picture Collection/Getty Images; posters warning of the threat of war, Enugu, 9 June 1967: Associated Press; bridge at Onitsha, June 1969: ©RIA Novosti/TopFoto; FF and Col. Emuka Ojukwu: David Cairns, London Daily Express; Col. Ojukwu giving a press conference during the war: AFP/Getty Images

David Ben Gurion at Sde Boker, October 1965: © David Rubinger/Corbis; Ezer Weizmann: UA/Israel Sun/REX Shutterstock; King David Hotel, 22 July 1946: Fox Photos/ Getty Images

Section two

Children, Biafra, June 1968: David Cairns, London Daily Express

Trip to Biafra with army escort, 1968; FF and Biafran, 1968; Biafran mother and baby, 1968; malnourished Biafran baby, 1968: all David Cairns, London Daily Express; protest rally, Speaker's Corner, Hyde Park, London, 1968: Evening Standard/

Getty Images; shell, Biafra, 1968: David Cairns, London Daily Express

FF and his parents; FF and sons hunting and scuba-diving: all *FF*; FF and his wife, Sandy, at Buckingham Palace, London, 4 April 1997: Fiona Hanson/Press Association; FF, Carrie Forsyth and their first son, Shane, 14 June 1979: Philip Jackson/ Associated Newspapers/Rex; FF, Carrie and their second son, Stuart, 1979: Mike Forster/Associated Newspapers/Rex

FF at his typewriter, c. 1970: Hulton Archive/Getty Images; FF and Michael Caine, 14 February 1986: Mirrorpix; FF in Guinea-Bissau, 4 March 2009: Associated Press; FF at a book signing, London, 25 September 1972: Wesley/Keystone/Getty Images; Edward Fox and Fred Zinnemann on the set of *The Day of the Jackal*, 1973: Snap/Rex

FF flying, August 2014: all *FF*

ABOUT THE AUTHOR

Former RAF pilot and investigative journalist, **Frederick Forsyth** defined the modern thriller when he wrote *The Day of the Jackal*, described by Lee Child as 'the book that broke the mould', with its lightning-paced storytelling, effortlessly cool reality and unique insider information. Since then he has written twelve novels which have been bestsellers around the world: *The Odessa File*, *The Dogs of War*, *The Devil's Alternative*, *The Fourth Protocol*, *The Negotiator*, *The Deceiver*, *The Fist of God*, *Icon*, *Avenger*, *The Afghan*, *The Cobra* and, most recently, *The Kill List*. He lives in Buckinghamshire, England.